Eyes on the Prize

Eyes on the Prize

Procedures and Strategies for Collecting Money Judgments and Shielding Assets

Jason J. Kilborn
Professor of Law
John Marshall Law School

Carolina Academic Press
Durham, North Carolina

Library of Congress Cataloging-in-Publication Data

Names: Kilborn, Jason J., author.
Title: Eyes on the prize : procedures and strategies for collecting money judgments and shielding assets / by Jason J. Kilborn.
Description: Durham, North Carolina : Carolina Academic Press, LLC, 2019. | Includes bibliographical references and index.
Identifiers: LCCN 2019016444 | ISBN 9781531016067 (alk. paper)
Subjects: LCSH: Executions (Law)--United States.
Classification: LCC KF9025 .K537 2019 | DDC 347.73/77--dc23
LC record available at https://lccn.loc.gov/2019016444
e-ISBN 978-1-5310-1607-4

CAROLINA ACADEMIC PRESS
700 Kent Street
Durham, North Carolina 27701
Telephone (919) 489-7486
Fax (919) 493-5668
www.cap-press.com

Printed in the United States of America

This book is dedicated to the memory of
Stefan A. Riesenfeld

We stand on the shoulders of giants

Contents

Foreword ix

Introduction 3

Chapter 1 · Ancestry 7

A. The Common Ancestor: Rome 7

B. Roman Influence and the Beginnings of English Law 9

C. Early American Inheritance and Revision of English Enforcement Procedure 12

D. New Primary Sources: The Field Code and Modern American Procedure 15

Chapter 2 · Locate 17

A. Registration and Domestication of "Foreign" Federal and State Judgments 18

B. Immigration of Non-US Judgments and Arbitral Awards 21

C. Timing . . . and the Time Value of Money 22

D. Discovery 26

1. Informal 26
2. Formal 28

Chapter 3 · Grab 33

A. Restrain 33

B. Record 36

C. Levy 38

1. Execution 38
2. Garnishment 40

a. Bank Accounts 43

b. Wages, Salaries, Commissions 45
c. Business Property, Receivership, and Investment Securities 50
d. Intangibles 53
3. Turnover 54
D. Monetize 56
E. Expand 58
1. Voidable Transactions 59
2. Veil Piercing 61

Chapter 4 · Shield 63
A. Shielding Substance — Property Exemptions 63
1. Texas 64
2. Pennsylvania 66
3. New York 66
4. California 69
5. Illinois 70
B. Shielding against Procedure — Fair Debt Collection Practices Act 72
C. Shielding Assets Ahead of Time — Asset Protection Schemes 74

Chapter 5 · Battle 79
A. Liens 80
B. Judgment/Execution Liens on Real Estate 81
C. Judgment/Execution Liens on Personal Property 82
1. Creation 82
2. Third-Party Effectiveness (and Priority) 84

Chapter 6 · Capitulate 87
A. Bankruptcy as Collection or Relief . . . and Collection 87
B. The Automatic Stay 89
C. Limitations on Relief: Objections and Exceptions to Discharge 90
D. Preference Clawback within 90 Days 92

Chapter 7 · Exercises 95

Appendix A · New York Civil Practice Law & Rules (CPLR) 101

Appendix B · California Code of Civil Procedure (CCP) 137

Appendix C · Illinois Code of Civil Procedure (735 ILCS 5/) & Supreme Court Rule 277 191

Index 209

Foreword

This is a book about the civil procedure that few talk about and many do not know exists. It charts the metamorphosis by which the caterpillar of a money judgment is transformed into the butterfly of ... money. Its primary audience comprises law students, to respond to the constant reproach in legal commentary that modern law schools do not teach students the methods and mechanics by which a money judgment is enforced. Designed to be inserted as a unit into a course on Civil Procedure, Remedies, Debtor-Creditor Rights, Bankruptcy, Secured Transactions, or perhaps other subjects, this book describes how lawyers achieve what civil litigation clients pay for—not a judgment declaring that the plaintiff is entitled to money, but actual money that the plaintiff can use to compensate for the contractual or tortious injury on which the lawsuit was based.

It is also addressed to practicing lawyers and even laypeople who want or need to understand the details of the critical point at which the rubber meets the road in a civil lawsuit. Most judgments in the US awarding money to a victorious plaintiff are not self-enforcing. Plaintiffs' lawyers and their clients need to have some sense from the very beginning of a lawsuit how a paper victory might ultimately (or not) be translated into lucre, most plaintiffs' real goal. Not to leave out the defense side, this book also describes the many ways by which defense counsel and their clients can invoke the law to protect themselves from expropriation of the defendant's assets by judgment creditors, not only while the judgment enforcement process is unfolding, but also in advance.

This book is a survey, not a treatise. It does not examine the multivariate laws of the 50 states, the District of Columbia, and the federal system. That being said, it does provide a detailed examination of the specific procedural rules implicated in the money judgment enforcement process, and it makes precise and fairly exhaustive reference to the statutes and jurisprudence of several key jurisdictions. Most references are to the state and federal law of three key, high-population states in which substantial collection activity takes place—New York,

California, and Illinois—but other states' laws figure prominently here as well—Texas, Florida, and Pennsylvania in particular. Not all of the minute details of the money judgment enforcement laws of any of these states or the federal system are presented here, but all of the fundamentals are covered and arranged in logical order to allow readers to proceed to enhance their understanding by (1) finding the relevant additional details in these states' laws, and/or (2) anticipating and finding the relevant provisions in states whose law is not specifically analyzed. This is a guidebook, leading the reader to and describing the highlights, but leaving some of the adventure to be undertaken independently.

For teachers inclined to drill students on what lawyers really do, a series of hypothetical problem exercises is included in the end. These problems are designed to allow students to cut their teeth on putting this material into action, applying the law to determine precisely which steps a plaintiff's lawyer would have to take to collect on a money judgment for a particular plaintiff, and how the law would or could protect the assets of a particular defendant (and the interests of third parties). These problems can be worked either by referring to the reading and the excerpts of the statutes included in the appendices, or by applying the rules of a different jurisdiction (state or perhaps non-US country) to which the commentary in this book will have guided the students—and to which a professor might make more precise reference.

Over my years of teaching this material to students in a one-week unit of my Civil Procedure course, I have been surprised at the degree of enthusiasm with which they have devoured the material. I have been equally surprised by the volume of gratitude expressed over the years as these students have encountered money judgment enforcement or defense issues in practice, either in a pre-graduation clerkship or in their later law practice. These students often report that they have been among the only members of their firms with any specific knowledge of these rules and their operation, knowledge that has served them and their clients well and frequently. I hope my publication of these materials arouses similar enthusiasm and provides similarly valuable knowledge to students, lawyers, and others whom I have not had the pleasure of meeting.

Jason Kilborn
Chicago, IL
2019*

---

* I am grateful for a research grant from the John Marshall Law School that supported some of the research for this book conducted during summer 2018. I am also very grateful to Sam Schumer, partner in the commercial litigation department at Meltzer, Purtill & Stelle LLC, for both his eagle-eyed proof of this book and his invaluable front-lines explanations of how things really work in Chicago collections actions.

Eyes on the Prize

Introduction

Congratulations! After a grueling multi-year odyssey through pleadings, motions, discovery, and a trial, you've just obtained a judgment declaring that the defendant owes your client $750,000, perhaps for breach of contract, a civil rights violation, or infringement of intellectual property rights. As you and your client toast your hard-fought victory, she asks you, "So when do I receive the money?" If this were a tort case involving a car crash, the answer would likely be, "The insurance company should send us a check in the next few weeks." Even more likely, the case would have ended like most do, not with a trial and verdict, but in a settlement, in which case the defendant would have agreed to send over money on an arranged schedule. But in the slightly fanciful, textbook case of an actual money judgment, the answer to your client's question is one that eludes many otherwise very talented and knowledgeable lawyers. The answer to this question has not been taught systematically in most US law school for over 40 years.

Despite what many lawyers and lay people believe, a money judgment is not an order to pay;[1] rather, it is a final determination of liability of defendant to plaintiff—now called *judgment debtor* and *judgment creditor*, respectively. To turn that judgment into money, someone has to be responsible for finding money's worth in valuable property belonging to the judgment debtor and transferring that value to the judgment creditor to satisfy the monetary demand awarded in the judgment.

From time immemorial, Western law has assigned this task to the judgment creditor, with only limited and legally constrained assistance from the court or other official authorities. The judgment creditor's task in enforcing a money

1. With the exception of family support orders and perhaps criminal fines/fees/penalties/ restitution orders, which are often *additionally* enforced by the court's contempt power.

judgment now poses several challenges that compose a new and discrete stage of civil procedure. As one commentary aptly puts it, "the entry of a judgment is often the beginning of a different process which can be just as arduous" as obtaining the judgment in the first place.[2]

A new series of questions now looms large. If the judgment debtor has valuable property or rights in property, how is the judgment creditor to find out about this? Once that property is located, can the creditor effectuate the forcible seizure and transfer of that value, or must the debtor be indirectly coerced into ceding that value "voluntarily"? What of intangible property rights and rights to property in the possession of third parties, perhaps located in distant fora—can the judgment creditor seize intangible property rights or intervene and seize value in a third party's hands, or must she wait until value has materialized and been turned over to the judgment debtor? And what of other creditors? If more than one creditor has current or contingent rights in the debtor's valuable property, how are those rights to be reconciled or prioritized to decide which creditor is entitled to that value if it is, as it often will be, insufficient to satisfy all claims?

Meanwhile, does the law have anything to say about protecting the judgment debtor? She might be suffering greatly from the siphoning off of all sources of value, including those needed to support a family. May all sources of value be coerced or seized, or does the law impose limits on the types of property that a creditor can pursue? Is there any check on the rapacious efforts of judgment creditors to pummel the debtor into submission? Indeed, anticipating these problems, can a defendant-to-be plan her affairs so as to put sources of value beyond the reach of judgment creditors?

The leverage effects of these complicating factors for both judgment creditors and judgment debtors—not only after, but crucially *before* a lawsuit is initiated—constitute a vital input into the decision to initiate a lawsuit or to settle one. Both sides (and their lawyers) need to have full information to assess these considerations accurately to gauge the value of pursuit or defense of a lawsuit. It makes little sense to commence a lawsuit against a debtor against whom a judgment cannot eventually be collected efficiently and effectively.

These and other issues will be examined here from the perspective of three modern, representative money judgment enforcement systems: New York, which has stuck fairly close to its historical roots; California, which came to the game a bit later and thus reflects a greater relaxation of historical

2. Robert L. Haig & Patricia O. Kahn, "Representing the Judgment Creditor," 16 *Am. J. Trial Ad.* 1, 1 (1992).

constraints; and Illinois, which has entirely revolutionized its money judgment enforcement system to overcome the principal historical challenges in this process. These three states have the virtues of hosting large population centers with significant money judgment enforcement activity. They represent fairly distinct paradigms of enforcement procedures, each of which is likely to be reflected in any given other state's money judgment enforcement system. When these states' laws are not representative, other states' examples (Texas, Florida, Pennsylvania, and others) will often be presented to complete this overview of modern US judgment enforcement law and practice.

A hypothetical problem exercise follows the discussion of the law and allows for focused reflection on how these rules operate together. Nothing concentrates the attention or sharpens understanding like applying law to concrete facts, and that, after all, is what lawyers need to be able to do (not simply memorizing rules, but applying them in context). Indeed, you might read the problem in the final chapter now to have in mind the specific types of factual challenges that the laws in the following detailed discussion attempt to solve.

Chapter 1

Ancestry

There are few places in modern law where the distant past is reflected more vividly than in the rules for enforcing money judgments. In this context in particular, modern procedures and terminology can be truly understood only by appreciating their origins. Western society has struggled with the same problems for millennia, and especially in the Anglo-American world, technical complications have prompted odd workaround solutions that make little sense without a bit of background knowledge of how this all began.

A. The Common Ancestor: Rome

The technical challenges of judgment enforcement rise from the earliest foundations of Western law. The structure of the earliest Roman dispute resolution system and the nature of a money judgment established a binary, bifurcated view of the process, distinguishing adjudication from collection. This approach would persist over the next 2500 years to the present.[3]

Roman procedure progressed through three stages, each with its own distinct approach to judgment enforcement. First, in the earliest Roman civil procedure of *legal actions* (*legis actiones*) from about 450–100 BCE, civil disputes between private parties were initiated by formalistic oral pronouncements that led to a hearing before a lay adjudicator nominated by the parties

3. This section is based primarily on Max Kaser and Karl Hackl's authoritative *Das Römische Zivilprozessrecht* (C.H. Beck 2nd revised ed. 1996), but see also J.H. Dalhuisen, *Dalhuisen on International Insolvency and Bankruptcy* (Matthew Bender 1986); Zachary Herz, "The Effect of Bankruptcy Law on Roman Credit Markets," 2 *Bus. & Bankr. L.J.* 207 (2015); and Rafael Domingo, "Civil Litigation in Roman Law. An Overview" (2017 online at http://ssrn.com/abstract=2942875).

to serve as their private judge, or *iudex*. Because the *iudex* was not a public official, his pronouncement of a judgment in favor of the complaining party was not backed by official force.

If the losing defendant refused to pay the amount awarded in the judgment within 30 days, the judgment creditor could only invoke the procedure called *nexum* (via the action of *manus iniectio*) to coerce the debtor into paying the judgment "voluntarily" by seizing the body of the judgment debtor and locking him in chains in the creditor's house! If the judgment were not satisfied during the next 60 days, the judgment debtor's situation took a dire turn. Though the particulars of what happened next remain shrouded in the mists of history, the earliest practices reportedly allowed the judgment creditor to sell the debtor into foreign slavery "over the Tiber" to raise money to be applied against the judgment. Alternatively, rather than selling the judgment debtor for a one-shot payout, the judgment creditor might continue to hold the judgment debtor as a domestic slave to work off the unpaid judgment over time. Whatever the largely lost specifics of this frightening procedure might have been, it is clear that the debtor's body in one way or another was the exclusive object of early Roman money judgment enforcement.

In the second, classical age of *formulary procedure* (*ordo iudiciorum*) from about 100 BCE to 200 CE, debtors still faced bodily seizure, but judgment creditors were granted direct access to the debtor's property as the preferred object of enforcement. The creditor on an unsatisfied judgment could now bring a new action, *actio iudicati*, before an official, the *praetor*. Unless the debtor established that the judgment was invalid, the *praetor* would issue a decree authorizing the now twice victorious judgment creditor to seize all of the movable goods of the judgment debtor (*missio in bona*) and, if the judgment were not paid within 30 days, to sell those goods (*venditio bonorum*) at public auction, though for the benefit of *all* of the debtor's creditors. While this procedure had the humane advantage of leaving the debtor's body and liberty intact, its overbroad application to the entirety of the debtor's movable effects, and its conscription of the enforcing creditor to vindicate the rights of free-riding other creditors, still left much to be desired.

The third, post-classical stage of Roman procedure introduced significant changes, foreshadowing modern approaches. In the first several centuries of the Common Era, *extraordinary cognition* (*cognitio extra ordinem*) gradually replaced formulary procedure, as the Emperor exerted greater control over the administration of justice via his magistrates and other public officers. One of these new public officers was the *exsecutor*, a court officer appointed later in this period to exercise exclusive administrative authority to enforce judgments. Individual creditors could now apply in writing to the imperial magistrate for an order directing the *exsecutor* to seize (*pignus in causa iudicati captum*) and sell (*distractio bonorum*) individual items of the judgment debtor's property at public auction. If movable property produced insufficient value, the *exsecutor* could now seize and sell immovable property (land), as well, but any value in excess of the judgment amount obtained at the auction would be returned to the judgment debtor, rather than distributed to other creditors.

B. Roman Influence and the Beginnings of English Law

Most of the complications of modern US enforcement law trace their roots directly back to the beginnings of English law and procedure, which were themselves influenced by the Roman foundations just described. When the Angevin-English kings established the earliest royal law courts in the 1100–1200s, they created a centralized and highly formalistic system with procedures along the lines of the late Roman extraordinary cognition, though with even more carefully circumscribed remedies.

Money judgments were the only judgments ordinarily awarded by these royal law courts. As in the late Roman period, these judgments could be enforced only in a separate, subsequent procedure requested by the judgment creditor's formal application for official action initiated by one of the many "writs" issued in the King's name by his royal Chancellor. While proceedings in the law courts were conducted orally in Norman French, the Chancellor and his officers were among the few literate members of early English society. They were principally Roman Catholic clerics and later others educated in Roman law in the first European universities in Bologna, Paris, and Oxford. These jurists thus wrote in the language of ancient Rome—Latin—leaving a linguistic imprint that persists to this day on Anglo-American law.

By the late 1200s, three writs had become the foundation of English enforcement law. In the King's name, they commanded action by the King's local officers, the sheriffs, to collect value from the judgment debtor with which that judgment could be satisfied. The Latin words that began the command in each writ came to be used as a shorthand reference to each.[4]

4. The remainder of this chapter is based largely on the landmark work of Stefan A. Riesenfeld, "Collection of Money Judgments in American Law—A Historical Inventory and a Prospectus," 42 *Iowa L. Rev.* 155 (1957), and "Enforcement of Money Judgments in Early American History," 71 *Michigan L. Rev.* 691 (1973).

The primary execution writ, *fieri facias*, directed that the local sheriff "cause to be made" (*fieri facias*) from the goods and chattels (*de bonis et catallis*) of the judgment debtor a sum of money by seizing and selling the judgment debtor's movable effects and applying that sum to satisfy the creditor's judgment. This writ is the only one to survive to modern times (often abbreviated "*fi fa*"). It emerged from ancient origins, doubtless inspired by the late Roman procedures of seizure and sale by the *exsecutor*. The process by which the sheriff seizes and sells property in execution of this writ is still today called *levy*, a word arising from the language of an even earlier writ of *levari facias* ("cause to be *raised*" or "levied"). The object of levy under *fieri facias* was limited to movable effects, not land. If the sheriff could not find sufficient chattels within a year and a day from the signing of the judgment, the creditor had to pursue a subsequent action (*debt*) or writ (*scire facias*, "make known" that the judgment remains unsatisfied) to renew the judgment or execution writ and obtain a new execution writ (called an *alias* or *pluries* writ). This process could go on indefinitely.

A second writ was a statutory innovation arising in 1285 aimed at extracting value not only from the debtor's movable property, but also from his interests in land. By the writ of *elegit* ("[he has] chosen"), the judgment creditor would literally elect to have the debtor's personal property transferred to him at an appraised value, and if this were insufficient to satisfy the judgment, to receive a tenancy in the debtor's interest in land entitling the creditor to collect one-half (a *moiety*) of the appraised value of the anticipated rents and fruits of the land for a period of time that would satisfy the judgment. In making this election, the judgment creditor had to forego other execution remedies, thereby running the risk that these dual appraisals might be depressed in comparison with what actual future sales of the debtor's movable effects might produce. Unlike the writ of *fieri facias* for movables, in no event could the judgment debtor's interest in land be forcibly liquidated by sale.

A final writ, *capias ad satisfaciendum* ("arrest in order to satisfy") offered the option of having the sheriff seize and jail the judgment debtor in order to coerce him into paying the judgment "voluntarily." The horrid conditions of English debtors' prisons are legendary, but while this writ might have satisfied judgment creditors' bloodthirsty desire to inflict suffering on their debtors, it did not satisfy many judgments. Imprisoned debtors, unable to earn a free living, were often unable to pay their judgments. This indirect coercion might have flushed out some hidden property or squeezed the debtor's family or friends to apply their property to pay the debtor's judgment, but it was productive in relatively few cases where *fieri facias* or *elegit* was not. Imprisonment for debt would eventually be abolished in the mid-1800s, but not before being exported to the American colonies, where it was also abolished at the same time and so will no longer be discussed in this book.[5]

As commerce and value in movable property grew, so did judgment creditors' challenges in locating tangible, movable effects on which to levy. Judgment debtors became more adept at concealing the location of movable property, and many sources of value (anything other than tangible goods) were simply beyond the reach of the execution writs. A particular problem was the practice by judgment creditors of conveying their property to friends or relatives, alienating it beyond the reach of creditors, since the law courts would authorize levy only on property to which the debtor held legal title.

From the mid-1300s, to soften the rigidities of the common law and afford more flexible remedies (e.g., injunction, specific performance) when the law courts' money judgments offered inadequate relief, a parallel justice system called *equity* grew out of the Chancellor's office, later called *Chancery*. While the development of these equitable remedies is generally well known, less well known is the crucial role that Chancery's equity jurisdiction played in assisting creditors in collecting their money judgments from hidden or otherwise unavailable assets.

If and only if creditors' remedies at law had proven inadequate (that is, the sheriff returned the writ of *fieri facias* indicating that he had attempted to levy but found "no property," *nulla bona*), equity offered additional recourse "supplementary to execution at law" in at least two crucial ways. First, by a late-1500s Statute Against Fraudulent Conveyances, judgment creditors were empowered to petition Chancery to use its equity power to seize movable property legally conveyed to third parties by judgment debtors fraudulently attempting to put value beyond the reach of a creditor executing a judgment. Second, around this same time, Chancery empowered judgment creditors to file *creditor's bills* in equity to gain access to equity's extraordinary discovery procedures to supplement the lack of such procedures at law. Only via such a *bill of discovery* could judgment creditors compel answers to questions posed to

5. For further exploration of the topic of imprisonment for debt, its 19th century abolition, and its 20th and 21st century reincarnation in limited but troubling contexts, see Peter J. Coleman, *Debtors and Creditors in America: Insolvency, Imprisonment for Debt, and Bankruptcy, 1607–1900* (State Historical Society of Wisconsin 1974); American Civil Liberties Union, *In for a Penny: The Rise of America's New Debtors' Prisons* (2010) (examining imprisonment of low-income debtors, principally racial and ethnic minorities, incident to collection of public debts for "legal financial obligations" relating to fines, fees, and costs associated with criminal sentences).

judgment debtors and third parties regarding the location of the debtor's assets, especially assets the debtor had concealed or transferred to avoid levy.

Equity's assistance only went so far, however. Jealous defense of the prerogative of the Common Law led Chancery to refuse assistance in extending the limited reach of the law writ of *fieri facias*. No seizure was possible, for example, of intangible and equitable interests in property (*choses in action*). This included increasingly common stores of value such as promissory notes, investments in business entities, and the judgment debtor's right to collect debts owed to him by his own debtors (eventually including, for example, the debt owed by a bank to return funds placed on deposit).

More fundamentally, equity's assistance came at great cost, as proceedings were infamously long, drawn out, and expensive. Like other proceedings in equity, discovery was conducted in writing. Judgment creditors could pose questions regarding the nature and location of assets and conveyances only by composing written *interrogatories*, which would be presented to the examinee in person by Chancery officials called examiners (or, outside London, by private commissioners), who recorded summarized answers to these questions in a document called a *deposition*. Only one set of these questions for all witnesses was allowed, and because lawyers thus could not supplement or clarify the record with further interrogatories once the answers in the deposition had been revealed through *publication*, lawyers felt compelled to pose countless "what if" and "suppose the following" interrogatories in an attempt to predict and respond to any eventual testimony relating to their or their opponents' interrogatories. In factually complex cases, the Chancellor might refer the matter to a master for more rounds of directed discovery and significant additional time and expense.[6] This laborious, time-consuming, and expensive process exacerbated rather than alleviated the challenges faced by creditors in finding value to apply in satisfaction of a judgment.

C. Early American Inheritance and Revision of English Enforcement Procedure

Before the American Revolution in the late 1700s, the American colonies were England (more or less), so the English law and practice just described ap-

6. For the source of these details and a fascinating exploration of the evolution of equity discovery procedures in the United States, see Amalia D. Kessler, *Inventing American Exceptionalism: The Origins of American Adversarial Legal Culture, 1800–1877* (Yale Univ. Press 2017).

plied (again, more or less) in the New World, as well. That would change after independence, of course, but even before then, significant differences in conditions in the New World would prompt substantial revisions to American execution procedure. And political independence did not mean necessary abandonment of longstanding English law and equity procedure; rather, the new United States began a never-ending process of tinkering with inherited common law and equity practices, including practices related to enforcement of money judgments.

With land being much more plentiful in America, the restrictive writ of *elegit* began to disappear almost immediately, as creditors were gradually allowed to seize not just a temporary tenancy, but ownership of land rights. Some colonies—and later, states—required creditors first to seek satisfaction from movable property, but if this proved insufficient, the execution writ of *fieri facias* was expanded to encompass execution against land, as well.

A British statute in 1732 provided more broadly that creditors could execute judgments in the American colonies in the same way against both chattels and realty, including forced sale by writ of *fieri facias*. Due to a severe shortage of money (*specie*), many colonies preferred to simply transfer either chattels or realty or both to creditors at an appraised value, rather than selling them at public auction. Both of these methods of value transfer continued to appear in later execution laws in various states. Alternatively, some colonies and later states modified the English rule to establish that a judgment gave rise to a *lien* on land (a concept discussed in more detail below in chapter 5). This lien was enforceable not only by collecting rents for a term of years, but by the ultimate equity procedure of foreclosure sale of the land.

In either case, some colonies and later states protected debtors' interests in land by allowing then to *redeem* (that is, repurchase) land lost through execution. Within, say, one year of the execution sale, debtors could pay the entire amount owed on the judgment and forcibly repurchase the land, even from a buyer at a sheriff's auction sale. These kinds of variations in state procedures would persist and grow in later years.

While land was perhaps less valuable in America, apparently time was more so. Another American innovation was a limitation on the effectiveness of a judgment, which soon after the Revolution several states began to limit to a maximum term of years. No longer could execution issue on a judgment indefinitely. Creditors were eventually restricted in many states by special statutes of limitations for judgments, such that after 10 or 20 years, for example, no further execution could issue on a judgment. These statutes were by no means uniform, and the limitations periods varied significantly among the states.

The most substantial American developments concerned equity proceedings. Until the mid-1800s, the states by and large retained the bifurcated justice system inherited from England, with law courts doling out money judgments at law and issuing execution writs, and chancery courts using their equity power to support creditors' efforts to find and seize sources of value not easily obtainable by execution writ. While English equity practice had been reticent to help creditors access value in judgment debtors' choses in action, such as business investments (e.g., stocks and bonds) and debts owed to them (e.g., bank deposits and later wages and salaries), American legislators provided a statutory impetus for such assistance.

The most direct response was simply to extend the scope of the execution writ to intangible choses in action. This worked fine for stores of value that had some sort of physical embodiment, such as a stock certificate or a promissory note, but for debts owed to the judgment debtor, a statutory procedure called *garnishment* (or *trustee process*) was recruited. This existing process allowed creditors to seize property, including the amount owed on a debt, from the in-state obligors of debts and custodians of property owed/belonging to out-of-state judgment debtors. Legislators reoriented and broadened this garnishment procedure, making it available for judgments against all judgment debtors (in-state and out-of-state), invoked either by ordinary *fieri facias* execution writ or in a separate garnishment proceeding.

A more aggressive response was a substantial expansion of the use of *equity receivership*. Statutes most notably in New York expanded this ancient procedure into a nuclear remedy for judgment creditors who had been unsuccessful in enforcing judgments in ordinary execution proceedings. In response to a rise in commerce and defaults in the 1830s, commercial creditors increasingly sought to impose equity receiverships over their defaulting judgment debtors, placing all of their property under the control of a court-appointed receiver and threatening debtors with contempt if they continued to conceal or transfer any property to anyone other than the judgment creditor.

This was an especially effective remedy against large business interests, whose complex business dealings could be maintained by a receiver, all for the judgment creditor's benefit. When directed aggressively against individual debtors—often individuals having fallen on hard times through no fault of their own in an increasingly impersonal, market-driven economy—it provided political impetus for a wave of debtor-protection legislation, including statutes exempting a broader range of property, especially wages and salaries, from execution, along with the first permanent US bankruptcy statute.

D. New Primary Sources: The Field Code and Modern American Procedure

The mid-1800s also saw a wholesale consolidation of the rules and practices of the judicial systems of most states, as law and equity were "fused" by statute into one unitary jurisdiction of courts of now both law and equity. An unruly mess of colonial and state statutes and centuries of both law and chancery precedents was consolidated and replaced, first by New York's 1848 adoption of David Dudley Field's organized code of rules on practice and pleadings in civil cases.

The organized elegance of the Field Code swept across the country like wildfire, adopted virtually verbatim by most states, especially those in the new West, by the turn of the next century.[7] For example, when California became the 31st state in 1850, it also adopted the Field Code at the urging of Stephen J. Field, a New York lawyer who moved to California in the Gold Rush, later justice of the California and US Supreme Courts, and brother of the principal author of the Field Code, David Dudley Field. While many variations can be observed in the Field Code provisions as adopted outside New York, the provisions on debt collection are quite uniform throughout the West, Midwest, and South, as the attraction of capital through powerful creditor remedies was the driving force behind the adoption of the procedural code of the great commercial center of New York.

In the new unitary system of the Field Code, proceedings formerly pursued by creditor's bill in equity to assist creditors in seeking judgment execution at law—such as discovery, garnishment, injunction, and receivership—were brought within the power of the unitary courts under the heading "proceedings supplementary to execution." These proceedings were designed to minimize the former expense and delay associated with equity proceedings, making *supplementary proceedings* (sometimes called *supplemental proceedings*) simpler, cheaper, more expeditious, and therefore more effective for judgment creditors. Until recently, such proceedings generally still required an unsuccessful attempt at ordinary execution (sheriff's return of the *fieri facias* writ *nulla bona*), but

7. For a revealing corpus linguistic study of the migration of the Field Code across the states in the 1800s, see Kellen Funk & Lincoln Mullen, "The Spine of American Law: Digital Text Analysis and U.S. Legal Practice" 123 *Am. Hist. Rev.* 132 (2018) (manuscript available online at https://ssrn.com/abstract=3001377). A map on page 12 of the manuscript reveals the years in which each state adopted a Code of Procedure modeled on the New York Field Code, as well as an indication of which states retained a traditional, local common law approach (e.g., Illinois, Pennsylvania, New Jersey, and Virginia) or adopted procedural reforms unrelated to the Field Code movement (e.g., Texas, Georgia, Massachusetts, Connecticut, and Louisiana).

eventually even this technicality would abate (though it is still a requirement in some states).[8]

The process of simplification and consolidation of judgment creditors' remedies continued in the 1900s and even 2000s, and it will doubtless continue to evolve as the cat-and-mouse competition between judgment creditors and debtors continues. The following chapters will examine the specifics of how that game plays out today as exemplified in the laws and procedures of several representative states.

While the following discussion will focus primarily on the fairly representative (and often governing) laws of New York, California, and Illinois, which are excerpted in the appendices to this book, it will also make reference to several other representative jurisdictions' rules (Texas, Florida, Pennsylvania), and you might want to find your state's version of these rules and see which of the various alternatives have been adopted. Today, most states' money judgment enforcement rules are readily available online, even without access to a paid database (we will see in the next chapter that there are no general federal enforcement rules).

These provisions might be divided among two principal sources: (1) state statutes, usually a code of civil procedure adopted by the legislature, arranged in the large state codifications under such headings as "justice and the judiciary," "legal proceedings," "judgments," or "civil procedure," and possibly also (2) rules of civil procedure in the trial-level courts, likely adopted by the state supreme court. Both of these sources, of course, have often been interpreted by the courts, so reference to the jurisprudence remains often necessary, as well. Forms are also readily available online, sometimes for a fee, so one no longer needs to go through the tedious process of transcribing the long notice-and-warning passages from the statutes or rules into the papers that launch this or that enforcement process. Always be sure to reference the latest versions of these statutes, rules, and forms, however, as revisions continue to pour in to a greater or lesser degree in various states virtually every year.

The essence of modern American money judgment enforcement is finding money's worth in valuable property in which the judgment debtor has at least some degree of rights that can be seized and monetized for the judgment creditor. However the specific rules and procedures in any given jurisdiction might vary, the process involves several discrete steps that can be broken out and examined more or less in the order of the following discussion.

---

8. *See, e.g.*, Iowa Code §630.1; *cf.* Fla. Stat. §56.29(1) (requiring an outstanding execution writ in order to initiate supplementary proceedings).

Chapter 2

Locate

The first step in the process of enforcing a money judgment is locating sources of value that might be forcibly transferred from judgment debtor to judgment creditor. As usual in the American tradition, this responsibility is not *sua sponte* fulfilled by the court or other official institution; rather, it falls squarely on the judgment creditor. Outside the context of child support orders and perhaps criminal fines and penalties (neither of which is specifically treated in this book), no official authority commands debtors to turn over all sources of value to a prevailing creditor. Imprisonment for debt was an institution that essentially did this, as it was designed to compel debtors to reveal and apply whatever property value they might have to satisfy the judgment debt and be freed from prison. With the abandonment of that enforcement technique in the mid-1800s, the judgment creditor now bears the initial burden of identifying fairly specifically the form and location of potential value and invoking a procedure to get that specific value conveyed to the judgment creditor so it can be applied to satisfy the monetary demand in the judgment.

Like the process of obtaining a judgment, the money judgment enforcement process requires us to return to square one and consider where the judgment can be enforced; that is, which precise court has the power (jurisdiction) to compel property to be seized and persons to cooperate. As a pronouncement of official sovereign power, a judgment can be enforced initially only by the sovereign whose territory currently hosts the value or person against whom enforcement is sought—and only using the enforcement techniques sanctioned by that sovereign.

This challenge is obvious when the judgment to be enforced within the US has been issued by a non-US sovereign (e.g., Canada or Germany). But also domestically, the American tradition of federalism raises issues of both interstate relations among co-equal state sovereigns and the delicate federal-state relationship that preserves the prerogatives of the state sovereigns in the face of encroachment by the federal union. Moreover, the states themselves also subdivide their territory into counties (and parishes), further delineating spheres of restricted authority of local courts and enforcement officers. Navigating the maze of potential enforcement sites and localizing a judgment in the proper site(s) is a crucial first step in the money judgment enforcement procedure.

A. Registration and Domestication of "Foreign" Federal and State Judgments

Until the introduction of the Federal Rules of Civil Procedure in 1938, the federal district courts followed the procedural rules of the various states in which they sat. The drafters of the new, unified federal rules must have been either tired after hammering out the dozens of rules regulating the process from pleadings to judgment, or they were overwhelmed at the challenge of unifying the widely disparate state rules on money judgment enforcement. For whatever reason, they left in place the old deference to state procedure for the post-judgment enforcement phase.

Federal Rule of Civil Procedure 69 directs that federal money judgments are to be enforced according to the procedure for both execution and proceedings supplementary to and in aid of execution of the *state* where the federal court is located.[9] Thus, money judgments of the US District Court for the Central District of California are enforced in that court, but according to the enforcement rules of the State of California—with the one major exception that the federal courts cannot commandeer state officials, so the US Marshals are in charge of doing things that the state sheriffs would otherwise do, as discussed in the next chapter.

If the persons or property against which the judgment creditor wishes to pursue an enforcement action are subject only to the jurisdiction of a federal court in a different district, especially a district in a different state, the judgment must be migrated to that other district. For example, if the judgment debtor

9. Federal statutes govern, if one applies, but this is uncommon except in one context: The United States as a judgment creditor (e.g., for judgments related to recovery of student loans and benefit overpayments) has its own exclusive execution statute, the Federal Debt Collection Procedures Act, 28 USC §§3001 *et seq*. This statute is largely consistent with state enforcement laws, though providing various forms of preferential treatment to the US as judgment creditor.

on the judgment from the US District Court for the Central District of California has a large bank account in a bank in New York City, enforcement proceedings against that bank and the account might have to be pursued in New York (given personal jurisdictional limitations).

This can be done relatively quickly and easily, however, by simple *registration* of a federal judgment in the target district. That is, a certified copy of the judgment can be filed in the US District Court for the Southern District of New York, and the "judgment so registered shall have the same effect as a judgment of the district court of the district where registered and may be enforced in like manner."[10] The judgment can now be enforced in the New York federal court, using New York state enforcement rules, by the California judgment creditor.[11] As this example illustrates, given how frequently wealthy individuals' and large companies' assets are located in New York, California, and Illinois, it is often useful for litigators even from outside these states to have some knowledge of the enforcement laws of these three states ... which is one reason why these laws are the primary focus of this book.

State court judgments can migrate to other states, as well, and the process is generally similar. The Full Faith and Credit clause of the US Constitution commands that states give the judgments of sister states the same effect such judgments would have in the state of origin. So no matter how bitter the rivalry between Ohio and Michigan or Wisconsin and Illinois or New York and New Jersey, these states all must recognize each other's courts' judgments as valid and subject to local enforcement. But this command is not self-executing. The states themselves decide what procedure they require for recognition of sister state judgments and the migration of those judgments into a new host state for enforcement using the latter's local rules.

The states are largely consistent in their adoption of the simple procedure under the Uniform Enforcement of Foreign Judgments Act[12] or an equivalent local rule.[13] First, a copy of the original state judgment has to be *authenticated*,

---

10. 28 USC § 1963.

11. A similar local registration process exists for intra-state migration of state court judgments, which usually must be registered in a court and enforced by an official in a county where the relevant property or person is located or domiciled. *See* NY CPLR § 5221; CA CCP §§ 699.510, 708.160; 735 ILCS 5/12-106; *but cf.* Tex. R. Civ. P. 622 ("execution ... shall not be addressed to a particular county, but shall be addressed to any sheriff or constable within the State of Texas"); Fla. Stat. § 56.031 (providing that writs of execution "shall be in full force throughout the state").

12. *See, e.g.*, NY CPLR art. 54.

13. *See, e.g.*, CA CCP §§ 1710.10 to 1710.65 (containing provisions almost identical to the Uniform Enforcement of Foreign Judgments Act, with minor modifications).

which involves having the issuing court's clerk attest to the genuineness of the copy, put a seal on it, and provide a certificate from a judge of that court attesting that the clerk's attestation is in proper form.[14] Next, the judgment creditor must swear or affirm in an affidavit that the judgment has not been stayed, how much of the judgment remains unsatisfied (perhaps among other things, varying by state), and the last known name and address of the judgment debtor. When these two items are properly filed in a court in the target state, that court's clerk either "shall treat the foreign judgment in the same manner as a judgment of [the relevant trial court] of this state" or might enter a judgment of that clerk's own target-state court on the basis of the authenticated sister-state judgment. In either case, persons and property under the jurisdiction of the target-state courts are at the judgment creditors' disposal only 30 days after the judgment creditor mails notice of the filing of the sister-state judgment to the judgment debtor's last known address and files proof of such service.[15]

An important non-uniform quirk appears in the law of New York, which refuses automatic recognition to default or confession judgments.[16] An original lawsuit must be brought on the basis of the sister state judgment, which will likely produce another quick, New York judgment, perhaps again by default or a quick summary judgment (on the basis of *res judicata*, claim preclusion), but a bit more process is required in New York to import judgments on disputes that were not actively litigated.

Finally, though state enforcement procedures apply as noted above in federal court, the judgment creditor might wish to domesticate a federal judgment in state court, so as to take advantage of the greater numbers, enthusiasm, or expertise of state sheriffs, as opposed to US Marshals. Here we begin to encounter significant non-uniformity. In Illinois, filing a certified copy of a judgment of a federal court *located in Illinois* gives rise to automatic recognition with the same effect as an Illinois state court judgment.[17] In New York and Illinois, in-state and out-of-state federal judgments can be domesticated in state court just as a sister-state judgment would be domesticated under the Uniform Enforce-

14. 28 USC § 1738. Alternatively, the target court's local rules might allow for simpler procedures.

15. This restriction does not seem to apply in the Illinois version of the law. 735 ILCS § 5/12-653(b). So much for the "uniform" statute.

16. NY CPLR § 5401.

17. 735 ILCS § 5/12-501. A similar rule in New York, California, and Illinois allows for filing of a transcript, abstract, or certified copy of a judgment of *any* federal court, which has the same effect as filing a state court judgment; i.e., creation of a judgment lien on real (and in California, personal) property, as discussed in the next chapter. NY CPLR § 5018(b); CA CCP § 697.060; 735 ILCS § 5/12-502; *see also* 28 USC § 1963.

ment of Foreign Judgments Act, described above.[18] In California, however, federal judgments—from California or elsewhere—are not entitled to registration and full recognition like sister-state judgments are. Instead, an ordinary action must be instituted in California state court on the federal judgment, which will in all likelihood result in immediate summary judgment on preclusion grounds and the entry of a full-fledged California state judgment. Here again, the end result is likely the same, but a bit more procedure is required. This is why procedural specialists get paid the big bucks!

B. Immigration of Non-US Judgments and Arbitral Awards

Yet more procedure is required for the importation of judgments of arbitral and non-US tribunals. Monetary awards of non-US courts are not entitled to full faith and credit and are generally importable only on the traditional basis of cooperation among nations, or *comity* (from Latin *comitas*, "courtesy").[19] The courtesy to be afforded by *state* courts to non-US money judgments is subject to another uniform statute with a title similar to the one relating to sister-state judgments, the Uniform Foreign-Country Money Judgments Recognition Act.[20] Its requirements are more rigorous, however, and the states have much more leeway in this context to refuse to grant comity to the judgments of foreign sovereigns whose courts are regarded, rightly or wrongly, as less reliable in terms of due process. Nonetheless, New York's highest court has announced that "New York has traditionally been a generous forum in which to enforce judgments for money damages rendered by foreign courts."[21]

A full-fledged civil action, complete with service of process, must be initiated on the basis of the non-US money judgment, which again might lead to an immediate motion for summary judgment (perhaps even in lieu of a complaint). But the plaintiff-judgment creditor must prove that the judgment is final, conclusive, and enforceable in its home country (and is not for taxes or

18. The uniform act includes orders of courts of the United States, as well as orders of sister-state courts entitled to full faith and credit. NY CPLR §5401.

19. The classic case on comity in the federal courts is *Hilton v. Guyot*, 159 US 113 (1895).

20. *See, e.g.*, NY CPLR art. 53. The title of the original uniform act was confusingly similar to that of the sister-state judgment recognition act, so a 2005 revision, adopted by both New York and California, added "-Country" after "Foreign" in the title to avoid this confusion.

21. CIBC Melon Trust Co. v. Mora Hotel Corp., 100 N.Y.2d 215, 221 (2003).

fines, which are not entitled to recognition due to the virtually universal so-called *revenue rule*, incorporated into the uniform statute). The defendant-judgment debtor can defeat recognition by establishing one of a number of grounds, such as entry of the original judgment despite lack of notice or personal jurisdiction, as defined in the statute, or that the non-US judgment "is repugnant to the public policy of this state" or "was rendered under a system which does not provide for impartial tribunals or procedures compatible with ... due process."[22] This topic is explored at greater length in a class on Conflicts of Laws, which is highly recommended.

Increasingly, monetary awards result not from litigation, but from arbitration, domestic or international. If coercive enforcement of an arbitral award is necessary, such awards must migrate to the courts and become money judgments. An arbitral award is imported into the judicial enforcement system by virtue of a process called *confirmation* by a state or federal court, following the procedure laid out in the Federal Arbitration Act or a similar state statute.

The original award and a copy of the arbitration agreement are filed with a petition (or motion) for confirmation in the relevant court having jurisdiction over the parties and the subject matter of the dispute. This petition must be served on the adverse party and should, and perhaps must, be filed within one year of entry of a domestic arbitral award. Petitions for confirmation of international arbitral awards must be filed within three years of the award.[23] The grounds for refusing confirmation are quite narrow, and the judgment confirming an arbitral award is enforceable just like any other judgment.[24]

C. Timing ... and the Time Value of Money

In addition to locating the geographical limits of enforcement, the money judgment creditor must be sure to locate and act within the time limits for enforcement within any given state. Enforcement efforts are often constrained

22. NY CPLR §5304. In a recent case, a guarantor of bank debt, adjudicated liable on this debt in a Moscow court, asserted this defense, charging the Russian process as being unfair and repugnant to the public policy of New York. This attempt to impugn the Russian judicial process was predictably unsuccessful. *See* VTB Bank v. Mavlyanov, No. 650245/2017 (N.Y. Sup. Ct., Jan. 30, 2018).

23. 9 USC §§9, 207.

24. 9 USC §§10–11, 13, 207–208.

by both a beginning and an end date, though the latter in particular often depends upon the creditor's timely action in extending a judgment's life.

The location of the start line is delineated by two sometimes surprising rules. First, unlike in much of the rest of the world, an appeal in the US does not automatically prevent enforcement of a money judgment. Registration of a federal money judgment in another federal district, as discussed above, does require that the judgment have "become final by appeal or expiration of the time for appeal,"[25] but outside this context, an appeal generally will not delay enforcement of a money judgment.

Anticipating a successful appeal and hoping to avoid the inconvenience of interim enforcement measures, a judgment debtor may file a motion and bond for an order of *supersedeas* (Latin, "you shall desist"; that is, desist enforcing the judgment). Federal Rule of Civil Procedure 62(d) obliquely refers to this process, but the specific requirements of this bond are generally found in local court rules, likely requiring a bond from an approved surety company in an amount sufficient to cover the amount of the judgment plus costs and some period of post-judgment interest (as discussed below). State rules are usually similar.[26] In California, for instance, the supersedeas bond must be for 150% of the judgment amount.[27] The bond may be subject to an upper limit, as in Texas, where supersedeas bonds are capped at the lesser of $50 million or 50% of the judgment debtor's net worth.[28]

Second, in part to allow the judgment debtor time to obtain a supersedeas bond and order, federal law imposes a waiting period on the commencement of enforcement proceedings after entry of a *federal* judgment. A specific federal rule—which thus governs over the ordinarily applicable state enforcement rules—proscribes enforcement proceedings for federal judgments until 30 days after entry of the judgment.[29] Texas imposes a similar 30-day waiting period,

25. 28 USC § 1963 (allowing the issuing court to override this delay by order for "good cause shown").

26. Statutes often allow an automatic stay for certain types of appeals or appellants (e.g., by state agencies) without the posting of a bond. *See, e.g.*, Fed. R. Civ. P. 62(e); La. Rev. Stat. § 13:4581. If such a non-bonded stay would be available to the appellant under state law, the appellant can take advantage of that stay in federal court via Fed. R. Civ. P. 62(f) if a judgment in that state is a lien on real property, which is quite common, as discussed in the next chapter.

27. CA CCP § 917.1(b).

28. TX Civ. Prac. & Rem. Code § 52.006(b); 735 ILCS 5/2-1306.

29. Fed. R. Civ. P. 62(a) (increased from 14 days, effective Dec. 1, 2018). The requirements and timing of "entry" of a federal judgment are described in Fed. R. Civ. P. 58(b)–(c).

as does California for small claims judgments.[30] Other state money judgments, in contrast, are ordinarily immediately enforceable upon entry unless the court grants a brief discretionary stay. Indeed, New York allows eager judgment creditors to apply for an order authorizing immediate examination and restraint of the debtor even before judgment is officially entered.[31]

The more important boundary is the finish line. At common law, there was no finish line, only a temporary roadblock. As mentioned in the previous chapter, after a year and a day, old English judgments became *dormant* and could no longer be enforced unless they were revived in a simple, special action called *scire facias*, but this process of dormancy and renewal could be repeated indefinitely.

Modern state laws take widely varying perspectives on the lifecycles of judgments. Texas continues to use the old English terminology and allow for immortal judgments, but for unwary creditors, judgments can expire. A Texas judgment becomes dormant ten years after it is rendered or after any execution writ is issued on that judgment, whichever is later, but a dormant judgment can be revived by a simple action of *scire facias* brought no later than two years after the judgment becomes dormant. The verb might as well be "must" be revived, however, as if ten years passes with no further execution writs, and another two years passes without a *scire facias* action, the judgment expires.[32] California has a similar system of dormancy and revival. California judgments become dormant after ten years, but they can be renewed for another ten years by filing a simple application with the rendering court (and mailing notice of renewal to the judgment debtor). Further renewal applications must be filed no earlier than five years—and no later than ten years—after the date the earlier renewal application was filed.[33] If ten years passes with no further renewal application, the judgment expires.

In Illinois, in contrast, judgments become dormant seven years after entry and can be revived for another seven years by petition (*scire facias* having been expressly abolished), but repeated revival is effective only for a maximum total life of 27 years (final renewal in year 20), after which Illinois judgments expire.[34] New York also imposes an outside limit of 20 years, but the clock is reset any time the judgment debtor acknowledges the debt in a signed writing or "makes

---

30. Tex. R. Civ. P. 627; *see also* Tex. R. Civ. P. 628 (allowing for earlier execution upon affidavit that debtor about to remove, transfer, or secrete property); CA CCP § 116.810.

31. NY CPLR § 5229.

32. TX Civ. Prac. & Rem. Code §§ 31.006, 34.001.

33. CA CCP §§ 683.010–683.200.

34. 735 ILCS 5/12-108, 5/2-1602(a) (allowing ongoing wage garnishment to continue post-expiration).

a payment" on the judgment, which is oddly defined to include any instance of the judgment creditor's acquiring property through the enforcement process.[35] And then there's Florida. Until the late 1960s, Florida law was clearly parallel to Illinois law in that judgments became dormant after three years but could be renewed up to a total of 20 years, after which they conclusively expired. This clarity was repealed along with the governing statute in 1967, leaving potentially expensive confusion as to the outer limits of enforcement of a Florida money judgment today.[36]

On a final time-related note, the law recognizes that time is money, so judgment creditors are compensated for the time spent looking for assets. Generally from the day on which a money judgment is entered, interest begins accruing on the unpaid judgment amount at a rate established by statute. New York and Illinois, for example, provide for flat 9% per annum simple interest, while California sweetens the offer to 10%.[37] Federal judgments accrue interest at a floating rate determined by reference to the "weekly average 1-year constant maturity Treasury yield" published by the Federal Reserve, and Florida judgments similarly bear adjustable interest (adjusted annually) at 4% above the one-year average discount rate of the New York Fed.[38] Complicated enough for you? Luckily the courts usually figure and publish these rates. To make things more complex, a judgment on a contract that itself calls for interest might accrue post-judgment interest at the contract rate, at least if it does not exceed a statutory ceiling.[39]

The more pressing question is whether the costs and fees, especially attorney's fees, incurred pursuing enforcement can be added to the judgment (or taxed to the judgment debtor, perhaps on noticed motion). California law is clear and sensible: costs (such as filing and application charges and other government fees) are recoverable from the judgment debtor and added to the judgment periodically, while the judgment creditor's attorney's fees for ongoing enforcement activity follow the American Rule; that is, creditors bear their

35. NY CPLR § 211(b). *See also* NY CPLR §§ 5014, 5203 (requiring renewal of the judgment by action 10 years after docketing of the judgment roll to renew the real estate lien effect of docketing of the original judgment roll).

36. Richard H.W. Maloy & Cynthia Lynne, "The Life of a Money Judgment in Florida Is Limited—For Only Some Purposes," *Fla. Bar J.*, July-Aug. 2005, at 20.

37. NY CPLR § 5004; 735 ILCS 5/2-1303; CA CCP § 685.010.

38. 28 USC § 1961; Fla. Stat. § 55.03.

39. *See, e.g.*, Fla. Stat. § 55.03(1) (deferring to the contract rate); TX Fin. Code § 304.002 (limiting post-judgment interest on judgments on interest-bearing contracts to a maximum of 18%).

own fees (reducing the net recovery on the judgment) unless the judgment includes a fee award (e.g., as a result of a contract).[40] The rule is likely the same in other states, which often mention "costs" to be charged to the judgment debtor, explicitly or implicitly excluding attorney's fees.[41] Texas, in contrast, defines "costs" for this purpose as including attorney's fees![42] Attorney-fee shifting rules could have a substantial impact on the judgment creditor's calculus as to the degree and nature of attorney action to authorize in pursuit of a money judgment recovery.

D. Discovery

Once a location is chosen, the judgment domesticated in that location's governing court, and the timing issues sorted out, at last the real process of finding and seizing value from the judgment debtor can begin. The finding part of that process is arguably the most important and the most challenging.[43] Just as effective discovery is a crucial aspect of effective pre-judgment litigation, effective discovery is also essential to effective post-judgment enforcement process. Before a judgment is obtained, formal discovery is generally unavailable to help plaintiffs plan for the collection of any eventual money judgment, since the ability of a defendant to fulfill a judgment is not "relevant to any party's claim or defense."[44] Liability insurance might have to be disclosed,[45] but beyond that, the nature and location of the defendant's property interests are beyond the scope of pre-judgment discovery.

1. Informal

Nonetheless, any competent plaintiff's lawyer will have evaluated the defendant's ability to pay a money judgment using whatever informal means

40. CA CCP § 685.040 (seeming to exclude recovery of attorney's fees provided by statute).

41. 735 ILCS 5/2-1402(h); *cf.* Fed. R. Civ. P. 54(d); 28 USC § 1920.

42. TX Civ. Prac. & Rem. Code § 31.002(e); *see also id.* § 38.001–006; Fla. Stat. § 56.29(8) (providing for reasonable attorney's fees for supplementary proceedings to be taxed to debtor).

43. Commentators have long recognized that discovery of the judgment debtor's assets "comprises by far the most important area of judgment collection." Isadore H. Cohen, "Collection of Money Judgments in New York: Supplementary Proceedings," 35 *Colum. L. Rev.* 1007, 1007 (1935).

44. Fed. R. Civ. P. 26(b).

45. Fed. R. Civ. P. 26(a)(1)(A)(iv).

might be at hand, to avoid wasting the lawyer's time and the client's money obtaining a practically unenforceable judgment. The plaintiff may have done business with the defendant for some time, and the documents and other disclosures related to those business dealings may reveal important information about, for example, the location of the defendant's bank account (e.g., checks and other forms of payment from the defendant), the location of business premises and other types of property the defendant might own in a variety of locations (e.g., addresses on letterhead, references in advertising or other media, and certainly in loan applications), and third parties who might be obligated to the defendant on business-related accounts (e.g., references to major customers in advertising or sales pitches). Public databases and records relating to land registration and personal property security interests, in particular, can reveal early on whether the defendant owns valuable real or personal (movable or immovable) property and whether that property is subject to major encumbrances (e.g., mortgages) that would stand in the way of a judgment creditor's seizing value (a battle discussed in chapter 5 below).

Both before and especially after the defendant becomes a money judgment debtor, a creditor might have fee-based access to an especially valuable source of information: credit reports detailing the debtor's other obligations and the banks and other businesses with whom the debtor has done business—and who might know something more about the debtor's property. Business entity credit reports can be purchased from companies like Dunn & Bradstreet, Paynet, Experian Business, and Equifax Small Business.

Individuals' financial information is protected, however, by the federal Fair Credit Reporting Act, which restricts the acceptable purposes for accessing consumer credit reports with agencies like TransUnion, Experian, and Equifax. Among the permissible purposes for accessing an individual's credit report, the statute lists "review or collection of an account of the consumer."[46] For years, debt collectors took this as authorization to access an individual debtor's credit report to assist with, for example, collection of a judgment. But a great controversy flared up around this topic in 2009 in light of other language, including a new definition, in the complex statute. The "review or collection of an account" language follows an introductory phrase, "in connection with a *credit transaction* involving the consumer."[47] The Ninth Circuit in a hotly contested ruling held that the definition of "credit transaction" (inserted in March 2004) requires the consumer to have been involved at least initially in a credit

46. 15 USC § 1681b(a)(3)(A).
47. *Id.* (emphasis added).

transaction—a loan or other voluntary credit extension—which in that case was held *not* to include the collection of towing and impound fees relating to the debtor's illegally parked car.[48]

Crucially in the Ninth Circuit's view, the debtor's obligation for these fees was not yet reduced to judgment; this was a pre-judgment debt collection case. Earlier Ninth Circuit precedent had explicitly allowed *judgment* creditors to access individual credit reports, even in judgments not pertaining to voluntary "credit transactions."[49] But this ruling predated a 2004 revision to the statute, now defining "credit" as "the right granted by a creditor to a debtor to defer payment of debt."[50] It is now not at all clear that a money judgment not related to an initial, voluntary "credit transaction" provides the basis for permissible access to an individual's credit report, and several courts have reasoned that it does not.[51]

2. Formal

Which makes formal discovery all the more important. Fortunately for judgment creditors, modern procedure offers a very effective array of coercive discovery options not only pre-judgment, but also (especially) post-judgment. Often, the same discovery devices that were available pre-judgment remain available post-judgment, with a scope of permissible inquiry now delimited by relevancy not to the parties' claims and defenses, but to the judgment creditor's wide-ranging search for value to collect the judgment. The federal rules make this explicit, as do the rules of, for example, California, Texas, and Florida.[52] In contrast to the ordinary limitations on pre-judgment discovery, these limits might be imposed or relaxed in the context of post-judgment dis-

---

48. Pintos v. Pacific Creditors Ass'n, 605 F.3d 665 (9th Cir. 2010). This is the final in a series of three opinions, however, in which the Ninth Circuit flip-flopped on this confusing issue, with the other opinions reported at 504 F.3d 792 and 565 F.3d 1106.

49. Hasbun v. County of Los Angeles, 323 F.3d 801 (9th Cir. 2003) (child support collection judgment).

50. 15 USC §1691a(d), incorporated by reference into §1681a(r)(5).

51. Miller v. Trans Union LLC, 2007 WL 641559 (N.D. Ill. Feb. 28, 2007) (child support); Rodriguez v. Experian Info. Solutions, Inc., 2016 WL 3976564 (W.D. Wash. July 25, 2016) (parking violations); Baron v. Mark A. Kirkorsky, P.C., 2017 WL 4573614 (D. Ariz. Oct. 13, 2017) (court costs imposed by judgment after dismissed case); *cf.* Middlebrooks v. Sacor Fin., Inc., 322 F.Supp.3d 1300 (N.D. Ga. 2018) (allowing credit card judgment buyer to access consumer credit report to aid collection).

52. Fed. R. Civ. P. 69(a)(2); CA CCP §§708.020, 708.030; Tex. R. Civ. P. 621a; Fla. Stat. §56.30(1).

covery. In California, for example, pre-judgment interrogatories are limited to 35 in *total*, but post-judgment interrogatories are limited to 35 per *set*, with another (perhaps verbatim repeat) set of interrogatories allowed every 120 days.[53]

New York, in contrast, slightly alters its post-judgment discovery regime by funneling all requests through three kinds of subpoenas (deposition or *ad testificandum*, production or *duces tecum*, and information).[54] These subpoenas achieve the same objectives as ordinary discovery, but now the debtor receives these subpoenas (rather than simple discovery demands) just like third parties. Abuse of scattershot subpoenas directed to masses of third parties is averted by requiring the judgment creditor or attorney to certify her or his reasonable belief, after reasonable inquiry, that the recipient possesses information about the judgment debtor's assets.[55] Mass-mailed subpoenas to every bank in New York City or every current or former customer, friend, or relative of the debtor are no longer allowed. Similar to California, New York limits these inquiries directed to the judgment debtor to once per year.[56]

Another approach is to make specific (sometimes exclusive) provision for a probing, in-person examination concerning assets, often followed by an opportunity to obtain a court order directing the debtor or third party to turn over the value thus discovered. Illinois takes this approach, imposing direct court control over an expansive post-judgment discovery process. Virtually the entire post-judgment process in Illinois is concentrated in supplementary proceedings initiated by one flexible device, the *citation to discover assets*, issued (signed and sealed) by the clerk of the circuit court (and a hearing date assigned) upon presentment by the judgment creditor or attorney. As we will see in the next chapter, this citation achieves far more than simple discovery, but that is its starting point.

Served upon the judgment debtor[57] or any other person, a citation hales the respondent to a citation hearing before the court (or more likely an interrogation in a jury room or the hallway outside the courtroom) for a sworn personal and documentary examination concerning the debtor's assets and income. An individual judgment debtor must receive an income and asset form, directing the debtor to reveal in writing the nature and location of all manner

53. CA CCP §§708.020; 2030.030.

54. NY CPLR §5223.

55. NY CPLR §5224.

56. NY CPLR §5224(f) (allowing more frequent repeated inquiry with leave of court).

57. Individual (natural person) debtor-respondents must receive personal or abode service. 735 ILCS 5/2-1402(b-1); Ill. Sup. Ct. R. 105(b).

of income and assets and directing him or her to bring documents evidencing employment and assets, including two years of tax returns (and other documents can be requested).[58] Third-party citations also request specific information regarding property and debts owed to the judgment debtor, and the debtor must be notified of such citations. Such a proceeding can be pursued only once per respondent, however, without special leave of court.[59]

California has a somewhat similar procedure, though it is an adjunct to the other, ordinary discovery devices, and it is somewhat limited with respect to third parties. The judgment creditor can apply to the court for an order for appearance and examination (OEX/ORAP) of any person, including the judgment debtor.[60] Once issued by the court, this order must be personally served on the respondent in the same manner as a summons, the debtor also must receive mailed notice, and the examination occurs in court (or before a court-appointed referee). Again to avert harassment and abuse, an order directed to a third party (or to the debtor within 120 days of a previous examination) is available only if the creditor submits an affidavit attesting that the third party has possession or control of property in which the debtor has an interest. A similar examination is an addition to the Florida rules of discovery, though the formalities for service and the details of the notice and procedure are less complex than in California and Illinois.[61]

While imprisonment for debt has been abolished in the US, one still hears stories about debtors being imprisoned in connection with civil money judgment enforcement proceedings. The explanation usually lies in this discovery stage.[62] Failure to comply with subpoenas, citations, and examination orders is punishable as contempt, eventually leading to the issuance of a bench warrant and the arrest of the contemptuously absent party. While many courts are reticent to engage their contempt authority in this context, some are not. Debtors

---

58. The officially approved forms are available online at http://www.illinoiscourts.gov/forms/approved/small_claims/post_judgment_collection.asp.

59. Ill. Sup. Ct. R. 277(a).

60. CA CCP §§708.110–708.170.

61. Fla. Stat. §56.30.

62. Sometimes incarceration is the result of a contempt ruling for the debtor's failure to comply with an order to turn over property, discussed at the conclusion of the next chapter. Some debtors can be quite obstinate. One debtor (a Pennsylvania lawyer) insisted that he could not produce $2.5 million awarded to his ex-wife in a divorce, because he had lost the money in bad investments. The judge disbelieved him, held him in contempt, and kept him in jail for 14 years (!) until another court held that further imprisonment was clearly ineffective to coerce the debtor into paying. Debra Cassens Weiss, "Lawyer Freed After Spending 14 Years in Jail on Contempt Charge," *ABA J.*, Jul. 13, 2009.

who are confused or afraid of the orders to appear at these examinations risk incarceration if they fail to respond properly, and the Illinois and California rules require explicit, large-type warnings on the citation or order warning respondents that failure to appear may lead to arrest and imprisonment for contempt. These warnings should be taken seriously. Debtors will have an opportunity to assert legal protections for their property at these examinations (as discussed below in chapter 4), they should be sure to do so, and if the debtor is found to have no assets not legally protected, the Illinois rules call for the immediate dismissal of the enforcement proceedings.[63]

Note that the scope of questioning here need not be limited to *current* assets and documents directly relevant to them. Questioning can and should extend also to *past* assets recently alienated, such as large payments made, as well as to value the judgment debtor expects to obtain in the *future*. Both of these kinds of value—past and future—might be recovered in enforcement proceedings, as discussed in the next chapter. Discovery should also encompass documents likely to make indirect reference to assets, such as home and business loan applications and tax returns, though the latter are often protected by privilege or other state law restrictions on access.[64] While the judgment debtor is likely *not* to answer these questions truthfully and fully, despite all the warnings about perjury, third-party testimony and documentary trails might lead more reliably to asset value that the debtor recently had or soon will have.

The judgment creditor can then seize this value using the techniques described in the next chapter. The scope and operation of the procedures for seizing value thus must be understood and borne in mind in formulating effective discovery questions. This requires a very different mindset, legal analysis, and skill set from the ones used to obtain the money judgment originally. For this reason, some lawyers specialize in enforcing money judgments on behalf of other lawyers' clients. This is an interesting practice area that few law students know exists but that can make for a very engaging and gratifying career.[65] Read on!

---

63. 735 ILCS 5/2-1402(d-5).

64. *See, e.g.*, Sav-On Drugs, Inc. v. Superior Court, 123 Cal. Rptr. 283, 286-87 (Cal. 1975, en banc).

65. An entertaining illustration of this appears in a guidebook that reads like a memoir by California debt collection lawyer David Cook, in which he revels in the drama of his pursuit of collection of the wrongful death money judgment obtained against O.J. Simpson by the family of Ron Goldman. David J. Cook, *The Debt Collector's Handbook: Collecting Debts, Finding Assets, Enforcing Judgments, and Beating Your Creditors* (ABA 2014).

Chapter 3

Grab

Once value has been located, it must be obtained and realized for the benefit of the judgment creditor. A multiplicity of strategic choices is available to judgment creditors here, differing based on the nature and location of the property, as well as the jurisdiction whose rules will govern seizure and turnover of the value of that property. Here, careful attention must be paid to the nature of the debtor's interest in any given type of property value and the appropriate procedural mechanism for reaching value in that form. Creditors also must be mindful of the protections afforded to the debtor's and other competing creditors' interests in certain kinds of property, to avoid wasting time pursing value that is not really available, but those topics will be discussed in later chapters.

A. Restrain

The power to grab the judgment debtor's property can be complicated or vitiated by a last-minute transfer of that property to a new owner or custodian who is more difficult to reach by ordinary process. Recognizing this problem, the law of most states provides for a means of restraining both debtors and third parties from alienating the debtor's property before a judgment creditor can take the steps to formally grab it.

This step is optimally taken at the same time as—if not before—the previous, discovery step. Once the debtor gets wind of a creditor's attempts to discover valuable property, evasive maneuvers are likely the next thought. If the judgment debtor is resisting turning over value to pay a money judgment, chances are the debtor is considering how to conceal or alienate any sources of such value to avoid having to give them up in the future. Third parties in possession of value likely do not want to get involved, preferring to pass the hot potato back to the debtor or on to a different third party.

In ancient times, when things like oxen and plows were the principal sources of such value, and most commerce was local, creditors could be less concerned about debtors' hiding these bulky things or alienating them to a distant new owner. Today, these are very real concerns, as bank account balances and investment securities can be transferred across the world instantaneously with a simple electronic command, and even more substantial assets can be sold and transported to distant buyers quite quickly and efficiently. Preventing both debtors and third-party custodians of debtors' property from conveying such value beyond the reach of a judgment creditor is a crucial prerequisite to effective money judgment enforcement.

New York law separates discovery from restraint. Good judgment creditor lawyers put them together.[66] Along with or perhaps even in advance of one of the discovery subpoenas mentioned above, the judgment creditor's lawyer can issue over her own signature, and serve like a summons or by registered or certified mail, a *restraining notice* on any person other than the debtor's employer.[67] This notice is essentially an injunction, enforceable by contempt,[68] enjoining the recipient from transferring (or allowing to be transferred) any property in which the judgment debtor has a non-exempt interest.

Directed to the debtor, such a notice is effective until the judgment is satisfied. Directed to a third party, however, a restraining notice is subject to a couple of sensitive timing issues. The notice is effective only if, at the time of receipt of service of the notice, the third party actually is in "possession or custody" of property in which the third party should know the debtor has an interest (including a debt owed by the third party to the debtor). If the recipient has no such property or debt at that time, the notice is ineffective and has no restraining power, then or in the future. Leave of court is required to serve more than one restraining notice on any given person, so creditors need to be fairly sure the recipient has seizable property before serving such a notice.

---

66. We might say "back together," since before the advent of the CPLR in the 1960s, a New York subpoena alone carried its own restraining effect. *See* David Gray Carlson, "Critique of Money Judgment Part Three: Restraining Orders," 77 *Albany L. Rev.* 1493, 1496-97 (2013).

67. NY CPLR §5222 (also requiring specific mailed restraint/exemption notice to the debtor). The effect of service of an income execution on the debtor's employer has a somewhat similar restraining effect, as discussed below, as failure to turn over the required amounts exposes the employer to a lawsuit for those amounts by the judgment creditor. NY CPLR §5231(f).

68. NY CPLR §5251.

If, however, at the time of service the recipient has any property in which the debtor has an interest, the restraining order enjoins transfer not only of that property, but any property in which the debtor has an interest that comes into the third party's possession within a year after service of the notice. If the third party has a lot of this kind of property or debt (for example, the debtor's bank), the third party can set aside value equal to twice the amount due on the judgment, which must be mentioned in the notice, and can transact normally with respect to other value belonging to the debtor.

Illinois reunites the discovery and restraint aspects of enforcement process and does away with the "currently in possession" nicety. A citation to discover assets served upon any person "may" (and invariably does) prohibit the recipient from making or allowing any transfer of property (or payment of a debt), then or thereafter within that person's control, in which the debtor has a non-exempt interest.[69] This restraint continues for any property coming into the person's possession until termination of the citation proceeding, which occurs automatically six months after the respondent's "first personal appearance" in response to the citation, though citation proceedings are often "continued" to prevent this lapse.[70] Here again, withholding double the amount due on the judgment satisfies this directive and allows free transfer and transaction in surplus value. Illinois law adds to the New York warning that violation of this restraining order can be punished as contempt, inviting the court instead to simply enter judgment against a third party for the amount due on the judgment or the value of any property improperly transferred, whichever is less.

California takes a less direct and probably less effective approach. Service of an order of examination on the debtor gives rise to a lien (a concept discussed below in chapter 5) on all of the debtor's personal property for a period of one year from the date of the order. If the order is served on a third party, a similar lien is created, but only on property or debts described in the required application for the order of examination.[71] Only this property is potentially subject to prior restraint, and the duty is enforceable only if the creditor ultimately initiates a creditor's suit against the third party seeking recovery of that property or debt. If the third party transferred away this property

69. 735 ILCS 5/2-1402(f).

70. Ill. Sup. Ct. R. 277(f). For respondents who simply answer the questions in the citation in writing and return it to the creditor's lawyer without a hearing, the date of these answers is generally construed to be the "first personal appearance" of the respondent. The court can extend the six-month termination date "as justice may require."

71. Compare CA CCP §§708.110(d) and 708.120(c).

subject to any lien or paid the identified debt, the court in such a creditor's suit "shall" enter a judgment against the third party for the lesser of the value of the debtor's interest in the property or the amount due on the judgment.[72] The only context in which a creditor could apply for a special prior restraining order (other than an ordinary TRO) is one of these creditor's suits, by which point the restraining order seems fairly superfluous.[73]

B. Record

One of the first simple steps a judgment creditor can take to prepare to seize value requires little effort for a potentially great return. Even before launching into formal discovery, the creditor can likely develop a sense of whether the debtor has an interest in any real property and, if so, where. Land is tied down and subject to public records, so this pursuit is more manageable than the hunt for personalty. No more detail than the county in which such property might be located is necessary. With that one piece of information, a judgment creditor can grab at least the debtor's attention (and willingness to pay voluntarily) if not some serious value in the debtor's interest in realty.[74]

In contrast to old English process, modern US judgment enforcement procedure generally makes realty interests an easy target. In most states, filing a certified copy (or sometimes transcript, abstract, memorandum, or other embodiment) of a money judgment in the county real property records (wherever a mortgage would be filed) creates a property interest called a *lien*—or more specifically, a judgment lien—as discussed in greater detail below in chapter 5.[75] New York does not require this recording step; rather, *docketing* of the judgment by the supreme court clerk of any county prevents effective transfer of the debtor's interest in any realty in that county to any third party.[76] Docketing occurs automatically in the court in which a supreme court or county court judgment is entered after the judgment creditor files the judgment

72. CA CCP §708.280(d).

73. CA CCP §708.240. The very next article creates a similar lien on the property that is the subject of the suit, so an application for a restraining order seems to accomplish quite little in any event.

74. Note that a short-term leasehold interest is likely a personal right, not realty, so pursuit of the debtor's right to occupy realty for a time-limited term might be a challenge. *See* CA CCP §695.035.

75. CA CCP §§697.310, 697.340; 735 ILCS 5/12-101.

76. NY CPLR §5203.

roll.[77] Other counties' supreme court clerks will do so upon the creditor's filing a transcript of the docket of a judgment of any other county (or a transcript of a New York federal judgment).[78] This judgment lien encumbers (affects) any interest of the judgment debtor in realty within the county of recording, both at that point and acquired in the future during the life of the lien.[79]

At the very least, this lien will *cloud title* to the debtor's realty and inhibit the debtor from transferring or borrowing money against that property without paying the judgment. In some states, the lien is enforceable just like a mortgage, leading to sale of the property. In Illinois, the judgment lien is explicitly equated with a mortgage and can be enforced by the same foreclosure procedure applicable to a contractual mortgage.[80] In New York, the effect of the judgment lien is described simply as preventing a transfer of the realty from being effective against the judgment creditor. The idea in both New York and California is that the lien simply preserves the priority of the creditor's interest in the property—much like a restraining notice—until the debtor sells the property or the creditor proceeds to the next step of having the property seized and sold by levy.

In California, Florida, and a few other states, a judgment lien can be created in personal property, as well, simply by filing a notice in the UCC records or similar database.[81] The range of personal property subject to this judgment lien is limited in California to business-related items, such as accounts, inventory, and equipment; not so in Florida.[82] Here again, this lien has the limited purpose of preserving the creditor's priority spot in line for distribution of the value of this property after it is seized and sold later through ordinary process, the topic of the next section.

---

77. These are unique New York concepts described in NY CPLR §§5017–5018; *see also* David Gray Carlson, "Critique of Money Judgment Part One: Liens on New York Real Property," 82 *St. John's L. Rev.* 1291, 1296-97 (2008).

78. NY CPLR §5203. A notation of any and all out-of-county docketings should appear on the docket in the original issuing county. *See also* Iowa Code §624.23(1) (creating judgment lien on realty in issuing court's county upon entry in docket and lien index, or after filing in other clerks' offices).

79. The life of the lien is generally coterminous with the life of the judgment, but both might have to be separately revived, preserved, or re-memorialized to avoid lapse.

80. Louisiana law is even more explicit about this, as the recorded judgment creates what is called a *judicial mortgage*. La. Civ. Code art. 3300.

81. CA CCP §§697.530–697.570 (notice of judgment lien on personal property, filed in UCC records); Fla. Stat. §§55.201–55.209 (judgment lien certificate, filed in Department of State database).

82. CA CCP §697.530 (also including farm products, chattel paper, and documents of title); Fla. Stat. §55.202 (all personal property except fixtures, money, negotiable instruments, and mortgages).

C. Levy

Which finally brings us back to the traditional method of enforcing money judgments. Imported from England, the writ of *fieri facias*—now almost universally called by its simpler English name, *writ of execution*, or simply, *execution*—remains the central enforcement tool in most of the US today,[83] though usually having shaken off many of the limitations of old English usage. Its cumbersome process and significant expense have led many states to implement more direct and effective procedures for commanding the transfer of identified value from debtors and third parties to judgment creditors, as discussed at the end of this section.

1. Execution

The judgment creditor remains responsible for obtaining or issuing a writ of execution and delivering it to a public officer, usually the county sheriff, for *levy*, the process of the officer's "raising" a sum of money from property found, seized, and sold. A New York execution, for example, can be issued over the simple signature of the judgment creditor's attorney as officer of the court to any county sheriff or New York City marshal (or US Marshal for federal courts).[84] California and most other states require the attorney to apply (in writing or orally) for a signature and perhaps a seal from the clerk of court to formalize the issuance of a writ of execution. Here again, the judgment creditor must deliver the writ to the executing officer for levy, again most likely a county sheriff but perhaps a registered process server or other official identified in the law.[85]

The officer will most likely demand upfront payment of a fee for performing this levy, probably between $50–$100, in addition to a deposit to cover any anticipated expenses of inventorying, transporting, and storing property recovered.[86] Moreover, the writ does not simply say "go find stuff"; the creditor

83. Illinois law contains vestiges of this earlier process, though a certified copy of the judgment is substituted for the execution writ as the document delivered to the public officer to initiate a levy. 735 ILCS 5/12-110, 12-111. Since the more comprehensive process of turnover orders in the citation to discover assets proceeding was significantly enhanced in 2008, levy has been less commonly used.

84. NY CPLR § 5230.

85. CA CCP §§ 699.080, 699.510; Tex. R. Civ. P. 627.

86. *See, e.g.*, CA CCP § 685.100 (deposit to cover 15 days of storage, with periodic further demands if storage time exceeds 15 days, and allowing officer to release levied property if fee not paid). Later, some officers collect a percentage commission from any recovery from an execution, for example the 5% so-called *poundage* for sheriffs and marshals in New York. NY CPLR § 8012.

bears the further responsibility of precisely locating and identifying property subject to levy. Texas law, for example, is particularly straightforward in clarifying that the officer receiving a writ of execution "does not have a duty to search for property belonging to the judgment debtor."[87] California law expressly prompts the judgment creditor's lawyer to "give the levying officer instructions in writing," including among other things, "[a]n adequate description of any property to be levied upon" including the precise address of any person to be served.[88] This directive is implicit in every state. The value and necessity of detailed asset discovery in advance should now be clear.

From the date of issuance of the writ (sometimes referred to as the *teste* of a writ), the sheriff is given a period of time during which to accomplish the levy. These periods vary greatly; e.g., 30, 60, or 90 days in Texas (at the judgment creditor's option),[89] 60 days subject to unlimited 60-day extensions by the creditor's attorney in New York,[90] 180 days in California,[91] and perpetual until the judgment is satisfied in Florida.[92] After the expiration of this period, the writ loses its force, but if the officer has levied during this period, the seizure, collection, or sale process usually may continue to completion. At some point, either upon expiration of the un-levied writ or perhaps completion of an execution sale, the officer must make a *return* (either of the writ itself or of a report) to the court with a notation of the sheriff's fees and an explanation of action taken and value seized. Additional writs may be issued until the period of enforceability of the judgment expires.

Unlike in old English execution practice, the writ extends to realty as well as most intangible property, especially debts owed to the judgment debtor, and the property need not be in the debtor's possession. A New York execution directs the officer to "satisfy the judgment ... out of the real and personal property of the judgment debtor ... and the debts due to him or her."[93] It used to be common for rules to require levy against personal property before realty, or vice versa, but such rules are rare exceptions today.[94] The levy process on land

87. Tex. Civ. Prac. & Rem. Code §34.071.

88. CA CCP §§684.130, 687.010.

89. Tex. R. Civ. P. 621, 629.

90. NY CPLR §5230(c).

91. CA CCP §699.530.

92. Fla. Stat. §56.021.

93. NY CPLR §5230. Forms of executions are available on the New York State Bar Association's website at https://www.nysba.org/ENFdown/ (see ENF014, 015, and 016).

94. *But see* 735 ILCS 5/12-113 (still requiring "personal property shall be last taken" after realty!) *and cf.* Tex. R. Civ. P. 637 (requiring levying officer to ask debtor to choose which property to be levied).

is quite similar to the judgment recording process mentioned above, except now, the officer generally records a copy of the execution writ (and perhaps notice of levy or other document) in the county land records.[95]

In the simple case of tangible personal property in the debtor's possession and "capable of delivery" (as the New York law puts it), levy simply involves the officer taking the property into custody, either physically or constructively.[96] In New York, the sheriff can do so regardless of the location of the property, while California explicitly allows sheriffs to avoid potentially explosive confrontations likely in this context. If the property is "located in a private place of the judgment debtor," a California officer need only demand that the debtor turn it over. If the debtor refuses, the officer "shall make no further effort to obtain custody of the property." The judgment creditor is then relegated to applying to the court for an order directing the officer to break open the debtor's "private place" and retrieve the property, or an order directing the debtor to turn over the property to the officer.[97]

2. Garnishment

The law historically has struggled with the special concerns raised by property of the debtor in the possession of a third party. This challenge has been especially acute in the context of property that has no physical embodiment, intangibles and especially debts owed by a third party to the debtor. The third party possessor/obligor has not been before the court and may have claims to the property or defenses to payment of the debt that have not been properly adjudicated. Seizing such property or debts from third parties is often still referred to by its historical name, *garnishment*, a statutory creation designed to fill a major gap in the common law.

The traditional garnishment procedure persists in some places, such as Texas.[98] As in Texas, garnishment is sometimes still subject to the traditional restriction of failure or impossibility of enforcement by the "normal" method

---

95. NY CPLR §§5235–5236 (sheriff's filing of notice of levy with county clerk after ten-year period of judgment lien expires, but allowing sale based on either judgment or execution lien after execution delivered to officer); CA CCP §§700.015–700.020; 735 ILCS 5/12-152, 12-153; *cf.* Tex. R. Civ. P. 639 (simply requiring the sheriff to "indorse such levy on the writ").

96. *See* NY CPLR §5232(b); CA CCP §§687.030, 700.030 (defining "take into custody" broadly to include "obtaining possession or control").

97. CA CCP §§699.030–699.040.

98. The largely abandoned Illinois garnishment procedure is similar. 735 ILCS 5/12-701 *et seq.*

of execution against property in the debtor's possession. For example, to obtain a writ of garnishment from a Texas court clerk, the judgment creditor must file an application supported by an affidavit swearing that the judgment debtor "does not possess property in Texas subject to execution sufficient to satisfy the judgment."[99] Once issued, the garnishment writ is again delivered to the sheriff for service on the third party (with notice to the debtor), but it does not command or empower the sheriff to collect the property or debt; instead, the third party (now a *garnishee*) is commanded to answer in writing (and theoretically to appear in court to testify) as to property or debts the judgment creditor might seize. If the garnishee fails to answer, a default judgment will enter for the entire amount of the original judgment![100] If any property or debts are revealed, a judgment for the creditor is entered against the garnishee for the amount of the debt (or commanding turnover of property to the sheriff for execution).[101] Though this seems to put the creditor right back where he or she started with an unenforced judgment, the garnishee is more likely to simply pay or turn over the value that belongs to the judgment debtor.

New York and California, in contrast, take a much more direct and efficient approach by simply extending execution to these third-party property rights and debts, leaving the resolution of any disputes to later litigation.[102] Levy simply requires the officer to make personal service of the writ of execution on the person in control of the property or who owes the debt (and provide notice to the debtor). Receipt of service of the writ of execution automatically obliges the third party (still often called the garnishee) to surrender the debtor's property, or pay the debt owed to the debtor, to the officer; otherwise, the third party might be punished for contempt and/or be held liable for the value of that property to the judgment creditor.[103]

---

99. Tex. Civ. P. & Rem. Code §63.001(2)(3); Tex. R. Civ. P. 658, 659.

100. Tex. R. Civ. P. 659-678.

101. If any adverse claims to the property are advanced, the process historically had to be dismissed and another suit filed to quiet these claims, though modern procedures often provide for the adjudication of adverse claims within the garnishment proceeding.

102. The garnishee or third-party claimant bears the burden of initiating a proceeding to determine adverse claims, if any, in New York. NY CPLR §5239 (requiring a special proceeding). In California, in contrast, the burden seems to be on the judgment creditor to challenge the garnishee's "good cause" for failing to turn over value, or to initiate a creditor's suit to seize such value. CA CCP §§701.020, 708.210–708.290.

103. NY CPLR §§5232(a); CA CCP §§700.040, 701.010–701.020, 701.050 (clarifying that paying debtor after service of writ no longer discharges debt); Tex. Civ. P. & Rem. Code §63.003 (same).

California preserves an important discovery aspect of the traditional garnishment proceeding by requiring the garnishee to deliver to the sheriff within 10 days after service a *garnishee's memorandum*. This memo catalogues the property of and debts owed to the judgment debtor in the garnishee's possession or control *not* delivered to the sheriff right away, including future debts not yet due, and the sheriff is supposed to mail a copy of this information gold mine to the judgment creditor.[104]

Though levy ordinarily only affects property held at the moment of service of the writ, a third-party levy might extend for some period of time after service. In California, if a debt levied upon becomes due over time, amounts due from the garnishee to the judgment debtor on *that debt* (though not other future debts) for two years after *issuance* (not service) of the execution writ remain subject to the levy.[105] The timing in New York is a bit quirky. A New York execution on property "not capable of delivery" is subject to varying timing requirements similar to those for a restraining order, discussed in the preceding chapter; that is, if the garnishee has no property of or debt due the judgment debtor at the time of service, the levy is ineffective. But if the garnishee does have such property or owe such a debt, the levy encompasses and imposes a restraining order on all property of or debts due to the judgment debtor coming into the garnishee's possession or control until all such property or debts are turned over to the levying officer (or for 90 days after service of the execution, after which the levy becomes void).[106] Further executions can be served on that same garnishee, however, whenever the creditor is willing to pay the officer's levy fees.

What are we talking about here? All of this ambiguous technical talk of debts due and property not capable of delivery most often implicates four kinds of value sources that are among the first and best targets of enforcement efforts: (1) the debtor's bank account, (2) the debtor's right to receive payment of wages, salaries, commissions, or other payment for personal services, (3) the debtor's rights in a business, and (4) intangibles, such as the debtor's causes of action against third parties, as well as licenses and rights related to intellectual property. These standout categories of property warrant a bit more concentrated attention.

---

104. CA CCP §701.030.

105. CA CCP §§697.710, 701.010(b)(2)(B).

106. NY CPLR §5231(a).

a. Bank Accounts

Perhaps the lowest-hanging fruits and probably the most common targets of judgment enforcement efforts are bank accounts. If the judgment debtor is foolish or unfortunate enough to have left a chunk of money sitting in a bank account, what better source of value to seize by way of simple third-party levy/garnishment against the bank? Actually, to be technical, a bank account is not a box of money, and it does not represent tangible property of the debtor; rather, a bank account is a debt owed to the judgment debtor. Banks do not hold very much money on deposit; instead, they make their profits in part by promising depositors to return an equivalent amount of value later, lending it in the meantime to borrowers and charging fees and interest. A bank account is the depositor's intangible right to enforce the bank's promise to return the equivalent value for any money placed on deposit (therefore, a bank account is also called more accurately a *deposit account*).

Bank accounts are classic "debts due" to the judgment debtor, and so they are subject to either levy or garnishment, as described above. A salient question here, though, is the reach of a levy or garnishment against a bank with many branches in many counties, states, or even countries. For example, JPMorgan Chase Bank has around 5100 branches in 26 states, over 300 branches in Chicago alone, and it is headquartered in New York City. Must the sheriff be directed to serve a writ of execution or garnishment on the precise branch where the judgment debtor opened an account, or on any branch, or on the headquarters, and if the debtor has many such accounts at branches of the same bank around the state or country, can they be levied or garnished all at once or only individually, one at a time?

The current rules on this issue sometimes persist from an era when bank account records were kept with quill pens, ink wells, and paper ledgers in one physical location of a given bank. These rules makes little sense today, when electronic records link together a bank's nationwide if not worldwide network of accounts, accessible by any bank branch location, and debtors can transfer money around the globe with the click of a mouse or tap on a smartphone screen. The execution writ must issue from a court with personal jurisdiction over the bank, an issue substantially complicated by the US Supreme Court's latest personal jurisdiction pronouncements,[107] but for national banks with headquarters and control centers in New York, could a judgment entered or

107. Daimler AG v. Bauman, 134 S. Ct. 746 (2014); Bristol-Meyers Squibb Co. v. Superior Court, 137 S. Ct. 1773 (2017).

domesticated in New York be the gateway to seizing nationwide branch bank account riches?

Perhaps not. New York's infamous "separate entity" rule is a common law doctrine that regards each branch of a bank as an entity entirely separate and apart from any other branch of that same bank. Adherence to this doctrine requires service of a writ on (issued from a court with personal jurisdiction over) the specific branch(es) maintaining the debtor's deposits. The doctrine was affirmed by New York's highest court, the Court of Appeals, in 2014 in invalidating process on a New York branch seeking to restrain assets in a non-US branch of that same bank.[108] Reflecting on developments in electronic bookkeeping, among other things, the dissent in that case observed that the "outmoded rule" had been developed "nearly a century ago based on a rationale that has no application to these modern times."[109]

The separate entity rule begs for exceptions in the digital age and has been rejected in at least some states. Lower courts in New York have fashioned exceptions over the years to make service on the bank's main office effective for other branches within the state,[110] and reports confirm that US banks consistently comply with enforcement orders served on their New York City headquarters (or even on other New York branches) to restrain and turn over value from deposits in branches located in other states.[111] Illinois rejected the separate entity rule over a century ago based on the advanced technological development of its day, as the *telegraph* (!) enabled any branch to inform another branch, even in another country, of the bank's receipt of and obligation to comply with a garnishment order.[112]

California has taken a much more sensible, modern approach. The default rule remains that levy on a bank account requires service on the "officer, manager, or other person in charge of the office or branch ... where the financial

108. Motorola Credit Corp. v. Standard Chartered Bank, 24 N.Y.3d 149 (NY 2014) (explicitly noting that the court was not deciding on application of the separate entity rule to US branches).

109. *Id.* at 163 (Abdus-Salaam, J., dissenting).

110. Digitrex, Inc. v. Johnson, 491 F. Supp. 66 (S.D.N.Y. 1980); *In re* Nat'l Union Fire Ins. Co. of Pittsburgh v. Advanced Empl. Concepts, Inc., 703 N.Y.S.2d 3 (N.Y. App. Div. 1st Dept. 2000); *see also* Carlson, above note 66, at 1594–95.

111. For a sobering account of aggressive judgment enforcement in New York against debtors and bank accounts outside the state, see the exposé on the merchant cash advance industry and confessions of judgment, Zachary R. Mider & Zeke Faux, "Sign Here to Lose Everything," *Bloomberg Businessweek*, Nov. 26, 2018, http://www.bloomberg.com/graphics/2018-confessions-of-judgment/.

112. Bank of Montreal v. Clark, 108 Ill. App. 163 (1st Dist. 1903).

institution maintains the account."[113] But notwithstanding this anachronistic default position, California invites financial institutions to designate a central location for service in the state.[114] A bank operating more than nine branches in the state, like Chase Bank, *must* designate one or more central location(s) for service in California; otherwise, *every* branch is a central location for effective service on all other branches simultaneously. At least within the enormous territory of California, one branch is often effectively all branches, at least for levies against accounts at large banks.

b. Wages, Salaries, Commissions

A second piece of low-hanging fruit, and many individuals' primary source of value, is the periodic debt due from an employer to pay wages, salary, commissions, or other compensation for personal services. This is also a "debt owed" to the judgment debtor, but at any given moment of garnishment, the debt is both future and recurring, neither of which was dealt with well by classical garnishment proceedings.

To overcome these complications, and in light of the central importance of this value to most working judgment debtors, most states developed special *wage garnishment* procedures, with special sensitivity for the protection of the debtor and employer. Note that the protections here apply only to debts for personal service compensation owed to natural persons, so debts owed to business entities on any sort of contract (and debts owed on non-personal service contracts even to natural persons) should be subject to ordinary levy/garnishment, with no special restrictions. Where wage garnishment is permitted, the process is slightly more complicated than for ordinary garnishment of a present debt owed to the judgment debtor. On the other hand, a wage garnishment order generally gives access to future such debts and is usually not a one-shot deal, remaining in effect in most states until the judgment is fully paid or the debtor's employment is terminated.[115]

---

113. CA CCP §684.110(b); *see also* CA CCP §700.140. This location might have no connection whatsoever to the debtor's current physical location, but it is presumably indicated by the ABA routing number associated with the account, the first, 9-digit series of numbers on the bottom of a personal check, the second series on a business check.

114. CA CCP §§684.110(c)–684.115. Such a designation allows individual branches to ignore service made on them, rather than at the central location, publicized on the Dept. of Business Oversight's website, http://www.dbo.ca.gov/Laws_&_Regs/legislation/service_of_legal_process/default.asp.

115. NY CPLR §5231(f); CA CCP §706.022; 735 ILCS 5/12-808(b).

A handful of states flatly prohibit wage garnishment, at least in most cases. In all cases not involving child support, Texas law emphatically prohibits the enforcement of any order that requires an employer to turn over wages to satisfy a judgment.[116] Pennsylvania also generally prohibits wage garnishment, but this prohibition is subject to a unique exception that appears to reflect the power of a particular industry lobby. The "wages, salaries and commissions of individuals" are not subject to execution or any other collection process in Pennsylvania "except upon an action or proceeding ... [f]or amounts awarded to a judgment creditor-landlord arising out of a residential lease."[117] Apartment building owners must make very substantial donations to the reelection campaigns of members of the Pennsylvania General Assembly!

New York has a unique face-saving procedure for wage garnishment involving two steps. An *income execution* must identify not only the debtor's employer to be served, but also the amount and frequency of payment and the amount to be garnished from each payment (subject to the limitations discussed below)—again, requiring careful planning and discovery in advance. It also must contain a notice to the judgment debtor to begin paying those installments (the amounts that would otherwise be garnished from each paycheck) to the sheriff immediately. The sheriff must first serve the income execution on the debtor, to allow the debtor to begin paying privately and avoid the embarrassment of what comes next. If the debtor fails to pay the garnishment installments "voluntarily" within 20 days, the sheriff serves the income execution on the employer. The employer must then deduct the stated installments from each future payment to the judgment debtor and instead pay those amounts over to the sheriff, who is required "from time to time and at least once every ninety days" to pay the garnished amounts over to the judgment creditor—less the sheriff's 5% fee and expenses, of course. If the employer fails to do this, the judgment creditor can collect the "accrued installments" only by initiating a special proceeding against the employer.[118]

In California, wage garnishment requires a slightly simpler two-step process. It begins, somewhat like in New York, with the issuance of an ordinary writ

116. Tex. Civ. Prac. & Rem. Code §§31.0025, 63.004. Indeed, this prohibition is written into the Texas Constitution, Article XVI, sec. 28 ("No current wages for personal service shall ever be subject to garnishment" except to enforce family support orders).

117. 42 Pa. Cons. Stat. §8127(a) (also allowing limited garnishment of wages for collection of support, restitution and fines, and state education assistance support).

118. NY CPLR §5231. A special proceeding is a summary lawsuit with a similar filing fee to an ordinary plenary proceeding, but with vastly simplified rules and accelerated timeframes (offering relief within as little as 8 days), somewhat similar to motions practice.

of execution (in the county where the employer is located), followed by an application for an *earnings withholding order* submitted to the levying officer. The required forms for the order and several other documents, including *employer's instructions*, are prescribed by the Judicial Council, available online.[119] The officer issues and serves the order on the "managing agent or person in charge" at the debtor's place of employment—without warning the debtor in advance. The employer is then required, as in New York, to withhold the portion of the debtor's wages not protected as discussed below and turn them over at least monthly to the levying officer, minus an inconvenience/processing fee of $1.50 per payment. The officer must then pay over the amounts to the judgment creditor, also at least once every 30 days. Only when the judgment is satisfied must the creditor notify the officer, who must terminate the order and notify the employer.[120] Just like in New York, if the employer fails to deduct and pay over any amount due, the creditor can sue to recover that amount from the employer.[121]

The ordinary process in Illinois is quite different, avoiding the sheriff entirely, and is discussed in the next section, on turnover orders. But the result is similar, with one notable distinction. If the employer fails to pay over any amount that was supposed to be deducted from the debtor-employee's wages, the court can enter a judgment against the employer not just for the missed payment, but for the entire balance due on the judgment, unless the employer can convince the judge that this draconian remedy should not be imposed.[122] A couple of less notable exceptions allow the employer to keep an inconvenience fee of 2% of any installment deduction, which is likely be larger than the $1.50 allowed by statute in California, and the creditor's attorney is required to account and report to the employer and the debtor quarterly as to the amount remaining unpaid; otherwise, the employer can hold the wage deductions and not pay them over until this certification is received.[123]

The older *wage deduction order* process in Illinois likely reflects other states' current approaches. It begins somewhat like an ordinary garnishment process, with the creditor submitting an application for a wage deduction order to the clerk of court with an affidavit attesting that an employer is believed to be in-

---

119. http://www.courts.ca.gov/forms.htm?filter=WG.

120. CA CCP §§706.025–706.027, 706.034; *see also* CA CCP §706.028 (providing for a separate "final earnings withholding order for costs and interest" to clean up any accrued cost/interest extras).

121. CA CCP 706.154.

122. 735 ILCS 5/12-808(f).

123. 735 ILCS 5/12-808.5, 12-818(c).

debted to the judgment debtor. Before this, though, the creditor must have mailed to the debtor a wage deduction notice, setting out the amount of the judgment and the amounts to be deducted from future paychecks (as determined by identified federal and state limitations, discussed below) and inviting the debtor to request a hearing if the deduction amounts exceed the applicable limits. Otherwise, the process unfolded like an ordinary garnishment proceeding, with the clerk immediately issuing a summons to the employer, who is required to answer written interrogatories concerning the debtor's wages. The employer has to begin immediately withholding the amounts to be garnished, to be paid over monthly to the creditor (notably, *not* the sheriff) once the court issues a wage deduction order on the basis of the employer's interrogatory answers.[124]

The principal difference between "ordinary" and "wage" garnishment is a set of restrictions on the amount of the debt—wages—that can be seized. A set of especially complicated provisions designed to protect particularly low-income debtors applies in fairly few cases (suing a minimum-wage defendant is a fool's errand) and the complex procedures for debtors to assert their rights in such cases are seldom invoked—because a combination of terror, denial, ignorance, complexity, and inconvenience effectively prevents these protections from being applied.[125] Consequently, these complex restrictions apply to only a relatively small subset of judgment debtors and will be mentioned here only in a footnote.[126] The discussion here will focus on debtors with moderate to higher incomes shielded by more straightforward garnishment limitations.

---

124. 735 ILCS 5/12-801 to 12-818.

125. You might read the following statutes in the appendices and consider whether a low-income debtor, probably without a college degree, would be able to read and understand their directions to invoke their protections: CA CCP § 706.105; NY CPLR §§ 5222-a, 5231(g).

126. For low-income debtors, federal and state laws protect 100% of wages up to a poverty-line level measured by a multiple of the federal or state minimum-wage; e.g., 30 or 40 times the minimum weekly wage multiplied by the number of weeks in a pay period. 15 USC § 1673(a)(2) (30 times); CA CCP § 706.050 (40 times). So if the current minimum wage is $7.25 per hour, no matter how many hours the debtor works, the first $217.50 per week ($435 for the standard every-two-weeks minimum-wage pay period) is 100% exempt under federal law, and possibly more under the state equivalent. Every dollar the debtor takes home beyond this is fully garnishable (in California, only 50%) until the garnishment amount reaches 25% of the debtor's disposable income, when the restriction discussed in the text kicks in. That is, the amount available to a garnishing creditor is the *lesser* of 100% (50% in California) of the excess of the debtor's take-home pay over 30 or 40 times the minimum wage, or 25% of her disposable income. Clear? (That's meant to be a joke …)

The amount of wages that can be expropriated from a working debtor is limited by both federal and state law. Whichever limitation allows the judgment creditor to collect *less* governs. In other words, whichever limitation provides greater protection to the debtor's wages is the one that controls how much of these wages are available to a garnishing creditor.

Federal law establishes the floor of wage protection. It restricts creditors' access to no more than 25% of the debtor's "disposable income," meaning the debtor's total (gross) salary minus any deductions "required by law to be withheld."[127] This might or might not be the equivalent of "take-home" pay, since if the debtor's paycheck is reduced for voluntary transportation or other deductions not required by law to be withheld, "disposable" income may be a bit higher.

For example, if the debtor earns $60,000 per year (gross), her paycheck will be not $5000 per month, but perhaps only about 70% of that ($3500) after required withholding for federal and state income taxes, Social Security and Medicare (often called FICA), and perhaps mandated retirement and healthcare premiums. If that employee also allows her employer to withhold $500 for "tax-sheltered" transportation expenses (the jury is still out on whether *voluntary* retirement savings are "required to be withheld"), the debtor's $3000 take-home pay after *all* deductions is not the basis for the federal 25% garnishment ceiling; rather, it is the $3500 net after *required* deductions. Note that the maximum garnishment amount of $875 (25% of $3500) is deducted from the employee's *take-home* paycheck, leaving the employee in our example with a reduced take-home pay of $2625 ($3500—$875)—the employee has had to pay tax and FICA on the amount garnished.

About half the states build up from this floor, providing greater protection. New York and Illinois are among them. Creditors can garnish only 15% of a debtor's gross wages in Illinois, 10% in New York.[128] So in the example above, a creditor could garnish a monthly maximum of only $750 per paycheck (15% of the gross, pre-deductions total of $5000) in Illinois and only $500 in New York, since both amounts are less than the federal maximum of $875. California takes a unique detour, allowing for greater protection only in cases where the debtor successfully navigates an adversary procedure for proving that the federal limits allow for garnishment beyond an amount "necessary for the support of the judgment debtor or ... family supported in whole or part by the judgment debtor."[129]

127. 15 USC §§1672(b), 1673(a).

128. 735 ILCS 5/12-803; NY CPLR §5231(b).

129. CA CCP §§706.051, 706.105. These complex procedures are laid out in Appendix C. Warning! Attempting to read these abstruse sections may lead to blindness or insanity.

c. Business Property, Receivership, and Investment Securities

Who is the debtor, and what is his/her/its relationship with the target property? These are questions that sometimes confound attorneys in cases involving business assets and business entities. Properly addressing this issue requires an understanding of the basics of business associations and asset-liability segregation, as would be covered in a class on Corporations or Business Organizations. Human beings can engage in business in a variety of ways that have very different implications for liability, property protection, and therefore judgment enforcement.

First, the simplest case. If one human being owns "the business" and has not organized a legal entity (e.g., corporation) to hold the business's assets and bear its liabilities, that human being (called a *natural* person, as opposed to a business entity, called an artificial, legal, or *juridical* person) is the business. Even if the owner, called a *sole proprietor*, conducts this unincorporated business under a separate trade name (often indicated by the prefix *d/b/a* or "doing business as"), the sole proprietor owns all the business's assets and bears liability for its debts. A judgment against such a business should be against the owner personally (if it is not, you have a problem), and all of the owner's property not otherwise protected (discussed in the next chapter) is liable to judgment enforcement proceedings.

If the business is operated through a limited liability legal entity (e.g., corporation, limited liability company, or limited liability partnership), and the judgment is against *that entity*, the situation is similar, with one major exception.[130] All of the property of the entity is liable to judgment enforcement, but even if the entity is owned by one natural person (human being), that natural person's assets are generally not subject to enforcement of the judgment. This is the primary purpose of an individual's organizing a legal entity through which to operate a business—shielding the individual's personal assets from the business's liabilities. As discussed below in section E.2. of this chapter, in some circumstances, the shield separating the individual's assets from the business's debts can be "pierced," making the individual's assets liable to enforcement of a judgment against the entity, but this requires a lawsuit to overcome a powerful presumption that the entity's debts are its and its alone, enforceable only against the entity's property.

---

130. If the entity is a partnership with no "L" in its name limiting its partners' liability—a so-called *general* partnership—all of the partners are secondarily liable for the partnership's debts, though such entities are fairly rare in the modern US.

If the business entity or sole proprietor is the judgment debtor, all of such a business's assets might be seized by the sheriff in an ordinary levy. The sheriff's fees for carting away, storing, and selling all of this tangible property, however, are likely to be substantial, and much of the value of the business as an ongoing, revenue producing entity will be lost. California law offers a better way to levy against such a business, by installing a *keeper*. While a so-called *till tap* involves the sheriff's simply seizing whatever cash is in the business cash register at the time of service of the writ of execution, a *keeper* seizes future receipts. The sheriff will, for a substantial fee, have someone sit in and conduct the business for a period of time, demand cash payment for all sales, and deliver that cash to the judgment creditor.[131]

An even more aggressive—and usually vastly more expensive—way to achieve a similar result is to petition the court to appoint a *receiver* to take charge of operating the business and turn over receipts to the creditor. Most states have a receivership statute,[132] but courts are reluctant to appoint a receiver in any but truly exceptional cases. Moreover, a receiver will charge substantial fees for undertaking this substantial responsibility, and the procedure for having one appointed is complex enough to be beyond the scope of this overview book. For a complicated and very valuable business or piece of property, though, a receiver can be a very effective way of extracting value without destroying the business.[133]

If, on the other hand, the judgment debtor is the owner of a business *entity* (as opposed to a sole proprietor), the separation of assets and liabilities goes the other way, too. That is, a corporation's or LLC's assets are not liable to enforcement of a judgment against its owner (shareholder or member). Nonetheless, the value of an investor's interest in a business entity can be seized to enforce a judgment against that investor, though careful thought should be given to the value of that interest before pursuing this path.[134]

The value is most clear and accessible when the judgment debtor is a shareholder of a publicly traded company, with share values quoted on an exchange

131. CA CCP §700.070(a).

132. NY CPLR §5228; CA CCP §708.610; Tex. Civ. P. & Rem. Code §§31.002, 64.001–64.108; Fla. Stat. §56.10 (specifically relating to receivership for corporate debtor's business).

133. Receivers are reportedly a more common and cost-effective remedy in Texas, even mentioned explicitly as an alternative to bank account garnishment. Tex. Civ. Prac. & Rem. Code §31.002(b)(3), (g), 31.010.

134. The odd concept of "reverse veil piercing" will not be discussed here, but beware that this corollary of traditional veil piercing, discussed in section E.2. of this chapter, might in rare cases allow access to the assets of a business entity to satisfy a judgment against an owner.

like the New York Stock Exchange or NASDAQ. These shares are quite liquid; that is, they are essentially a money substitute, because they can be readily sold on the exchange for cash. An investment in either the equity (stock) or debt (bonds, debentures, notes) of such a company is called an *investment security*, and the means of enforcing a judgment against such securities are outlined in section 8-112 (formerly 8-317) of the Uniform Commercial Code, as adopted by every state.

Levy on investment securities differs among three different ways in which an investment might be held. First, if the security is represented by an individual paper certificate (e.g., 100 shares of ABC, Inc.), levy on a *certificated security* requires actual seizure of the certificate (e.g., from the debtor or investment broker). In today's electronic world, especially for public companies, it is actually more common for a security to be represented either actually or practically in electronic form only. Thus, second, an *uncertificated security*, for which no certificate has been issued (e.g., investments in a mutual fund, and increasingly in operating companies, as well) can be seized only by levy/garnishment on the issuing company at its chief executive office in the US, according to the rules in that state (probably delivery of the execution or garnishment writ to the company's registered agent for service of process). Third and finally, a *security entitlement* is a fractional interest in a jumbo certificate, issued and subdivided electronically as part of the so-called *indirect holding system* of securities broker-dealers like Charles Schwab, Fidelity, TD Ameritrade, E*Trade, and Scottrade. Levy/garnishment on such an investment is accomplished by service on the broker (the *securities intermediary*) with whom the securities account is maintained (reintroducing the "separate entity" complication for branches of large, nationwide brokerages, though the precise location of the debtor's securities account branch is likely easier to establish).

The value of a judgment debtor's interest in a business entity is less clear when the entity is a non-public, closely held company or partnership. Little or no market exists for most such investments, so their value inheres in the governance power they confer over the entity and its assets. If the judgment debtor is a sole or supermajority owner, business law likely empowers the holder of such a stake to control or even liquidate the entity and its assets. If the judgment debtor is a minority owner, however, obtaining this stake might simply be buying a liability, with little power to control the entity, and potential exposure to tax liability for a pass-through entity's undistributed income. It might be difficult to find a willing buyer at a sheriff's sale of such a stake, and the judgment creditor is well-advised to think twice about bidding. The details of this analysis are beyond the scope of this book, but one final note is pertinent here: A special enforcement mechanism called a *charging order* allows a judgment creditor to seize the debtor's *financial* interest in a partnership or LLC.[135] Because this confers no governance or management authority, a charging order may do the judgment creditor little good unless the entity's governing documents require distribution of value to the partners/members.

d. Intangibles

Investments in business entities are intangible, rights-type property, thus beyond the reach of old English law and equity proceedings and even many classical US garnishment proceedings. Today, in most states, execution or garnishment easily reaches investment property thanks to the Uniform Commercial Code provision just described. With respect to other kinds of intangibles, some antiquated state laws still preserve old restrictions on access to contingent, future, and intangible property.[136] In many if not most states, however, such value is seizable, if not by execution or garnishment, then likely by one of the other enforcement mechanisms discussed here (receivership or, as discussed below, assignment/turnover order).

For example, the debtor's causes of action against third-party defendants for money damages for violation of contract, tort, civil rights, and other laws are potential debts owed to the debtor, albeit unmatured and unliquidated rights to payment. Judgment creditors might have access to the potential money recovery in a lawsuit via execution/garnishment, and perhaps control over the lawsuit itself, depending upon how state law defines "debts due."[137] It might be quite difficult to pursue such a cause of action without the debtor's cooperation, but one clever use of this enforcement power involves acquiring a cause of action not to pursue it, but to kill it. If the debtor happens to have a cause of action against the judgment creditor, the creditor might have this cause of action seized and sold, the only likely buyer would be the creditor, who could then dismiss the action, avoiding liability to the debtor in exchange for very little consideration.[138]

---

135. *See, e.g.*, CA CCP §708.310; 805 ILCS 180/30-20.

136. *See, e.g.*, Juliet M. Moringiello, "False Categories in Commercial Law: The (Ir)relevance of (In)tangibility," 35 *Fl. St. U. L. Rev.* 119 (contrasting capacious Illinois law with narrow Massachusetts and Virginia laws, which allow garnishment only of the "goods, effects, or credits" of and "liability owed to" the debtor, respectively).

137. NY CPLR §5201(a); CA CCP §§708.210–708.290; *cf.* CA CCP §§695.030 (subjecting only pending actions to enforcement), 699.720 (making such actions not subject to execution), 700.190 (levy on a final money judgment by filing writ and notice of levy with clerk of court that issued final judgment), 704.140–704.150 (making personal injury claims exempt).

138. *See, e.g.*, Arellano v. Clark County Collection Service LLC, 2017 WL 5505117 (9th Cir. 2018) (rejecting such a gambit by a debt collector facing a cause of action for violation

A more likely valuable intangible target is rights associated with intellectual property; e.g., patents and copyrights. In light of the requirements in (preemptive) federal law for transferring intellectual property rights,[139] the most likely, and perhaps only, effective state law method of seizing IP rights is not execution, but a *turnover order* (discussed immediately below) directing the debtor to convey those rights in writing to a receiver or execution sale buyer.[140] The patent or copyright holder's rights to receive royalties, however, might be distinguished and pursued separately by simple execution/garnishment on any current debt owed for these payments, and the right to receive future payments might be forcibly assigned in advance via a special *assignment order*.[141] If the debtor is not the owner of the IP, but just a licensee of those rights, enforcement is likely futile against these rights, as most valuable IP licenses contain a clause allowing the licensor to cancel the license upon voluntary or involuntary assignment, and even if the license does not say this, federal law might still allow the licensor to refuse a re-assignment.[142]

3. Turnover

There must be an easier way, you say. Levies and garnishments and receivers, oh my! Lawmakers in Illinois and an increasing number of other states have agreed, developing streamlined procedures in recent years to remove much of the complexity—and often the sheriff—from the process.

Recall that, in Illinois, post-judgment discovery is initiated by the judgment creditor's service of a simple *citation to discover assets* on either the debtor or any third party, including a bank or employer. Once the debtor or third party has responded to this citation, either in writing or by appearing and testifying at a citation hearing, if that process reveals property or debts subject to enforce-

---

of the Fair Debt Collection Practices Act!); Criswell v. Ginsberg & Foreman, 843 S.W.2d 304 (Tex. Ct. App. 1992) (creditor's acquisition with intent to dismiss debtor's cause of action violated open courts doctrine).

139. *See* Ager v. Murray, 105 US 126 (1881) (reasoning patents and copyrights assignable only by a writing executed by rights holder, so simple execution could not transfer, but acknowledging that court could order rights holder or trustee on his behalf to execute such a written assignment).

140. CA CCP §§708.620, 708.630 (also requiring receiver for debtor's interest in alcoholic beverage license); David J. Cook, "Post-Judgment Remedies in Reaching Patents, Copyrights and Trademarks in the Enforcement of A Money Judgment," 9 *NW J. Tech. & Intellectual Prop.* 128 (2010).

141. CA CCP §708.510 (specifically mentioning royalties and payments on patents and copyrights).

142. Non-assignable rights are not subject to enforcement at all. *See, e.g.*, CA CCP §695.030(a).

ment, the judgment creditor's attorney simply requests that the court issue an order "compelling the application of [precisely identified] non-exempt assets or income discovered toward the payment of the amount due under the judgment."[143] *Et voilà!* This can often be done by walking back into the courtroom and requesting the order on the spot. Judges are accustomed to these requests, Cook County has judges dedicated to just such procedures, and such orders are routinely entered against debtors and third parties, including banks and employers, producing swift and effective judgment enforcement and ensuring close court scrutiny of enforcement actions (and minimizing abuse) in most cases.

Such a turnover order can accomplish essentially everything that any other enforcement device could accomplish, as part of one concentrated procedure. The debtor can be compelled to relinquish any property, including "choses in action," for sale by the sheriff or other agent (see the section immediately below), or to pay directly to the judgment creditor installments of income (so long as the payments do not exceed the applicable state and federal wage garnishment limits discussed above) and even to execute documents to convey title to land or other property or assign (or resign) rights in tangible and intangible property (including memberships in clubs or exchanges, such as the Chicago Mercantile Exchange[144]). Third parties can be similarly compelled (e.g., banks and employers directed to turn over money directly to the judgment creditor). With the citation to discover assets procedure, Illinois has transitioned from a multi-stage enforcement process run by sheriffs to a single-stage procedure directly supervised and controlled by the courts and their much more direct power to resolve disputes and punish for contempt.

New York and California have statutes offering similar turnover procedures, though they are slightly more cumbersome, less expansive, and seem to be used less frequently than the Illinois citation process.[145] In New York, a creditor can upon noticed motion request a turnover order directing the debtor to relinquish to the sheriff personal property in his or her "possession or custody" or to relinquish money or make installment payments directly to the judgment creditor, and a simple special proceeding can be initiated to obtain such an

143. 735 ILCS 5/2/1402(a), (c).

144. *Cf.* Haig, above note 2, at 28 (suggesting garnishment under New York law might reach the debtor's right to occupy a seat on the New York Stock Exchange).

145. Texas provides for turnover orders, as well, only expressly directed at the judgment debtor (though appellate courts disagree on whether such orders can be directed at third parties). Tex. Civ. Prac. & Rem. Code §§31.002(b)(1), 31.010 (referring to turnover order directed to a financial institution). Florida's supplementary proceedings seem to be limited to discovery of property "to be levied upon." Fla. Stat. §56.29(6). No turnover order possibility is mentioned.

order against a third party.[146] California also provides for examination hearings and turnover orders somewhat like in Illinois, though like New York's procedure, limited to personal property and requiring a noticed motion and hearing for orders directing the judgment creditor to assign future rights to payment. Moreover, unpaid wages remain subject exclusively to the separate "earnings withholding order" process.[147]

Local legal culture does not seem to have embraced the turnover order as broadly in New York and California, perhaps because turnover hearings are slower than sheriff's process (in states that do not require multi-stage garnishment procedures), because judges are hesitant to enter "extraordinary" turnover orders, or because such lawyer-driven proceedings are more expensive than simple service of executions and collection via the sheriff (again, where garnishment summons is not otherwise required). The resistance to concentrating all possibilities in one proceeding (like the Illinois citation process) seems to have distracted attention from the newer, turnover order possibility in cases not involving debtors' hiding assets or keeping them offshore (outside the US) where ordinary execution cannot reach them. This last circumstance, however, is a perfect context for the use of turnover orders as a last resort when all other enforcement measures have failed.

D. Monetize

The Achilles heel of the execution/turnover process is the means by which the debtor's property is ultimately transformed into money. If the levy itself produces a sum of money, such as by garnishment of a debt/wages, the sheriff can simply turn that money over to the judgment creditor, though minus a transaction cost that is arguably unnecessary. For liquid assets, the turnover-order process avoids this sheriff transaction cost by allowing transfer directly from employer or other third party to judgment creditor.

But if the levied property is land or illiquid property, real or personal, tangible or intangible, it has to be monetized, and enforcement laws generally provide little flexibility in the liquidation process.[148] The property must be

---

146. NY CPLR §§5225–5227 (seemingly allowing court to require payment of more than 10% income).

147. CA CCP §§699.040, 708.205, 708.510, 706.020–706.021.

148. Compare the flexibility in the foreclosure process in Article 9 of the UCC, which allows a secured creditor who has repossessed collateral to "sell, lease, license, or otherwise dispose of any or all of the collateral in its present condition or following any commercially reasonable preparation or processing," so long as the disposition is "commercially reasonable." UCC §9-610(a)-(b).

sold, most likely by the sheriff at a public auction, literally or figuratively on the courthouse steps.[149] Even a turnover order ordinarily will direct turnover of illiquid property to the sheriff for liquidation at public auction.[150]

Despite elaborate rules requiring the sheriff to provide broad and repeated notice to the bidding public,[151] these sales are infamous for producing very depressed sale proceeds.[152] The value even of land is reduced by the existence in about half of the states of a post-sale right of *redemption*, by which the debtor can repurchase the land from the auction buyer for the price paid (with interest) within a period of six months to a year.[153] Except in auctions involving items like cars with a robust secondary market, few public sheriffs' auctions produce spirited bidding at all, much less bidding by people expecting anything other than a "fire sale" bargain-basement discount. The most likely outcome of this public auction façade is that the judgment creditor will win the auction by bidding in a credit of a certain amount due on the judgment,[154] pay the sheriff's fees and expenses for conducting the auction, and then resell the land/item later in a more commercially reasonable, privately negotiated sale for something approximating market value. The antiquated sheriff's auction procedure benefits only sheriffs and auctioneers; experts have long recognized that it harms everyone else involved, both debtors and creditors and potentially even the communities in which auctioned realty is located.[155]

While it might have been common in 14th-century Italy to see public execution auctions of household items like clothing, bedding, and furniture,[156]

---

149. Tex. R. Civ. P. 646a-650 (calling for sale of land on first Tuesday of each month, and personalty at time determined by sheriff, both by public auction "at the courthouse door," and carefully defining "courthouse door" to mean literally the entrance to the district court); NY CPLR §§5233, 5236; CA CCP §§701.510, 701.570; Fla. Stat. §56.22.

150. NY CPLR §5225; CA CCP §708.205 (ambiguously directing property "to be applied toward the satisfaction of the money judgment"); Fla. Stat. §56.29(6); 735 ILCS 5/2-1402(e).

151. *See, e.g.*, NY CPLR §5233(b), 5236(c)-(d); CA CCP §§701.530–701.560; Tex. R. Civ. P. 647; Fla. Stat. §56.21.

152. William C. Whitford, "A Critique of the Consumer Credit Collection System," 1979 *Wisconsin L. Rev.* 1047 (noting prices at sheriff's auctions are "notoriously low" aside from automobile auctions).

153. New York and California abolished redemption rights in the mid-1900s, but Illinois has not. 735 ILCS 5/12-122 (6 months).

154. *See, e.g.*, CA CCP §701.590(b).

155. Cohen, above note 45, at 1026; Ann M. Burkhart, "Fixing Foreclosure," 36 *Yale L. & Pol'y Rev.* 315 (2018).

156. *See* Daniel Lord Smail, *Legal Plunder: Households and Debt Collection in Late Medieval Europe* (Harvard Univ. Press 2016).

such items in the modern US are likely to produce either no bidding or insufficient bids to cover the costs of sale. Ethical sheriffs will avoid levying on low-value items, and creditors achieve little more than wasted time and money pursuing levy on such items (the evil pleasure of seeing the judgment debtor's personal effects squandered is not a legitimate aim). Execution is thus effective only in situations involving money (garnishment of bank accounts and wages), property with a recognized and easily accessible secondary market (automobiles, investment securities) and fairly high-value land and personal property (yachts, airplanes, and the like).

The Illinois citation to discover assets process contains a provision to avoid both the destruction of value in a public auction and the diversion of value to sheriffs and auctioneers. While the original, and still default, rule is that property will be ordered turned over to the sheriff for sale at public auction, the statute as of 2008 allows the court to order a sale "by the debtor, third party respondent, or by a selling agent other than the sheriff" in any case where "another method of sale is more appropriate."[157] This still does not make for profitable pursuit of low-value personal items, but it does increase the efficiency and effectiveness of the property execution process involving items of moderate value.

E. Expand

A particularly savvy or wily judgment debtor might own no property that can be seized, but the search might be expanded beyond the debtor's property in a few cases. A low-income individual's property may be protected by the "shield" exemption laws discussed in the next chapter, and no one should be surprised that such a debtor is *judgment-proof*. But a moderate- to high-income debtor, whether individual or business entity, may seem to be operating quite well and still be judgment-proof due to clever asset planning strategies, also introduced in the next chapter.[158] Sometimes these strategies can be thwarted, however, by unwinding the asset protection strategies, recovering value alienated earlier, or seizing value in some other person's hands. These complex topics can only be introduced here, but a treatment of judgment enforcement would not be complete without some mention of recovering fraudulent conveyances and piercing veils.

---

157. 735 ILCS 5/2-1402(e).

158. For the classic work on this, see Lynn LoPucki, "The Death of Liability," 106 *Yale L.J.* 1 (1996).

1. Voidable Transactions

For hundreds of years, wily debtors have attempted to put their property beyond the reach of creditors by transferring it to friendly third parties for safekeeping. Such transfers might be formal and complete, conveying ownership of the property, or informal or incomplete, simply shifting the appearance of ownership—possession being nine-tenths of the law in the eyes of the public. Often, this allows the judgment debtor to continue to enjoy the benefits of owning the property without facing the danger of potentially losing it to an executing judgment creditor. In any event, such transfers harm creditors by making value that would otherwise be available to them unavailable, either technically or practically.

Also for hundreds of years, lawmakers have armed creditors with the ability to challenge these transfers and recover the value improperly alienated. The earliest iterations of these statutes in England were designed to address outright fraud by debtors lying about the true ownership of property, so they were styled laws on "fraudulent conveyances." Later, they were expanded to encompass debtors' transfers of their property that were not so much technically fraudulent, but had the intended or inadvertent effect of reducing the value of the debtor's property reachable by executing judgment creditors. Today, state laws on "fraudulent transfers" are fairly uniform, but since these laws apply to many situations involving no real fraud, the latest version of the statute is called the Uniform Voidable Transactions Act (adopted in California in 2016 and introduced into the New York, Florida, and Pennsylvania legislatures, among others, in 2018).[159]

The first thing to note about these statutes is that they create a cause of action against *third-party transferees* of the debtor's property, not against the debtor. A judgment against the debtor would do the creditor little good—the creditor already has a judgment against the debtor, who has thwarted its enforcement by transferring away property. These statutes expand the range of property reachable by enforcement by (1) treating property conveyed to third parties as still belonging to the debtor, (2) treating the conveyance as "avoided" so the property can be seized in the execution proceedings, or (3) awarding the creditor a money judgment against the third party for the value of the property the debtor conveyed away.[160]

---

159. CA Civ. Code §§3439–3439.14. The previous version of the law, with largely parallel provisions, is called the Uniform Fraudulent Transfer Act and is still the law in Illinois. 740 ILCS 160.

160. CA Civ. Code §§3439.07, 3439.08(b).

Effective discovery is especially vital here. The judgment creditor bears the practical and eventually legal burden of establishing that property in a third party's possession or control was improperly transferred away by the debtor, and it or its value should be recovered for the creditor's benefit. This will not be obvious to a casual observer, so careful digging into the debtor's recent history of transferring real and personal property is required to reveal these questionable dealings. The look-back period—that is, the statute of limitations for an action to recover the transferred property or value—is usually four years after the date of the transfer.[161] Before this time runs out, an action must be commenced (either in supplementary proceedings or in a separate lawsuit[162]) against the third-party recipient of the property.

Two kinds of transfers are "voidable," and notably neither depends on any culpable actions or state of mind of the (possibly quite innocent) recipient third-party defendant. The outcome is determined only based on the *debtor's* state of mind in making the transfer, or the objective factors surrounding the transfer. First, reaching back to the fraud-based origins of these laws, a transfer is voidable if the debtor made it "with actual intent to hinder, delay, or defraud any creditor of the debtor."[163] This implicates the classic case of a judgment debtor transferring property to a relative or friend to keep it out of the hands of pursuing creditors. The debtor's culpable state of mind might be established based on a series of factors helpfully enumerated in the statute, such as (1) transfer to an insider (related party), (2) after being sued or threatened with suit, or shortly after incurring a substantial debt, or (3) for unreasonably little value in exchange.[164]

The second kind of transfer is voidable based on its objective terms, which inevitably injured existing creditors because the debtor transferred away property (1) in exchange for less than reasonably equivalent value in return (2) at a time when the value of the debtor's remaining assets no longer covered the burden of all of the debtor's debts; that is, the debtor was *insolvent* (or rendered insolvent).[165] This implicates a situation where the debtor sees the walls closing in and sells property in haste for insufficient consideration, intentionally

161. CA Civ. Code §3439.09 (in cases involving late-discovered actual fraud, up to 7 years).

162. *See* Guy Macarol, "Veil-Piercing and Fraudulent Transfer Avoidance in Supplemental Proceedings: How Expanding Statutory Remedies and Enforcement Jurisdiction Can Promote Judicial Economy and Facilitate Judgment Collection," 50 *J. Marshall L. Rev.* 279 (2017).

163. CA Civ. Code §3439.04(a)(1).

164. CA Civ. Code §3439.04(b).

165. CA Civ. Code §3439.05; *see also* 3439.04(a)(2) (identifying shaky business dealings equivalent to insolvency).

or unintentionally reducing the total value of property on hand available to creditors. Here, though, no evidence of either the debtor's or the third-party recipient's state of mind is necessary. A wide variety of fact patterns potentially give rise to such a claim, but they and other details in the UVTA are well beyond the scope of this book. A course in Bankruptcy or Debtor-Creditor Law is highly advised.

For now, just recognize that the scope of discovery and the range of available property value is not limited to land, things, and rights in the debtor's current possession. Significant value previously transferred away (alienated) might be recovered in a UVTA action to recover value related to "voidable" transfers to third parties—if the potential return warrants the substantial expense and effort of such a further adversary lawsuit.

2. Veil Piercing

As mentioned in the previous chapter in the discussion of business property, one of the primary purposes of forming a legal entity through which to conduct business is to shield the assets of the owner (a natural person, or perhaps another business entity) from debts arising in the operation of that particular company. A judgment against a business entity thus may be enforced only against the company's property, not the property of its owner(s), even if a sole individual. This limited liability is freely granted by states to encourage entrepreneurial risk-taking activity.

The states offer this privilege, however, subject to an implicit requirement that business owners respect the company's own separate existence and invest sufficient capital to allow the entity to function properly and meet its expected obligations. State courts have developed a doctrine to address owners' irresponsible and "unfair" abuse of the privilege of segregating the owner's assets from the business entity's operational liabilities. Explored in greater depth in a class on Business Associations, Enterprise Organizations, Corporations, or a variety of other names, the doctrine can again be introduced only briefly here.

Called either "alter ego" or "veil piercing,"[166] the jurisprudential doctrine applies all but exclusively to companies owned by fewer than two or three persons. If the trigger factors of the doctrine are established in a lawsuit against

---

166. Not "piercing the corporate veil" because the limited liability "veil" of LLCs, not just corporations, is increasingly being subjected to piercing, as well. Also not mentioned or dealt with here is the conceptually equivalent doctrine of "enterprise liability," extending the debt of one member of a corporate family to its parent and/or sibling companies for reasons similar to veil piercing.

a dominating owner, the court is said to pierce through or disregard the veil of limited liability and hold the owner liable for the company's debts.

Various state courts have developed hugely varying numbers of supposed factors leading to veil piercing, but two types of factors stand out. The first applies to an owner who treats the company like a personal piggy bank, commingling owner and company money freely, or who fails to observe the requisite formalities for the company's separate existence (proper corporate governance and recordkeeping). In such cases, courts might view the company as the owner's "alter ego," not worthy of recognition as a separate entity with liabilities separate from the owner's.

More important, and probably required in any case, is a second factor: that the owner has perpetrated some degree of "unfairness" or even fraud on an innocent third-party claimant, who faces limited recourse to an insufficient corporate asset base to cover the claim. The most likely source of such fraud or unfairness is the owner's failure to properly support the company's business by investing sufficient capital, or at the very least purchasing sufficient insurance. In extreme cases of so-called *undercapitalization*, courts might again pierce through the liability veil and hold the owner personally liable for the emaciated corporation's debts. The likelihood of this piercing depends in part on the claimant's "clean hands," however, so it may well not be successful in cases in which the claimant might be expected to have foreseen or forearmed against the possibility of a loss (e.g., in a contract situation, by availing of contractual hedges, such as security interests or a personal guarantee from the company's owner).

Again, the details here must be left for later. In fact, the details are arguably unimportant, as one commentator echoes the common characterization of courts' approach to this doctrine: "their opinions are nearly always simply gestalt results rather than genuinely articulated decisions."[167] For now just recognize that a judgment against a business entity usually can be enforced only against its own assets, not its owner's, but in exceptional cases, the asset-segregating veil of limited liability might be pierced, exposing the owner's assets to enforcement, as well.

167. Eric A. Chiappinelli, *Cases and Materials on Business Entities* 328 (4th ed. 2018).

Chapter 4

Shield

Collecting judgments against individual, natural persons is complicated by a pair of important protections the law provides only to such people. In addition, sophisticated individuals and business entities can make special arrangements to shield their assets from judgment creditors in advance. First, a range of property owned by individuals is shielded from the effects of judgment enforcement, *exempt* from seizure and sale. Second, enforcement efforts directed at collection of *consumer debts* are restricted by a regulation designed to avert abusive behavior by the debt collection industry. In cases involving individual judgment debtors, navigating the maze of substance and procedure restrictions is a vital part of gauging the power and limits of judgment collection activity. Finally, a sub-industry of lawyers and accountants markets techniques for putting assets of high-net-worth debtors beyond the reach of creditors ahead of time. These asset protection schemes represent a final shield that should be borne in mind by creditors and debtors alike.

A. Shielding Substance—Property Exemptions

The state is willing to underwrite the collection of private money judgments, but it is also concerned about judgment debtors being denuded of all assets and becoming public burdens. Long ago, a compromise emerged in Europe and has continued to this day to extend some degree of protection to judgment debtors to prevent their utter destitution at the hands of avaricious creditors. For reasons of both political expediency and moral conviction, all states place a range of any individual judgment debtor's property outside the reach of enforcement by private money judgment creditors. Such property is generally said to be *exempt* from actions to enforce a money judgment. Generally, only the property of natural individuals is protected; because business entities do not have families or souls, their property can be seized in its entirety and the entity brought to its bitter end.[168]

While most of the exemption action is at the state level, federal law skims a range of liquid value sources off the top with preemptive exemptions of a wide variety of benefits payments. Essentially any portion of an individual's bank account that is attributable to federal benefits of any kind is exempt from creditor process, and federal law requires banks to track two months of electronic deposits of these benefits and sequester the funds, safe from private execution.[169] The list includes payments related to the following: (1) social security old age, survivors, and disability insurance benefits, (2) retirement benefits for federal employees and railroad workers, (3) lighthouse keepers' surviving spouse benefits, (4) longshore and harbor workers death and disability benefits, (5) military pay, retirement, and survivors benefits, and (6) veterans benefits.[170] Most states similarly exempt state benefits of a variety of kinds, such as unemployment benefits, workers compensation, and public assistance such as aid to families and children. There is an especially hot corner of Hell reserved for ordinary money judgment creditors who would pursue people reliant on these sorts of hardship aid, anyway.

The great majority of real and personal property exemptions are found in state law. The scope of these exemptions varies greatly from state to state, reflecting often deep-seated local political sentiment regarding debtors and creditors. A few examples are offered here, and excerpts of the New York, California, and Illinois exemption statutes are set out in the appendices. Other states' approaches are likely to resemble one of these, but the possible variations are virtually endless.

1. Texas

To attract and provide refuge to debtors fleeing from their creditors in the East, the frontier Republic of Texas offered significant enticements in the form of very generous property protections. Those protections persist today. The notion of

168. *See, e.g.,* CA CCP §703.020(a); Tex. Prop. Code §42.001(a); 42 Pa. Cons. Stat. §§8123(b)(2); 735 ILCS 5/12-1001(j) (excluding property used for business purposes or not owned by an individual).

169. 31 CFR §212.1–212.12; 76 Fed. Reg. 9939 (Feb. 23, 2011), 78 Fed Reg. 32,099 (May 29, 2013).

170. *See* 5 USC §§8130, 8346, 8470; 10 USC §§1440, 1450; 22 USC §4060; 28 USC §376(n); 33 USC §§771–775, 916; 37 USC §701; 38 USC §5301; 42 USC §§407, 1383; 45 USC §§231m, 352(e).

exempting a debtors' real property *homestead* from the reach of creditors began in Texas in 1839[171] and spread to most other states thereafter. Today, Texas debtors enjoy an exemption in real property of unlimited value used as a home, preventing money judgment creditors from seizing up to 10 acres in an urban area, 100 or 200 acres in the country (for a single or family debtor, respectively).[172]

Personal property exemptions are much older, dating back millennia in some cases, but modern exemptions have become more and more generous in a few states in particular. The range of personal property value exempted from judgment enforcement in Texas is vast. Professionally prescribed health aids and the debtor's "religious bible or other book containing sacred writings of a religion" are exempt without value limitation, as are retirement savings and benefit plans of all kinds, as well as the benefits and cash value of any insurance policy (e.g., life insurance).[173] Other personal property is exempt subject to an aggregate value limit of $50,000 if owned by a single adult, $100,000 if "provided for a family," including the following:[174]

> (1) home furnishings, including family heirlooms;
> (2) provisions for consumption;
> (3) farming or ranching vehicles and implements;
> (4) tools, equipment, books, and apparatus, including boats and motor vehicles used in a trade or profession;
> (5) wearing apparel;
> (6) jewelry not to exceed 25 percent of the aggregate [value] limitations ... ;
> (7) two firearms;
> (8) athletic and sporting equipment, including bicycles;
> (9) a two-wheeled, three-wheeled, or four-wheeled motor vehicle for each member of a family or single adult ... ;
> (10) the following animals and forage on hand for their consumption:
> (A) two horses, mules, or donkeys and a saddle, blanket, and bridle for each;
> (B) 12 head of cattle;
> (C) 60 head of other types of livestock; and
> (D) 120 fowl; and
> (11) household pets.

171. Lena London, "The Initial Homestead Exemption in Texas," 57 *Sw. Hist. Q.* 432 (1954).

172. Tex. Prop. Code §§41.001–41.002.

173. Tex. Prop. Code §§42.002, 42.0021; Tex. Ins. Code §1108.051.

174. Tex. Prop. Code §42.001–42.002.

The expansive protections of Texas exemption laws have led some to query whether the state is in fact serious about supporting the collection of debts from moderate-income people.

2. Pennsylvania

Contrast this with the exemptions provided by a more traditional, creditor-oriented Eastern state. On the one hand, Pennsylvania's modern retirement plan and insurance policy exemptions are similar to the total exemption of these plans and policies in Texas.[175] On the other hand, Pennsylvania has no homestead exemption. It provides only one set of austere exemptions, setting aside only the debtor's "(1) wearing apparel, (2) Bibles and school books, (3) sewing machines…, [and] (4) uniforms and accoutrements," along with an extra $300 (!) of any other real or personal property of the debtor's choosing.[176] This monetary kicker that can be applied to any property is often called a *wildcard* and is quite common in state exemptions laws. The reference to $300 also reflects another common characteristic of these statutes, in that they often have not been indexed for inflation since the early- to mid-1800s when they were adopted (and when $300 was real money).

3. New York

New York's exemption statute, in contrast, is indexed for inflation every three years,[177] though it also retains the traditional flavor of a rural, religious, Eastern state. Borrowing from Texas, New York offers a homestead exemption, but only as to a certain amount of the debtor's *equity* in the property, depending upon its location.

For both real and personal property, *equity* is the value in property that is not encumbered by another third-party interest. Exemption laws often apply only to a limited amount of this equity value, rather than to an item or series of items themselves, as we will see below. For example, most people buy their home with money borrowed from a bank, and to secure their promise to repay that money, they grant the bank a mortgage (or deed of trust), a property interest that allows the bank to seize the property if the loan is not timely paid. The amount of the unpaid bank loan backed by this mortgage is value the

175. 42 Pa. Cons. Stat. §§8124(b)–(c).

176. 42 Pa. Cons. Stat. §§8123(a), 8124(a).

177. NY CPLR §§5205(*l*)(3), 5253.

property owner has reserved for the mortgagee bank (temporarily, on a contingent basis). Any unreserved value in excess of the mortgage encumbrance (and any other similar temporary giveaways or *liens*, as discussed in the next chapter) is the debtor's equity. Any equity in excess of a value-limited exemption is consequently unprotected and available for judgment creditors.

For example, New York exempts $170,825 in equity in real or personal property "owned and occupied as a principal residence" in the New York City area, and either $142,350 or $85,400 in specified counties with (and without) smaller cities.[178] If equity in excess of these amounts is present, the judgment creditor can force a sale only by commencing a special proceeding and convincing the court to order a sheriff sale of the property. After such a sale, the cash proceeds (net of the sheriff's and auctioneer's expenses) are distributed in order of priority of the claimants (as discussed in the next chapter). The first proceeds would be distributed to any prior claimants (e.g., the mortgagee, or if that party is not paid, the rights of the senior mortgagee pass along with the property sold), then the debtor's exemption amount, and only then any remainder to the judgment creditor.

The fairly generous New York personal property exemptions, with indexed dollar figures including a wildcard exemption of $1150,[179] are set forth in the appendix, but notable quaint exemptions include "all stoves and home heating equipment ... and necessary fuel" for 120 days, sewing machines (as in Pennsylvania), religious texts and "a seat or pew ... in a place of public worship" (judgment creditors would seize such things?!), "domestic animals with the necessary food for those animals" for 120 days, and 90% of any money or amount due the debtor "for the sale of milk produced on a farm operated by him."[180] Here again, retirement plan trusts are exempt without value limitation,[181] and New York has adopted some much more modern exemptions covering such items as "one computer and associated equipment, one cellphone," and up to $4550 of the debtor's equity value in a vehicle ($11,375 if the vehicle has been equipped for use by a disabled person).

These exemptions are supposed to be obvious and self-executing; that is, without debtors needing to assert these exemptions, the sheriff is simply expected not to levy on exempt property (though one wonders how often exempt property is levied on without debtors realizing and invoking their rights to a

178. NY CPLR § 5206.

179. The New York wildcard is available only if the debtor does *not* take advantage of the homestead exemption. NY CPLR § 5205(a)(9).

180. NY CPLR § 5205.

181. NY CPLR § 5205(c).

protective order). A pair of exemptions relating to individual debtors' bank accounts are clearly self-executing in part but require notice and opportunity for the debtor to assert further exemption.

First, as mentioned above, federal and state statutes exempt a variety of benefits payments, as well as child support payments and a percentage of wages. If such "statutorily exempt payments" were directly (electronically) deposited into the debtor's bank account within 45 days before service of a restraining order or execution (which the bank can tell from the electronic notations on the deposits), then a minimum of $2850 in that account is exempt and cannot be restrained or seized.[182] Woe to wage earners who deposit paper checks!

Second, in addition, service of either a restraining notice or execution affecting any natural person's bank account requires the bank to serve notice on the debtor of the right to assert a total exemption if *any* funds in the account are from exempt sources.[183] If the debtor follows instructions and signs and serves the exemption claim form on the bank and creditor's attorney within 20 days, indicating that the account contains exempt funds (deposited electronically or otherwise), the judgment creditor bears the burden of establishing (using an accounting tracing mechanism) what portion of the funds on deposit are exempt and should be released. If the creditor asserts that a portion of the funds are not exempt, the creditor must object to the exemption by noticed motion served on the bank and the debtor within eight days of the postmark on the debtor's exemption claim. At the motion hearing, the creditor must overcome a presumption that all funds in the account are exempt, showing by affirmation or affidavit that "shall not be conclusory, but is required to show the factual basis" that a certain amount of non-exempt funds are in the account. The likely intended effect of this extraordinarily burdensome and hurried back-and-forth is that any individual bank account into which wages or benefits have been deposited is entirely exempt from creditor process in New York (unless the debtor ignores or responds improperly to the exemption notice).

---

182. NY CPLR §§5205(*l*)(1), 5222(h); *see also* §5222(i) (exempting from the effect of a restraining notice an amount in an individual's bank account equal to 240 times the minimum wage, $1740, unless the court finds some or all of these funds to be "unnecessary for the reasonable requirements of the judgment debtor" and family).

183. NY CPLR §5222(d)-(e), 5222-a (outlining required exemption notice to be served with restraining notice or execution, as well as process for debtor to claim exemption and creditor to object by motion).

4. California

California's exemptions[184] are particularly notable not so much for the substance (which is similar to New York's, including indexing for inflation triennially[185]) but for the procedure for claiming them. Many of these exemptions are effectively affirmative defenses—the debtor must claim them timely or waive them.[186] The exemption claim procedure for all California property resembles the one in New York for bank accounts containing exempt funds, but the burden falls doubly on the debtor. The debtor-claimant must file a claim of exemption, including a citation to the specific applicable exemption statute, with the levying officer within 10 days after service of the notice of levy. If the creditor opposes this claim, it must within 10 days file a noticed motion of opposition with the court. At a hearing within 30 days, the debtor-claimant bears the further burden of establishing the exemption (in contrast to New York, where the creditor bears this burden), including the value of the property if the exemption is limited to a certain amount of equity value.[187]

Likewise, while California also preserves the exemptions relating to a month's wages and all public benefits deposited into a bank account, it again places a burden on the debtor to invoke and defend the exemption. For exempt wages deposited in the preceding 30 days, California again places the burden of tracing those funds and establishing the exemption on the debtor-claimant, rather than the creditor as in New York.[188] For electronically direct-deposited public benefits, California like New York exempts a base amount (depending upon the type of benefit and number of beneficiaries) and invites the creditor to file a notice of opposition in court to claim the excess *non*-exempt. Once again, if such an opposition is filed, the debtor bears the burden of establishing the extent of exempt funds remaining on deposit.[189]

The dollar limitations on exempt equity in real and personal property are also not as generous as those in New York. California's vehicle exemption protects only $3325, and its homestead exemption preserves home equity of only

---

184. CA CCP §§704.010–704.850.

185. CA CCP §703.150.

186. CA CCP §703.030 (allowing court to relieve a person from failure to claim an exemption).

187. CA CCP §§703.510–703.590.

188. CA CCP §703.080 (mandating the same "lowest intermediate balance" tracing test as New York), 704.070, 704.080(f).

189. CA CCP §704.080.

$75,000 for a single person and $100,000 for a family unit, a small fraction of the skyrocketing property values in most regions of the Golden State.[190] Like New York, California requires a creditor application and court order to proceed to an execution sale of a homestead with surplus non-exempt equity, and if an auction produces insufficient bidding to cover the exemption and *all* liens and encumbrances in full, the sale is cancelled and cannot be ordered again for at least a year.[191]

California also carefully limits the degree to which debtors can claim exemptions in ordinary household items that are not so ... ordinary. For example, household furnishings, appliances, clothing, and other personal effects are exempt without a specific value limitation, but only if they are "ordinarily and reasonably necessary" for the debtor and family. Items of "extraordinary value" do not fall within this protected category.[192] Similarly, while retirement savings and pension accounts are exempt without any specific dollar limitation, the debtor must claim the exemption, and the creditor can oppose the claim for any amount beyond "the extent necessary to provide for the support of the judgment debtor when the judgment debtor retires."[193]

5. Illinois

The outdated exemptions[194] in Illinois are fairly middle of the road,[195] not as generous as New York's, not as miserly as Pennsylvania's. The homestead exemption covers only $15,000 in equity value ($30,000 if two or more judgment debtors own the property) in real or personal property "occupied by him or her as a residence."[196] If the property is owned by a married couple who have planned ahead and hold title specifically "in tenancy by the

---

190. CA CCP §704.730 (raising homestead exemption to $175,000 for elderly and disabled debtors). Unlike the personal property exemptions, the homestead exemption is not automatically indexed for inflation every three years; instead, the Judicial Council reports to the legislature on the adjustment that would be appropriate in light of inflation, but the legislature must act to increase the homestead exemption. It has not done so since 2010, despite the fact that the consumer price index used to increase the other exemptions has risen more than 21% in the ensuing years.

191. CA CCP §§704.010, 704.740–704.970.

192. CA CCP §704.020.

193. CA CCP §704.115.

194. For a scathing indictment of outdated enforcement laws, including exemption laws that have long trailed economic developments, see Alfred F. Conard, "An Appraisal of Illinois Law on the Enforcement of Judgments," 1951 *Univ. Ill. L. Forum* 96.

195. 735 ILCS 5/12-901, 12-1001.

196. 735 ILCS 5/12-901.

entirety," however, the property is fully exempt unless both spouses are liable on the judgment.[197]

The Illinois personal property exemption statute has no provisions for tracing and safeguarding exempt public or private benefits (or wages) deposited directly or otherwise into a bank account (though federal law accomplishes this for *federal* benefits now, as described above),[198] and it has no burden-shifting provisions for the debtor to claim or the creditor to oppose any exemptions. The exemptions not limited by dollar value are self-executing, imposing a duty on the sheriff (or court) to disregard such things as necessary wearing apparel, bibles, school books, family pictures, and professionally prescribed health aids, along with several sources of benefit funds.[199]

But three exemptions are limited by dollar value of equity (not indexed for inflation), including $2400 in a motor vehicle, $1500 in tools of the debtor's trade, and a $4000 wildcard exemption in any other property.[200] For these, the debtor might have to choose which item(s) to exempt. The statute suggests the sheriff will select the property to exempt unless the debtor files "a schedule of all of his or her personal property of every kind and character," prompting the court to "summon 3 householders [to] impartially appraise the property of the debtor," from which the debtor must choose the item(s) she or he wishes to exempt and retain.[201] In light of the paltry values and the complex procedure involved here, it seems highly doubtful that this process ever unfolded as described in the statute with any regularity. With the advent of the citation to discover assets, the debtor's assertion of exemptions now usually occurs at the citation hearing, under court supervision.[202]

---

197. 735 ILCS 5/12-112.

198. Illinois law exempts payments of retirement benefits, as in New York, 735 ILCS 5/12-804; *cf.* NY CPLR §5203(d)(1) (same); CA CCP §§704.115(d) (same, though allowing garnishment of periodic payments within the limits applied to wage garnishment), the proceeds of the sale of exempt property also remain exempt, 735 ILCS 5/12-1001(j), but the statute makes no reference to tracing exempt funds once deposited into a bank account. Many other states' statutes reflect this ambiguity. Likewise, the "right to receive" a series of other benefits is exempt, but no reference is made specifically to any exemption for the money received by the debtor after those benefits are paid, except in the case of a series of enumerated awards for crime victims, certain wrongful death and personal injury claims, and certain life insurance contracts, which are exempt for a limited time along with "property that is traceable to" any of them. 735 ILCS 5/12-1001(h).

199. 735 ILCS 5/12-1002.

200. 735 ILCS 5/12-1001(b)-(d).

201. 735 ILCS 5/12-1002.

202. 735 ILCS 5/2-1402(b), (c-5), (*l*) (noting the debtor's opportunity to assert exemptions).

B. Shielding against Procedure—Fair Debt Collection Practices Act

Particularly if creditors know most of the debtor's property of any value is protected from judgment enforcement, they might choose to pressure the debtor into voluntarily turning over exempt funds (or selling exempt property) by making the debtor's life miserable. Debt collectors have long engaged in behavior that spans a broad spectrum from light persuasion to outrageously coercive abuse, and in the 1960s, Congress reacted and passed a federal law to restrict abusive debt collection behavior. The Fair Debt Collection Practices Act[203] prohibits a variety of behaviors—procedures, we might say—connected to the process of "debt collection."

The scare quotes indicate a series of important limitations on the scope of the FDCPA's reach, stemming from the definition of "debt collection." First, the statute regulates only the collection of "debts," which are defined restrictively to include only monetary obligations of a consumer incurred in connection with the consumer's personal, family, or household purposes. "Consumer" is also defined to mean a natural person.[204] Similar statutes passed by some state legislatures tend to be similarly limited to the collection of consumer debts.[205] These statutes thus do not regulate the enforcement of money judgments and other debt collection activities directed at artificial, juridical business entities (e.g., corporations, LLCs) no matter how small, nor do they apply to judgments or debts related to the judgment debtor's business dealings (that is, not personal, family, or household affairs) and perhaps tort and other judgments not involving voluntary "transactions."

In addition, the federal statute restricts the conduct of "debt collectors," defined as those who "regularly" collect debts "due another."[206] That is, it does not inhibit the conduct of the owners of debts—creditors—collecting debts owed to *themselves* (including debts purchased from an original creditor[207]).

---

203. 15 USC §§1692–1692p. Do not confuse this FDCPA with the other FDCPA, the Federal Debt Collection Procedures Act, the federal government's preferential enforcement law. See above note 9.

204. 15 USC §1692a(3), (5).

205. Tex. Fin. Code §392.001; NY Gen. Bus. Law §600; CA Civ. Code §1788.2.

206. 15 USC §1692a(6).

207. Henson v. Santander Consumer USA Inc., 137 S.Ct. 1718 (2017). If collecting consumer debts is "the principal purpose" of its business, however, even a debt buyer's activities collecting *its own* debts are subject to the FDCPA. *See* Tepper v. Amos Fin. LLC, 898 F.3d 364 (3d Cir. 2018).

Some state statutes do regulate the conduct of creditors themselves,[208] also, but in the judgment enforcement context, most activity will be conducted by lawyers on behalf of judgment creditors, and lawyers who "regularly" collect judgments and other debts owed by consumers are squarely within the ambit of the statute.[209]

Most ethical lawyers engaging in the procedures discussed in this book would come nowhere near a violation of the primary restrictions in the FDCPA.[210] Some are quite technical, though. The most glaring example is a requirement of a "validation notice" sent within five days after the "initial communication" with the debtor.[211] Especially if the lawyer enforcing the judgment was not trial counsel, the "initial communication" with the judgment debtor may occur in the post-judgment stage (service of a subpoena or citation, for example), and the validation notice is so utterly ridiculous and unnecessary in this context that no lawyer would naturally think to send such a thing to the debtor within five days, but it is required.

Other potential technical violations include, for example, in drawing up a writ of execution or affidavit, a judgment creditor's lawyer might slightly misstate the amount of the total judgment debt and thereby attempt to collect an unpermitted amount ("including any interest, fee, charge, or expense incidental to the principal obligation").[212] Or in the course of strategic discovery, the attorney might overcome evasion and dissimulation by using a "false representation or deceptive means to collect or attempt to collect any debt or to obtain information concerning a consumer."[213] Small slips in the collections process

---

208. Tex. Fin. Code § 392.001. California's Rosenthal Act definitions might also encompass creditors.

209. Heintz v. Jenkins, 514 U.S. 291 (1995).

210. *See* 15 USC §§ 1692c–1692f (prohibiting abusive and inconvenient communication with debtor, as well as abusive, false or misleading, and unfair practices, such as threatening violence, using profane language, falsely threatening imprisonment or claiming that the debtor has committed a crime).

211. 15 USC § 1692g (requiring express statement (1) of amount of debt, (2) of name of creditor, (3) that "unless the consumer, within thirty days after receipt of the notice, disputes the validity of the debt ... the debt will be assumed to be valid," (4) that "if the consumer notifies the debt collector in writing within the thirty-day period that the debt, or any portion thereof, is disputed, the debt collector will obtain ... a copy of a judgment against the consumer and a copy of such ... judgment will be mailed to the consumer," and (5) that, upon the consumer's written request within the thirty-day period, the debt collector will provide the consumer with the name and address of the original creditor, if different from the current creditor).

212. 15 USC §§ 1692e(2), 1692f(1).

213. 15 USC § 1692e(10).

might lead to legal exposure for up to $1000 statutory damages and attorney's fees and a big headache at the very least.[214] There is a "clean heart, empty head" defense that the violation was inadvertent, as well as a *de minimis* defense,[215] but these are not airtight, they require effort to advance, and they do not prevent a lawsuit in the first place.

Those "regularly" engaged in the collection of consumer debts, including judgments based on such debts, must be wary of the traps laid by the FDCPA. Proposals have been advanced repeatedly to provide an exemption for lawyers representing clients in litigation, but these efforts have so far failed.

C. Shielding Assets Ahead of Time—Asset Protection Schemes

A small subset of judgment debtors will have anticipated the challenge of facing down judgment creditors, and they will have attempted to avert the negative effects of judgment enforcement in advance. These are people with substantial assets and/or income—sufficient both to be worth protecting from creditors and to warrant the substantial expense of paying a lawyer to set up and maintain special asset protection arrangements. They also tend to be people who face higher than average litigation risk, such as doctors, corporate executives, and perhaps husbands planning on dumping their spouses without dividing their substantial wealth.

For these people, an industry of lawyers offers to set up *asset protection* schemes of a variety of kinds. The basic idea here is to separate legal ownership and control of assets from most of the benefits of the value of those assets. That is, make someone else the owner of the property with the legal power of control, but retain practical control and enjoyment of the benefits of that property to a greater or lesser degree.

Once again, the complex and varying details are far beyond the scope of this overview, but the common point of departure is the creation of an artificial entity, such as a limited partnership, LLC, or more commonly a trust, and a transfer of assets (usually liquid, like money or investment securities) to the entity, to be controlled by a managing partner or an "independent" trustee. The transferor (a limited partner or *settlor* of a trust) retains little or no legal right to manage or control the assets—though perhaps maintaining practical

214. 15 USC § 1692k.

215. 15 USC § 1692k(b)-(c).

control if the manager is a friend or relative—ostensibly retaining only a beneficial interest in a stream of limited payments to be distributed from the partnership or trust from time to time.

If the custodian is a business entity (e.g., LP, LLC), the concepts of limited liability and asset segregation discussed in the preceding chapter put the entity's assets legally beyond the reach of the investor-transferor's creditors, and the entity's governance rules likely make seizure of the transferor's management power either impossible or fruitless. If the custodian is a trust, the key restriction on the settlor-beneficiary's access to the *corpus* (body) of the trust makes this a *spendthrift* trust (originally designed to prevent spendthrift rich children from wasting their future by spending or promising away the assets placed in the trust). Though highly controversial and an exception to the common law rule, several US states' laws respect the spendthrift transfer restrictions even on trusts that are self-settled (i.e., the settlor-transferor is also a trust beneficiary), making them effective insulators of the value held in such trusts. The fact that creditors can seize only dribs and drabs of income distributions from the business entity or trust from time to time makes it time-consuming, troublesome, and (the transferor hopes) not worth it for judgment creditors to lay claim to the distributions as they are made.

This is a fascinating and creative area of law practice that can draw on the laws of many jurisdictions and sometimes call for visits to interesting and beautiful places like Aruba, Bermuda, and the Cayman Islands, or at least electronic communication with even more exotic locales, such as the tiny South Pacific Cook Islands—all of which are (in)famous havens for asset protection trusts. Less costly and complex asset protection schemes also abound closer to home, using simple domestic entities, perhaps managed by friends or family members.

Because these schemes are designed to put property beyond the reach of creditors, they are susceptible to being unwound as fraudulent conveyances, as discussed in the preceding chapter.[216] But if the custodian of the property is in a jurisdiction that refuses to cooperate with US authorities, much less

216. *See, e.g.*, Bruce A. Markell, "Comments on Selfishly-Settled Trusts: Fulminations Over Fraud and Asset Protection Trusts," 37 *Bankr. L. Letter*, No. 11, Nov. 2017 at 1. A much simpler form of asset protection for the other 99% is simple exemption planning; that is, a debtor anticipating a judgment might sell non-exempt assets and invest the proceeds to buy exempt property, thus laundering the non-exempt value and shielding it from judgment creditors. Some states explicitly label this fraud and deny the debtor the benefit of an exemption so obtained. 735 ILCS 5/12-1001(j). Elsewhere, less aggressive and obvious exemption planning is often accepted if it withstands application of the aphorism, "when a

judgment creditors, the risk of legal unwinding can be minimized. And increasingly, US states are enacting statutes that insulate certain asset protection trusts from the precise danger of fraudulent conveyance (today, UVTA) attack. To attract out-of-state capital investment to in-state asset-protection trusts, 17 states, most recently Michigan, have adopted *domestic asset protection trust* (DAPT) legislation.[217] These laws explicitly validate self-settled trusts as discussed here, and so long as a few key terms are observed, they insulate transfers into these trusts by heightening the burden of proof of fraudulent intent (clear and convincing, rather than preponderance) and reducing the statute of limitations from the usual four years to two (with no tolling for the creditor's late discovery of a preexisting transfer).[218]

Moreover, to execute on assets or engage a fraudulent conveyance action, one has to know that the assets exist in third-party custody, and one has to finance the pursuit of expensive and possibly complex litigation to retrieve that value, either domestically or abroad. Sometimes ownership of assets need not even have been relinquished. It might be sufficient simply to park value in a jurisdiction whose banking and other authorities assiduously refuse to cooperate with or provide information to foreign interlopers, like foreign tax authorities, but especially judgment creditors. Simple moves that make information gathering more challenging, and especially strategies that require expensive litigation, are often practically sufficient to defeat judgment creditors even if the strategies are built on a legally vulnerable foundation.[219] These hurdles alone are often sufficient for asset protection schemes to achieve their creditor-rebuffing goal.

The creditor parry to this debtor dodge is to engage the coercive power of the court against the judgment debtor. If the property cannot be retrieved without the debtor's consent, that consent can be compelled via a *turnover order* directed at the judgment debtor, as discussed in part C.3. of the preceding chapter. If information will be released by foreign banking or other authorities

pig becomes a hog, it gets slaughtered." In other words, debtors who don't push it might get away with a bit of asset shielding in this way.

217. *See, e.g.*, Mich. Comp. Laws §§ 700.1041–700.1050; Robert Tiplady, "Michigan Asset Protection Trusts," *Mich. Bar J.*, Nov. 2018, at 30. For a powerful critique of these laws, see James J. White, "Fraudulent Conveyances Masquerading as Asset Protection Trusts," 47 *UCC L.J.* 367 (2018). None of the other states mentioned in this book has such a DAPT law.

218. Mich. Comp. Laws § 700.1045.

219. *See* Cook, above note 140, at 150 n.97 (noting that OJ Simpson conveyed the copyright to his book, *If I Did It*, to a corporation owned by his children, in part to evade enforcement of the wrongful death judgment obtained by the parents of Ron Goldman, the victim of the murder described in the book).

only with the debtor's consent, the debtor can be compelled to sign a *consent directive*,[220] authorizing foreign authorities to release the sought after information. Even if the debtor actually lacks the legal and practical ability to retrieve the assets themselves, a judgment creditor might access the future payment stream in advance by obtaining an *assignment order*, similar to a wage garnishment order, directed not at the payor, but rather directing the debtor to make an advance assignment of rights to payment in the future.[221] The effectiveness of any of these techniques depends on the state and the judge involved, but for every evasive maneuver today, many states continue to develop countermeasures to leverage courts' authority (and contempt power) over any persons within the ambit of their personal jurisdiction.

220. *See* Doe v. US, 487 US 201 (1988).

221. CA CCP §§708.510.

Chapter 5

Battle

If the debtor has plenty of easily accessible property to cover all claims, no battle need arise among claimants. But if the judgment debtor is not paying one judgment creditor, there is a fair chance that other creditors are similarly being left unpaid. It is highly likely in most coercive judgment enforcement scenarios that the enforcing creditor will face competition from *other* creditors for the limited value in the debtor's property. The outcome of such battles hinges on the *order of priority*—the place in line—of the various competing claims with respect to various sources of value. Another vital aspect of money judgement collection, then, is to understand how creditors arm themselves for this battle and how their priority is determined.

Note that the battle here is over value in specific items of the debtor's property. A judgment creditor has no rights in any specific property simply by virtue of having recovered a money judgment.[222] The creditor has to legally connect the *in personam* rights represented by a judgment to *in rem* rights in a specific item or source of value belonging to the judgment debtor. The legal connection established between a judgment or other debt and a property interest is called a *lien* (pronounced "leen"), a word deriving from the French word *lien*, meaning tie, binding, or connection.

222. Though note that the judgment lien against realty in New York arises upon docketing of the judgment, which happens automatically in virtually every case in a supreme court or county court, and a few other states provide for automatic liens on some types of property in some circumstances.

A. Liens

Liens come in several varieties. The one discussed here is called a *judgment lien* (or *execution lien*), created by the judgment creditor's enforcement action to bind an unpaid judgment debt to an interest in specific property that was the object of the enforcement action. Many other liens are consensual; that is, the debtor grants the lien to a creditor, usually a bank lender, in a contract to bind a debt, usually a loan, to an interest in specific property. For example, a debtor who borrows money from a bank to buy a house might grant the bank a lien to tie the debt to the house—if debtor fails to repay the loan, bank can follow the lien to grab the house. This lien is called a *mortgage*. If the property tied to a loan debt is personal property (including intangibles), the lien is called a *security interest*, governed by Article 9 of the Uniform Commercial Code (UCC), as adopted by every state. Finally, the law sometimes imposes a lien on some item(s) of the debtor's property automatically whenever the debtor enters into a credit transaction. For example, if the debtor buys an item on credit, or rents an apartment or office space, or has a car repaired without paying in advance, the law automatically grants a lien to tie some item(s) of the debtor's property (the purchased item, all personal property in the rented space, the repaired car) to the debt for the price of the sale, lease, or repair. This lien arises automatically by statute or common law and so is called a *statutory lien* or *common law lien*. Public authorities also often impose a lien on *all* of a taxpayer's property, tied to many unpaid public debts, especially federal taxes.

In addition to tying a debt to specific property, a lien reserves a place in line if more than one claimant is pursuing value in that item of property. A lien is like a reservation at an exclusive restaurant with only a few seats. Seats are generally allocated in the order in which reservations are received in time (though some VIPs can get special priority even if they call in late). If 12 parties of two, or one large party of 24, have already reserved all the seats, no dinner for you! If only one seat remains unreserved when you call, you can take that seat if you are willing to ditch your dinner partner—you can make it up to him or her later at a different restaurant. Likewise in property execution, if a valuable item, like a bank account, is already encumbered by liens for claims exceeding its value, that bank account is unavailable for late-arriving lien claimants. But if a bit of value is unencumbered by previous liens, a late-arriving judgment creditor can collect a partial recovery from that value, and the remainder can be pursued by making connections—liens—to other items of value using the techniques discussed in this book.

Any lien must be analyzed in terms of three steps: (1) creation (or *attachment*), (2) effectiveness against other third parties with various types of claims to the specific property subject to the lien (or *perfection*), and (3) *priority* of the liens on that specific property. A lien that has first (or higher) priority is called *senior*, whereas a lien with lower priority is called *junior* or *subordinate*.

Many of the enforcement procedures examined in this book create liens on some or all of a judgment debtor's property, as discussed below. Effectiveness against third parties often occurs at the moment of creation, especially against claimants whose liens are not connected to value given to the debtor (e.g., tax liens). But with respect to competing claimants who have given value in exchange for a lien or other interest in the property (secured lenders, buyers, lessees, most statutory and common law lienholders), effectiveness usually requires the competing third party to have some type of notice or knowledge of the existence of the judgment creditor's lien. Effectiveness also often has a limited duration; the lien must be carried through to enforcement by sale/collection of the property before this expiration date, or it is lost. Note that the debtor's equity exemption, discussed in the preceding chapter, is a special set-aside that stands before judgment liens, but behind contractual liens like mortgages and security interests. The proceeds of the sale/collection of the liened property are distributed to the claimants and the debtor in the order of priority of their liens and exemptions. Priority among liens is usually a simple matter of timing: the first lien or other interest that is effective against a particular third party has priority over that third party's claim or lien.[223]

B. Judgment/Execution Liens on Real Estate

This three-step analysis is quite simple for liens on realty. Real property judgment liens are created by recording or docketing the judgment as described in section B of chapter 3 above. The effective date of the lien is the moment of recording of the operative document (abstract of judgment, docket, memorandum) and it reaches all rights of the debtor in real property in the county of recording, not only rights existing at that time, but also rights acquired any time in the future for the life of the lien, which is generally coterminous with the life of the judgment.[224] This recording provides record notice

223. The few complex exceptions to these rules, especially in the context of contractual security interests, are beyond the scope of this book—they are covered, e.g., in a Secured Transactions class.

224. NY CPLR §5203 (not using "lien" language, but describing a similar effect); CA CCP §§697.310–697.340 (excluding rental payments and leasehold interests for a term less than two years); 735 ILCS 5/12-101. Note that an execution lien on realty, as opposed to a

of the judgment creditor's lien to the world, so these liens on realty are immediately effective against all other claimants. With few exceptions, the first recorded documents create the higher priority, senior liens; in other words, first in time, first in right.[225]

C. Judgment/Execution Liens on Personal Property

The analysis for liens on personal property (tangible and intangible) is slightly more complicated. Such liens can be created in a variety of ways, their third-party effective dates vary depending upon the competing claimant, and their durations vary. But if the three-part creation-effectiveness-priority analysis is conducted step-by-step, the analysis flows quite logically.

1. Creation

Liens on personal property are created by one or another action on a writ of execution or by service of a few of the various enforcement orders discussed in chapter 3 above (e.g., order for examination, turnover order, summons, citation). California law is representative. It creates a lien on personal property at the moment when the officer levies execution on a particular item or items of property. The lien binding this specific property lasts for two years after the date of issuance of the writ and so must be enforced by proceeding to an execution sale (or collection) of that property within that period; otherwise, the lien is lost.[226] New York takes a somewhat unique approach, creating an exe-

---

judgment lien, is often of limited duration. NY CPLR §5203 (lien expires upon return of execution); CA CCP §697.710 (lien expires 2 years after issuance of execution writ).

225. CA CCP §697.380. A major exception to the first-recorded, first-priority rule is the choateness doctrine, which gives a later (properly recorded) IRS tax lien priority in property the debtor acquires after the recording of the competing judgment lien. *See* US v. McDermott, 507 US 447 (1993).

226. CA CCP §697.710; *see also* 700.140(b), (d) (preventing check and withdrawal payment during two-year lien period unless sufficient funds remain in account to cover original levied amount). Also, in the context of an earnings withholding order, a lien attaches only if earnings are not paid by the employer as required to the sheriff, in which case the lien attaches for one year to those unpaid earnings *and* to *all* "property of the employer subject to the enforcement of a money judgment" to secure recovery of the unpaid earnings. CA CCP §§706.029. A lien arising from service of a charging order attaches for the life of the order. CA CCP §708.320(a).

cution lien on *all* of the judgment debtor's personal property at the moment of delivery of an execution to the officer.[227] Remember that creation is only the first step, however; the effectiveness of this lien against third-party claimants must also be considered, and at this later point, New York's law will turn out to be very similar to other states'.

Various enforcement actions not involving execution also give rise to liens. In New York and California, from the moment of issuance, a turnover order or an order appointing a receiver for specific property creates a lien on the property subject to the order.[228] In California and Illinois, which have broader supplementary proceedings, service of the document initiating such proceedings (order for examination, summons for creditor's suit, citation to discover assets) creates a lien on *all* of the debtor's *personal* property in the possession or control of the respondent (debtor or third party), as well as in all debts owed by a third-party respondent to the judgment debtor.[229]

The California OEX/ORAP lien is of limited duration, lasting one year by default.[230] The lien of an Illinois citation to discover assets also lasts only until disposition of the citation (six months, though often continued), but this lien also encumbers any such property acquired later during the citation lien period.[231] Both of these one-year (CA) and six-month (IL) durations can be extended by the court; otherwise, specific property must be located and subjected to a turnover order within these periods, or the liens are lost. To avoid a citation lien expiring, Illinois allows the judgment creditor to request that the court "impress a lien against a specific item of personal property" with a duration just like the judgment lien of a recorded judgment, coterminous with and renewable for the life of the judgment.[232]

Another option unique to California, Florida, and a few other states is a long-term, renewable judgment lien that attaches to later acquired property, as well, just like the one created in realty by the recording of a judgment in the county land records. In these few states, a judgment creditor can file a notice of lien in the UCC records or other central database, which creates a lien on

227. NY CPLR § 5202(a)(not using "lien" language, but providing for the functional equivalent).

228. NY CPLR § 5202(b); CA CCP § 708.205 (with a duration equal to life of judgment per § 697.030).

229. CA CCP §§ 708.110(d), 708.120(c), 708.250; 735 ILCS 5/2-1402(m) (including "choses in action").

230. CA CCP §§ 708.110(d), 708.120(c).

231. 735 ILCS 5/2-1402(m).

232. 735 ILCS 5/2-1402(k-10).

specified categories of personal property in which the debtor has an interest, both at the time of filing and acquired thereafter during the life of the lien. The California statute extends this lien only to business-related property; e.g., accounts, equipment, farm products, inventory.[233] The Florida statute extends to all personal property, with a few odd exceptions.[234] This personal property recording statute, unique to California and Florida and a few other states, creates a personal property judgment lien treated in most respects according to rules paralleling those in Article 9 of the UCC.

2. Third-Party Effectiveness (and Priority)

Recall that one of the twin purposes of a lien is to reserve a place in a line of claimants all clamoring for the value of an item of the debtor's property. For a lien to do this job, the law sometimes requires that third-party competing claimants have some way of knowing that the lien exists and stands before them; otherwise, the lien is not effective as to such claimants. Only effective liens reserve a space in line for the value of liened property, in chronological priority order. Timing is everything; first effective interest in line, first (and perhaps only) seat at the table.

Recall that liens on realty are generally created by recording just such notice in the public (land or court) records, so creation equals third-party notice and therefore immediate effectiveness as to the world. This is true also of the unique California and Florida personal property judgment lien filing in the UCC records or other public database. This is the way contractual security interests are generally made effective against third parties, by *perfection* by filing a notice document in the UCC records. Tax liens are made effective against third parties in this same way.

Execution liens, however, often involve no filing or other public notice. If the lien is created when the sheriff takes tangible property into custody, that overt act creates notice to the world and effectively reserves the judgment creditor's claim to the seized item(s). But the world receives no notice when execution is carried out privately by serving the debtor or a third party with an execution writ (e.g., garnishment), or if the lien is created by service of a turnover order or, worse yet, an all-encompassing order for examination or citation to discover assets.

---

233. CA CCP §§697.510–697.620 (also including tangible chattel paper and documents of title, but excluding vehicles and vessels required to be registered).

234. Fla. Stat. §§55.201–55.204 (excluding fixtures, money, instruments, and mortgages).

In such cases, enforcement lien statutes generally (though not in all states) divide the world of competing claimants into two groups, "not favored" and "favored." Against the former, creation of a judgment enforcement lien is automatically effective, regardless of whether the competing claimant could or did receive notice. This "not favored" group consists of other judgment lien creditors, the trustee in the debtor's bankruptcy case, and perhaps other claimants who have given no value to the debtor directly in exchange for their lien interests. These people's claims line up in the order received; that is, created.[235]

As against the second, favored group, judgment enforcement liens are generally effective only if the competing claimant received actual or at least constructive notice of the lien (and in some cases, had actual knowledge of the lien). Without this notice or knowledge on the part of a later-arising competing claimant, a judgment enforcement lien is not effective as to a favored group member, and interests in the debtor's property acquired by such a later combatant will beat the judgment creditor in the battle for that property's value.

The favored group includes those who have voluntarily given money or other value to the debtor in exchange for their competing lien claim.[236] For example, lenders who give the debtor money and receive a security interest in items of property are members of this favored group, since their lien interests in the property were transferred to them by the debtor in exchange for fair loan value given. Likewise buyers and lessees of the debtor's property are favored group members, since they too received a transfer of an interest in the debtor's property in exchange for fair value given. So long as these favored group members have no notice of the existence of a judgment creditor's competing lien, their interests—even if arising later, after creation of the execution lien—are often effective against and stand ahead of a judgment creditor's lien.

However, if at the point when these competing claimants obtained their interests in the debtor's property, they had notice (or again, in some cases, actual knowledge) of the judgment creditor's existing competing lien, their interests are subject to and stand behind the judgment creditor's lien. In other words, if they knew the judgment creditor already had made a reservation for a seat, these late-comer VIPs are not allowed to exercise their "favored" rights and occupy the earlier judgment creditor's reserved seat. How would they receive

235. NY CPLR §§5231(j), 5234(b); CA CCP §§697.740, 697.910–697.920.

236. NY CPLR §5202 ("transferee ... for fair consideration" (1) before levy, (2) without knowledge of prior levy on property not capable of delivery, or (3) without notice of turnover or receivership order); CA CCP §§697.740(a)-(k); 697.920 (interests acquired "for reasonably equivalent value without knowledge of the lien"); 735 ILCS 5/2-1402(m) ("bona fide purchasers or lenders without notice of the citation").

such notice? Rarely. But a recent amendment to the Illinois citation lien statute suggests an answer. If the temporary citation lien has been perpetuated on specific property by the court's "impressing" a lien on that property, as discussed above, such a lien "may ... be recorded" in the UCC records "filed as an informational filing."[237] This presumably provides constructive notice to the world, making such a lien effective just like a filed California or Florida notice of judgment lien on personal property. For detailed examination of this challenging and intellectually stimulating topic, take Secured Transactions.

237. 735 ILCS 5/2-1402(k-10).

Chapter 6

Capitulate

The topic of money judgment enforcement has not been taught in US law schools for decades largely because, as soon as judgment creditors begin to turn up the heat, debtors since the late 1960s have increasingly retreated into the air-conditioned comfort of federal Bankruptcy Court. The relief provided by the federal Bankruptcy Code[238] has long provided a powerful safe haven to struggling debtors—both individuals and businesses. As a matter of federal law, it legally supersedes and has thus all but displaced the state law of money judgment enforcement in regulating the distribution of value in strained debtor-creditor relationships. Consequently, judgment creditors must understand at least a few basic concepts about the potential effects of a bankruptcy filing before, during, or even after the initiation of judgment enforcement efforts. This is an exceptionally technical area of law, so a course in Bankruptcy is highly recommended, but the key highlights are as follows.

A. Bankruptcy as Collection or Relief ... and Collection

For about 2000 years since its inception in ancient Rome, bankruptcy was considered a collective creditors' weapon to be used against defaulting debtors. It was designed to prevent any one creditor from seizing all of the debtor's property and leaving others with nothing, instead equitably distributing the

238. The US Bankruptcy Code is codified in Title 11 of the US Code, 11 USC §§ 101 *et seq.*, not to be confused with Chapter 11 of the Bankruptcy Code, 11 USC §§ 1101 *et seq.*, which famously governs business reorganization.

debtor's property among all creditors. In much of the world today, bankruptcy is still viewed and used in this way, as a collection tool.[239]

Not so in the US. In 1898 the US adopted the first bankruptcy law in the world with a primary aim to offer relief to "honest but unfortunate" debtors. Not only creditors, but debtors could initiate a case, and the result of a bankruptcy case was not only distribution of the debtor's current assets among creditors, but also *discharge* of those creditors' unpaid claims to the debtor's future assets and income. This discharge relief is the *sine qua non* of modern bankruptcy law and has come to dominate US bankruptcy policy. Creditors are able to initiate bankruptcy cases against debtors today—to prevent other creditors from advantaging themselves in the debtor's moment of weakness—but this is extremely rare.

Instead, debtors initiate the overwhelming majority of bankruptcy cases, choosing among three principal *chapters* that provide discharge relief on very different terms. Chapter 7 is the dominant choice among individual debtors. In exchange for relinquishing their non-exempt property (usually nothing of any value) to a trustee for distribution among all creditors, individual debtors receive an immediate "fresh start" in the form of relief from creditor pursuit, and long-term discharge relief after a case administration period of about four months. Chapter 13 offers an alternative for debtors with valuable non-exempt property they wish to preserve. Debtors choosing chapter 13 agree to abide by a statutorily-determined payment plan by which they relinquish all of their disposable income for three to five years (almost always 60 months) to a trustee, who again distributes this value among all creditors. The discharge relief offered by chapter 13 is slightly broader than in chapter 7, as discussed below. Finally, chapter 11 is the ultra-sophisticated and vastly more expensive cousin of chapter 13. It is available to high-income and high-debt individuals, but it is used most often and most effectively by large business entities to rearrange and restructure their legal and business affairs pursuant to a plan of reorganization approved by creditor vote. Chapter 11 is a hugely complex procedure, but the basics from a judgment creditor's perspective are largely the same as the other two chapters. Beyond the basics, good legal counsel is essential in any bankruptcy case, but especially in a chapter 11 proceeding.

While the generous default position is that individual debtors can choose either a fairly easy, asset-turnover chapter 7 "fresh start" or a more arduous, 60-month-payment-plan chapter 13 "earned start," since 2005 that choice has been constrained by the so-called *means test.* Many in Congress were led to believe that too many individual debtors were choosing the easy way out and not

---

239. *See, e.g.,* Jason Kilborn & Adrian Walters, "Involuntary Bankruptcy As Debt Collection: Multi-Jurisdictional Lessons in Choosing the Right Tool for the Job," 87 *Am. Bankr. L.J.* 123 (2013).

doing their best to use future income to satisfy their responsibilities. Thus, the extraordinarily technical and complex means test was designed to identify those individuals who, if they only abided by a reasonable household budget, would have sufficient future disposable income to fund a reasonable payment plan.

The reality was and is that few "can-pay" individuals choose bankruptcy, and few debtors who choose bankruptcy can pay. Only about 1–3% of individuals seeking bankruptcy relief are denied chapter 7 relief, though these high-income, asset-rich people are the most likely group against whom it makes sense to have obtained a substantial money judgment. But chapter 13 is no panacea for judgment creditors, either. Of those choosing a chapter 13 payment plan, the vast majority offer payment primarily or only to secured creditors (those with liens, as discussed in the preceding chapter, that are not destroyed as discussed below in this chapter). Chapter 13 cases generally distribute little or nothing to judgment creditors and other "general unsecured creditors" like them.

The bottom line here is that bankruptcy is a real danger for creditors who push their debtors too far. Chapter 7 is available to most individual debtors, and unsecured creditors tend to collect very little in any form of bankruptcy, though perhaps slightly more in a chapter 13 case. Business entities can freely chose chapter 7 if pushed too hard, which generally means shutting down and producing no future income and little if any distribution to judgment creditors. Chapter 11 is an expensive rarity that usually results in conversion to chapter 7 and again paltry returns to judgment creditors. For high-net-worth individuals and asset-rich businesses, bankruptcy is unnecessary, disruptive, and unhelpful, but it is difficult for a judgment creditor to discern whether a non-paying judgment debtor is just being obstinate or is in real financial distress. The latter case will likely lead to a bankruptcy filing, in which case the music stops for state judgment collection.

B. The Automatic Stay

The very first thing that occurs immediately and automatically upon the filing of a bankruptcy case is the imposition of a stay, an injunction, on any further collection actions.[240] This stay applies to all creditors, secured and unsecured, those with and without judgments, and even those with unmatured and unliquidated potential claims and causes of action. In terms of judgment collection, the stay clearly and in virtually all cases prohibits any further enforcement efforts of any kind against the debtor or the debtor's property. Vi-

240. 11 USC § 362(a).

olation of this stay is taken very seriously by the Bankruptcy Courts and can lead to severe sanctions against creditors.

Lesson number one about bankruptcy is this: The moment a judgment creditor learns of the judgment debtor's bankruptcy filing, *all collections activity of any kind must cease.* No formal notice is required for this stay to operate, and debtors need not offer creditors any proof or other information concerning their case to enjoy the stay's protection. Debtors are required to file lists and schedules that will result in notification to creditors mailed from the Bankruptcy Court, but even before receipt of this notice, any hint of a debtor's bankruptcy filing should bring any collections efforts to a halt. This includes not only formal but also informal action, including putting pressure on the debtor orally and even indirectly to try to get the debtor to pay the judgment debt. It also includes passive action, such as holding the debtor's property, which by law must be turned over to the trustee or, in chapters 11 and 13, to the debtor, such as cars and other property seized but not yet sold before the bankruptcy filing.[241]

Judgment creditors often believe their actions are excepted from this automatic stay. They are almost always wrong. There are a few collections-related actions that fall within explicit exceptions to the stay, but these are largely limited to government or police actions and family-support related collections.[242] Once again, if a money judgment creditor learns that the judgment debtor has initiated a bankruptcy case under any chapter, any further action to enforce that judgment (or even inaction, such as by allowing the sheriff to continue to execute a writ or an employer to withhold or pay over garnished wages) is likely a violation, will be void, and will expose both creditor and attorney to sanctions, possibly severe. Don't do it.

C. Limitations on Relief: Objections and Exceptions to Discharge

In the usual case, the automatic stay will become permanent when the case ends. Whether or not a distribution of any value is made to creditors, a bankruptcy case ordinarily concludes with a discharge of any unpaid liability of the debtor on monetary claims. The discharge is not universal, however, and

241. 11 USC § 542.

242. 11 USC § 362(b). A creditor can also request that the Bankruptcy Court grant "relief" from the stay, but the bases for such relief are almost entirely limited to secured creditors pursuing the collateral securing their claims. 11 USC § 362(d). Unsecured judgment creditors in particular are unlikely to have any basis on which to credibly request relief from the stay.

the chapter 7 discharge can be challenged in appropriate cases. This relief is designed to be offered to "honest but unfortunate" debtors, so in chapter 7 cases involving dishonesty and other bad behavior, the discharge can be denied. It is automatically denied to any debtor who has received discharge relief under a previous chapter 7 (or 11) case within the past eight years, or after completion of a previous chapter 13 payment-plan case filed within the past six years.[243]

The other bases for the Bankruptcy Court to deny a chapter 7 discharge are mainly related to misconduct by the debtor during the bankruptcy case (failing to cooperate with the trustee, failing to keep proper records, destroying property, etc.), but one retrospective basis in particular is relevant to judgment creditors. A chapter 7 discharge can be denied if the debtor made an *actual* fraudulent transfer of property (as discussed in section E.1. of chapter 3 above) within the year preceding the bankruptcy filing.[244] Any creditor can object to discharge on this basis, though the evidentiary burden of proving the debtor's actual fraudulent intent is quite heavy and will likely fall on the creditor. The expense of pursuing such an objection is seldom worth the investment, especially since the debtor will emerge from the bankruptcy case denuded of assets and no more able than before to satisfy the judgment.

A more fine-tuned limitation on discharge is a range of debts that are excepted from discharge, either automatically or upon an objection and evidentiary showing by the affected creditor. Most of these are related again to government- and family-related debts, but a few could be the subject of an ordinary money judgment. Some of these debts are excepted only from a chapter 7 discharge, but some are excepted from *any* discharge at all. The latter group include debts for (1) money, property, services, or an extension, renewal, or refinancing of credit, obtained by the debtor's fraud, (2) "fraud or defalcation while acting in a fiduciary capacity, embezzlement, or larceny," (3) death or personal injury as a result of the debtor's operating a vehicle under the influence of drugs or alcohol, (4) public and private student loans and other "educational benefits," and (5) money judgments for restitution or damages for "willful or malicious [personal] injury" by the debtor to an individual person.[245] Only excepted from the chapter 7 discharge, in contrast, are debts for "willful or ma-

243. 11 USC § 727(a)(8)–(9).

244. 11 USC § 727(a)(2).

245. 11 USC §§ 523(a), 1328(a). The fraud exception in particular is quite complex and subject to numerous conditions and exceptions, and an objection to discharge on this and a few other bases must be timely made in order for these exception to apply in chapter 7—unlike most, these few exceptions are not self-executing. 11 USC § 523(c).

licious injury" to an entity or property—as opposed to an individual person.[246] This expansive notion has been held to encompass virtually any intentional tort, including violation of intellectual property rights. Collection of even these claims is temporarily stayed by the filing of a bankruptcy case, but collection on a non-dischargeable claim can resume after the case is closed. Knowing that a money judgment is for a non-dischargeable claim certainly changes the leverage dynamic in dealing with a debtor threatening bankruptcy.

D. Preference Clawback within 90 Days

For creditors whose claims are discharged at the conclusion of the case, it gets worse. Bankruptcy is designed to distribute among all creditors whatever non-exempt value the debtor has. One provision expands this pain/benefit equalization to transfers of value occurring in the period shortly *before* the bankruptcy filing. Any creditor who has received a transfer of an interest of the debtor in property within 90 days before the bankruptcy filing might have to give back that interest for redistribution among all creditors. Such a transfer has *preferred* one creditor over others, offering value to one and not all. Therefore, bankruptcy law provides for recovery by the trustee (or in chapter 11 and possibly 13, by the debtor) of any such *preferential transfer*, now preserved for the benefit of the *estate* and all creditors.[247]

The specifics here are eye-wateringly complex, but the basic idea is easy and important to comprehend: If a judgment creditor receives a transfer of *any* interest in the debtor's property within 90 days of a bankruptcy filing, that interest is likely to be pursued and recovered in the bankruptcy case. It is impossible at the time of a transfer to predict whether or when the debtor might file for bankruptcy, but if the debtor seems financially wobbly, an imminent bankruptcy filing is always a possibility. What kinds of transfers are implicated? Once again, *all* transfers, voluntary and involuntary, affecting all kinds of property. This includes both payments of money and voluntary transfers of other property, as well as the involuntary transfer of a lien on the debtor's property that occurs when a judgment creditor engages in collection efforts (as discussed in the preceding chapter). This is one of the most commonly litigated aspects of bankruptcy law, and judgment creditors lose recently acquired payment and lien rights regularly in contests with bankruptcy trustees and chapter 11 debtors-in-possession.

---

246. 11 USC § 523(a)(6).

247. 11 USC §§ 547, 550, 551.

The proper strategic choices here are difficult to gauge. Act too quickly and aggressively, and you'll push the debtor into bankruptcy and put recently acquired value in jeopardy. Move too slowly, and any transfer of value is more likely to have occurred within the 90-day lookback period before a bankruptcy filing. Careful evaluation of the debtor's financial stability and willingness ultimately to seek bankruptcy relief is crucial and very difficult to judge. *Caveat creditor!*

Chapter 7

Exercises

Having covered a broad terrain of information, the time has come to look back and put that information to use. The following exercises are designed to illustrate how the elements discussed in this book come together, to concentrate your attention on a few key details of law-fact interaction, and to provide a basis for active review of the material by placing it in a practical context. Answer these questions by referencing the general discussion in this book and the details in the law of one of the states whose relevant provisions are excerpted in the following appendices (New York, California, or Illinois) or find the corresponding laws of another state, perhaps the one in which you are studying or practicing (or hope one day to study or practice) and apply that law to the degree it provides answers. Note well: any given state's law might *not* provide clear answers to some of these questions, much less to any number of other questions that could be spun off from the simple hypothetical.

Your client, Paula Plaintiff, has obtained a $750,000 federal judgment against David Defendant for copyright infringement. David's lawyer has ignored all of your calls inquiring as to a timetable for payment of this judgment. You know nothing about David other than his home address and telephone number (which you found on the internet). What, if anything, can you do to effectively enforce your judgment against David?

1. Can you ask the court to put him in jail for contempt for failing to fulfill the judgment?
2. You want to find out what sources of value David might have against which you could enforce your judgment.
   a. Can you ask David questions (preferably under oath) about the existence and location of any such sources of value?
   b. Can you ask other people (again, preferably under oath) if they know of any sources of value belonging to David?

c. If you are able to question David under oath about the location of his assets, and he fails to appear for the examination, what then?

3. You discover that David owns the following valuable assets. What can you do to have them seized and their value applied to your client's judgment? In answering this question, consider what else you need to know about these assets, whether (and how) any of these assets might be protected from creditors by law, and what, if anything, David would have to do to take advantage of that protection. Consider in particular if it matters whether or not David is married, with or without children.

a. a four-bedroom home in your county/parish, valued at $750,000 and subject to a $735,000 recorded mortgage

b. a two-year-old Lexus ES350 sedan, Kelly Bluebook value about $26,000

c. a bank account at JPMorgan Chase Bank with a current balance of $7854.19 (you know the routing number and account number but are unsure exactly where the money is held)

d. a series of retirement accounts with a total current market value of $1.5 million, managed by various investment companies, along with an ordinary (non-retirement) investment account with E*Trade, currently worth $150,000

e. antique bedroom, dining room, and living room furniture likely to be worth at least $25,000

f. the copyright to several books that, though not blockbusters, seem to have been selling well in recent years (around the order of $3000 in royalties each)

4. You are concerned that the actions you might need to take to seize the value in the preceding question could take some time, and David might spirit away the assets in the meantime. What if anything can you do to prevent David or anyone else from transferring away these assets while you are preparing the action to seize them?

5. You have heard from friends that it is important that you "put a lien on" David's property. Which of the enforcement actions you've mentioned above "puts a lien" on some or all of David's property, and what generally does that mean?

6. You take legal action to enforce Paula's judgment against David's bank account by taking the proper actions, and a representative of the bank responds that, as of that day, the balance in David's account is $3765.23.

a. How much of this—at most and at least—will your client be able to seize?
b. One month later, you discover that David recently deposited $10,000 more into that same account. Can you seize any of this?
c. Must you renew your enforcement efforts against this account to seize the $10,000? May you do so?
d. What if another $20,000 is deposited six months later?
e. Suppose you served the papers necessary to seize the $10,000, but the bank paid out that $10,000 on several checks presented against David's account a few days later, before responding to the papers you served on the bank.
   i. Can you take any action to recover that money for Paula?
   ii. Would it matter if the bank argued that these payments were made in the "ordinary course of business" for both David and the bank?

7. You learn that Teresa Parks owes David $2500 for some manuscript editing work that David performed for Teresa a few weeks ago.
   a. Can you do anything to compel Teresa to make that payment to you rather than to David?
   b. Can you demand that the payment be made directly to Paula, or must some enforcement officer intervene, and what impact might that have on the costs involved in seizing this value?
   c. Can David invoke any legal protection for his right to receive this payment?
8. You learn that David has started working for a large corporate employer for a gross salary of $120,000 per year ($10,000 per month). You eventually discover that, after taxes and other required withholding, David's net take-home pay is $7000 per month, paid twice monthly (on the 15th and last day of each month).
   a. Can you do anything to compel David's employer to turn over all or some portion of David's recurring salary to Paula—or to an enforcement officer?
   b. If so, does the law protect any portion of this salary for David? If so, what, if anything, must David do to take advantage of this protection?
   c. How much, at most, can you collect from David's salary if you can collect anything, and on what timetable will you receive payments?
   d. How much will David's take-home pay be reduced while this procedure is in effect?

e. Must you renew your efforts to seize David's salary every pay period, or will the action you've taken continue in effect for some time? How long?
f. Suppose David deposits his take-home pay in his bank account—can you seize that money using the techniques you used against the bank before?
g. If David's employer ignores your enforcement efforts, what remedy do you have, if any, against the employer?

9. Can you add to the judgment any of the ongoing expenses your client is incurring for all of this enforcement activity? In particular, what about your fees? Can you add any other amounts to the judgment as time passes?
** Note that this lawsuit was based on the Copyright Act, § 505 of which gives the court discretion to award reasonable attorney's fees to a prevailing plaintiff, which you were savvy enough to request and obtain for Paula. Nice!
10. Suppose the judgment debtor were not David, an individual, but David's business, a single-member limited liability company called David, LLC. How, if at all, would your answers to the preceding questions change, particularly questions 3, 7, and 8 with respect to the protections for the debtor's assets?
11. If you represent David or David, LLC, and your client tells you that the burden of Paula's enforcement actions has become too great to bear (destroying David's family life, business, etc.), is there an inexpensive and effective form of relief available to put an end to Paula's collection efforts? What form(s) of relief might be available, and what generally will David (or David, LLC) be required to do to obtain such relief? Would you advise David to seek that relief or not?

Appendices

Appendix A · New York Civil Practice Law & Rules (CPLR)
Appendix B · California Code of Civil Procedure (CCP)
Appendix C · Illinois Code of Civil Procedure (735 ILCS 5/)
& Supreme Court Rule 277

NB: Dollar figures in square brackets indicate values indexed for inflation in New York as of April 1, 2018, and in California as of April 1, 2019, to be indexed again in each case at later three-year intervals.

Appendix A

New York Civil Practice Law & Rules (CPLR)

Article 51
Enforcement of Judgments and Orders Generally

§5101. Enforcement of money judgment.... A money judgment and an order directing the payment of money, including motion costs, may be enforced as prescribed in article fifty-two. ***

*** [*special provisions on child support enforcement omitted throughout*]

§5106. Appointment of receiver. A court, by or after judgment, may appoint a receiver ... to carry the judgment into effect....

Article 52 Enforcement of Money Judgments

§5201. Debt or property subject to enforcement; proper garnishee.

(a) Debt against which a money judgment may be enforced. A money judgment may be enforced against any debt, which is past due or which is yet to become due, certainly or upon demand of the judgment debtor, whether it was incurred within or without the state, to or from a resident or non-resident, unless it is exempt from application to the satisfaction of the judgment. A debt may consist of a cause of action which could be assigned or transferred accruing within or without the state.

(b) Property against which a money judgment may be enforced. A money judgment may be enforced against any property which could be assigned or transferred, whether it consists of a present or future right or interest and whether or not it is vested, unless it is exempt from application to the satisfaction of the judgment....

(c) Proper garnishee for particular property or debt.

1. Where property consists of a right or share in the stock of an association or corporation, or interests or profits therein, for which a certificate of stock or other negotiable instrument is not outstanding, the corporation, or the president or treasurer of the association on behalf of the association, shall be the garnishee.

2. Where property consists of a right or interest to or in a decedent's estate or any other property or fund held or controlled by a fiduciary, the executor or trustee under the will, administrator or other fiduciary shall be the garnishee.

3. Where property consists of an interest in a partnership, any partner other than the judgment debtor, on behalf of the partnership, shall be the garnishee.

4. Where property or a debt is evidenced by a negotiable instrument for the payment of money, a negotiable document of title or a certificate of stock of an association or corporation, the instrument, document or certificate shall be treated as property capable of delivery and the person holding it shall be the garnishee; except that section 8-112 of the uniform commercial code shall govern the extent to which and the means by which any interest in a certificated security, uncertificated security or security entitlement (as defined in article eight of the uniform commercial code) may be reached by garnishment, attachment or other legal process.

§5202. Judgment creditor's rights in personal property.

(a) Execution creditor's rights. Where a judgment creditor has delivered an execution to a sheriff, the judgment creditor's rights in a debt owed to the judgment debtor or in an interest of the judgment debtor in personal property, against which debt or property the judgment may be enforced, are superior to the extent of the amount of the execution to the rights of any transferee of the debt or property, except:

1. a transferee who acquired the debt or property for fair consideration before it was levied upon; or

2. a transferee who acquired a debt or personal property not capable of delivery for fair consideration after it was levied upon without knowledge of the levy.

(b) Other judgment creditor's rights. Where a judgment creditor has secured an order for delivery of, payment of, or appointment of a receiver of, a debt owed to the judgment debtor or an interest of the judgment debtor in personal property, the judgment creditor's rights in the debt or property are superior to the rights of any transferee of the debt or property, except a transferee who acquired the debt or property for fair consideration and without notice of such order.

§5203. Priorities and liens upon real property.

(a) **Priority and lien on docketing judgment.** No transfer of an interest of the judgment debtor in real property, against which property a money judgment may be enforced, is effective against the judgment creditor either from the time of the docketing of the judgment with the clerk of the county in which the property is located until ten years after filing of the judgment-roll, or from the time of the filing with such clerk of a notice of levy pursuant to an execution until the execution is returned * * *

* * *

§5205. Personal property exempt from application to the satisfaction of money judgments.

(a) **Exemption for personal property.** The following personal property when owned by any person is exempt from application to the satisfaction of a money judgment except where the judgment is for the purchase price of the exempt property … :

1. all stoves and home heating equipment kept for use in the judgment debtor's dwelling house and necessary fuel therefor for one hundred twenty days; one sewing machine with its appurtenances;
2. religious texts, family pictures and portraits, and school books used by the judgment debtor or in the family; and other books, not exceeding five hundred dollars [**$575**] in value, kept and used as part of the family or judgment debtor's library;
3. a seat or pew occupied by the judgment debtor or the family in a place of public worship;
4. domestic animals with the necessary food for those animals for one hundred twenty days, provided that the total value of such animals and food does not exceed one thousand dollars [**$1150**]; all necessary food actually provided for the use of the judgment debtor or his family for one hundred twenty days;
5. all wearing apparel, household furniture, one mechanical, gas or electric refrigerator, one radio receiver, one television set, one computer and associated equipment, one cellphone, crockery, tableware and cooking utensils necessary for the judgment debtor and the family; all prescribed health aids;
6. a wedding ring; a watch, jewelry and art not exceeding one thousand dollars [**$1150**] in value;

7. tools of trade, necessary working tools and implements, including those of a mechanic, farm machinery, team, professional instruments, furniture and library, not exceeding three thousand dollars [**$3400**] in value, together with the necessary food for the team for one hundred twenty days, provided, however, that the articles specified in this paragraph are necessary to the carrying on of the judgment debtor's profession or calling;

8. one motor vehicle not exceeding four thousand dollars [**$4550**] in value above liens and encumbrances of the debtor; if such vehicle has been equipped for use by a disabled debtor, then ten thousand dollars [**$11,375**] in value above liens and encumbrances of the debtor; ... ; and

9. if no homestead exemption is claimed, then one thousand dollars [**$1150**] in personal property, bank account or cash.

* * *

(c) Trust exemption.

1.... [A]ll property while held in trust for a judgment debtor, where the trust has been created by, or the fund so held in trust has proceeded from, a person other than the judgment debtor, is exempt from application to the satisfaction of a money judgment.

2. For purposes of this subdivision, all trusts, custodial accounts, annuities, insurance contracts, monies, assets or interests established as part of, and all payments from, either any trust or plan, which is qualified as an individual retirement account under section four hundred eight or section four hundred eight A of the United States Internal Revenue Code of 1986, as amended, a Keogh (HR-10), retirement or other plan established by a corporation, which is qualified under section 401 of the United States Internal Revenue Code of 1986, as amended, or created as a result of rollovers from such plans pursuant to sections 402 (a) (5), 403 (a) (4), 408 (d) (3) or 408A of the Internal Revenue Code of 1986, as amended, or a plan that satisfies the requirements of section 457 of the Internal Revenue Code of 1986, as amended, shall be considered a trust which has been created by or which has proceeded from a person other than the judgment debtor, even though such judgment debtor is (i) in the case of an individual retirement account plan, an individual who is the settlor of and depositor to such account plan, or (ii) a self-employed individual, or (iii) a partner of the entity sponsoring the Keogh (HR-10) plan, or (iv) a shareholder of the corporation sponsoring the retirement or other plan or (v) a participant in a section 457 plan. * * *

(d) Income exemptions. The following personal property is exempt from application to the satisfaction of a money judgment, except such part as a court determines to be unnecessary for the reasonable requirements of the judgment debtor and his dependents:

1. ninety per cent of the income or other payments from a trust the principal of which is exempt under subdivision (c); provided, however, that with respect to any income or payments made from trusts, custodial accounts, annuities, insurance contracts, monies, assets or interest established as part of an individual retirement account plan or as part of a Keogh (HR-10), retirement or other plan described in paragraph two of subdivision (c) of this section, the exception in this subdivision for such part as a court determines to be unnecessary for the reasonable requirements of the judgment debtor and his dependents shall not apply, and the ninety percent exclusion of this paragraph shall become a one hundred percent exclusion;

2. ninety per cent of the earnings of the judgment debtor for his personal services rendered within sixty days before, and at any time after, an income execution is delivered to the sheriff or a motion is made to secure the application of the judgment debtor's earnings to the satisfaction of the judgment; * * *

(e) Exemptions to members of armed forces. The pay and bounty of a non-commissioned officer, musician or private in the armed forces of the United States or the state of New York; a land warrant, pension or other reward granted by the United States, or by a state, for services in the armed forces; a sword, horse, medal, emblem or device of any kind presented as a testimonial for services rendered in the armed forces of the United States or a state; and the uniform, arms and equipments which were used by a person in the service, are exempt from application to the satisfaction of a money judgment; ...

(f) Exemption for unpaid milk proceeds. Ninety per cent of any money or debt due or to become due to the judgment debtor for the sale of milk produced on a farm operated by him and delivered for his account to a milk dealer licensed pursuant to article twenty-one of the agriculture and markets law is exempt from application to the satisfaction of a money judgment.

(g) Security deposit exemption. Money deposited as security for the rental of real property to be used as the residence of the judgment debtor or the judgment debtor's family; and money deposited as security with a gas, electric, water, steam, telegraph or telephone corporation, or a municipality rendering equivalent utility services, for services to judgment debtor's residence or the residence of judgment debtor's family, are exempt from application to the satisfaction of a money judgment.

(h) The following personal property is exempt from application to the satisfaction of money judgment, except such part as a court determines to be unnecessary for the reasonable requirements of the judgment debtor and his dependents:

1. any and all medical and dental accessions to the human body and all personal property or equipment that is necessary or proper to maintain or assist in sustaining or maintaining one or more major life activities or is utilized to provide mobility for a person with a permanent disability; and

2. any guide dog, service dog or hearing dog, as those terms are defined in section one hundred eight of the agriculture and markets law, or any animal trained to aid or assist a person with a permanent disability and actually being so used by such person, together with any and all food or feed for any such dog or other animal.

(i) Exemption for life insurance policies. The right of a judgment debtor to accelerate payment of part or all of the death benefit or special surrender value under a life insurance policy … is exempt from application to the satisfaction of a money judgment.

(j) Exemption for New York state college choice tuition savings program trust fund payment monies. Monies in an account created pursuant to article fourteen-A of the education law are exempt from application to the satisfaction of a money judgment …

* * *

(*l*) Exemption of banking institution accounts into which statutorily exempt payments are made electronically or by direct deposit.

1. If direct deposit or electronic payments reasonably identifiable as statutorily exempt payments were made to the judgment debtor's account in any banking institution during the forty-five day period preceding the date a restraining notice was served on the banking institution or an execution was served upon the banking institution by a marshal or sheriff, then two thousand five hundred dollars [**$2850**] in the judgment debtor's account is exempt from application to the satisfaction of a money judgment….

2. For purposes of this article, "statutorily exempt payments" means any personal property exempt from application to the satisfaction of a money judgment under any provision of state or federal law. [**earnings?**] Such term shall include, but not be limited to, payments from any of the following sources: social security, including retirement, survivors' and disability benefits, supplemental security income or child support payments; veterans administration

benefits; public assistance; workers' compensation; unemployment insurance; public or private pensions; railroad retirement; and black lung benefits.

3. (i) Beginning on April first, two thousand twelve, and at each three-year interval ending on April first thereafter, the dollar amount of the exemption provided in this section, subdivisions (e) and (h) of section fifty-two hundred twenty-two, subdivision (a) of section fifty-two hundred thirty and subdivision (e) of section fifty-two hundred thirty-two of this article in effect immediately before that date shall be adjusted [and published by the superintendent of financial services] ...

* * *

§5206. Real property exempt from application to the satisfaction of money judgments.

(a) **Exemption of homestead.** Property of one of the following types, not exceeding one hundred fifty thousand dollars [**$170,825**] for the counties of Kings, Queens, New York, Bronx, Richmond, Nassau, Suffolk, Rockland, Westchester and Putnam; one hundred twenty-five thousand dollars [**$142,350**] for the counties of Dutchess, Albany, Columbia, Orange, Saratoga and Ulster; and seventy-five thousand dollars [**$85,400**] for the remaining counties of the state in value above liens and encumbrances, owned and occupied as a principal residence, is exempt from application to the satisfaction of a money judgment, unless the judgment was recovered wholly for the purchase price thereof:

1. a lot of land with a dwelling thereon,
2. shares of stock in a cooperative apartment corporation,
3. units of a condominium apartment, or
4. a mobile home.

* * *

(e) **Sale of homestead exceeding [the limits mentioned in (a)].** A judgment creditor may commence a special proceeding in the county in which the homestead is located against the judgment debtor for the sale, by a sheriff or receiver, of a homestead exceeding [the values listed in (a)]. The court may direct that the notice of petition be served upon any other person. The court, if it directs such a sale, shall so marshal the proceeds of the sale that the right and interest of each person in the proceeds shall correspond as nearly as may be to his right and interest in the property sold. Money, not exceeding [the exempt amounts] paid to a judgment debtor, as representing his interest in the proceeds, is exempt for one year after the payment, unless, before the expiration of the year, he acquires an exempt homestead, in which case, the exemption ceases with respect to so much of the money as was not expended for the purchase of that property; and the exemption of the property so acquired extends to every debt against which the property sold was exempt....

(f) Exemption of burying ground. Land, set apart as a family or private burying ground, is exempt from application to the satisfaction of a money judgment, upon the following conditions only:

1. a portion of it must have been actually used for that purpose;
2. it must not exceed in extent one-fourth of an acre; and
3. it must not contain any building or structure, except one or more vaults or other places of deposit for the dead, or mortuary monuments.

* * *

§5221. Where enforcement proceeding commenced.

(a) Court and county in which proceeding commenced.

1. If the judgment sought to be enforced was entered in the city court of any city outside the city of New York, and the respondent resides or is regularly employed or has a place for the regular transaction of business in person within the county in which the court is or was located, a special proceeding authorized by this article shall be commenced in that court or in the county court of that county.

2. If the judgment sought to be enforced was entered in a district court, or by a justice of the peace whose office has been or is by law to be abolished and whose jurisdiction has been or is by law to be superseded by a district court, and the respondent resides or is regularly employed or has a place for the regular transaction of business in person within the county in which such district court is established, a special proceeding authorized by this article shall be commenced in such district court.

3. If the judgment sought to be enforced was entered in the municipal court of the city of New York, the city court of the city of New York or the civil court of the city of New York, and the respondent resides or is regularly employed or has a place for the regular transaction of business in person within that city, a special proceeding authorized by this article shall be commenced in the civil court of the city of New York.

4. In any other case, if the judgment sought to be enforced was entered in any court of this state, a special proceeding authorized by this article shall be commenced, either in the supreme court or a county court, in a county in which the respondent resides or is regularly employed or has a place for the

regular transaction of business in person or, if there is no such county, in any county in which he may be served or the county in which the judgment was entered.

* * *

§5222. Restraining notice.

(a) **Issuance; on whom served; form; service.** A restraining notice may be issued by the clerk of the court or the attorney for the judgment creditor as officer of the court.... It may be served upon any person, except the employer of a judgment debtor ... where the property sought to be restrained consists of wages or salary due or to become due to the judgment debtor.... It shall be served personally in the same manner as a summons or by registered or certified mail, return receipt requested.... It shall specify all of the parties to the action, the date that the judgment ... was entered, the court in which it was entered, the amount of the judgment ... and the amount then due thereon, the names of all parties in whose favor and against whom the judgment ... was entered, it shall set forth subdivision (b) and shall state that disobedience is punishable as a contempt of court, and it shall contain an original signature or copy of the original signature of the clerk of the court or attorney....

(b) Effect of restraint; prohibition of transfer; duration. A judgment debtor ... served with a restraining notice is forbidden to make or suffer any sale, assignment, transfer or interference with any property in which he or she has an interest, except as set forth in subdivisions (h) and (i) of this section, and except upon direction of the sheriff or pursuant to an order of the court, until the judgment ... is satisfied or vacated. A restraining notice served upon a person other than the judgment debtor ... is effective only if, at the time of service, he or she owes a debt to the judgment debtor ... or he or she is in the possession or custody of property in which he or she knows or has reason to believe the judgment debtor ... has an interest.... All property in which the judgment debtor ... is known or believed to have an interest then in and thereafter coming into the possession or custody of such a person, including any specified in the notice, and all debts of such a person, including any specified in the notice, then due and thereafter coming due to the judgment debtor..., shall be subject to the notice except as set forth in subdivisions (h) and (i) of this section. Such a person is forbidden to make or suffer any sale, assignment or transfer of, or any interference with, any such property, or pay over or otherwise dispose of any such debt, to any person other than the sheriff..., except as set forth in subdivisions (h) and (i) of this section, and except upon direction of the sheriff or pursuant to an order of the court, until the expiration of one year after the notice is served upon him or her, or until the judgment ... is satisfied or vacated, whichever event first occurs. A judgment creditor ... which has specified personal property or debt in a restraining notice shall be liable to the owner of the property or the person to whom the debt is owed, if other than the judgment debtor..., for any damages sustained by reason of the restraint. If a garnishee served with a restraining notice withholds the payment of money belonging or owed to the judgment debtor ... in an amount equal to twice the amount due on the judgment..., the restraining notice is not effective as to other property or money.

(c) **Subsequent notice.** Leave of court is required to serve more than one restraining notice upon the same person with respect to the same judgment.... A judgment creditor shall not serve more than two restraining notices per year upon a natural person's banking institution account.

(d) **Notice to judgment debtor**.... [A] copy of the restraining notice together with the notice to judgment debtor ... shall be mailed by first class mail or personally delivered to each judgment debtor ... who is a natural person within four days of the service of the restraining notice. Such notice shall be mailed to the defendant at his or her residence address; or in the event such mailing is returned as undeliverable by the post office, or if the residence address of the defendant is unknown, then to the defendant in care of the place of employment of the defendant if known, in an envelope bearing the legend "personal and confidential" and not indicating on the outside thereof, by the return address or otherwise, that the communication is from an attorney or concerns a judgment ... ; or if neither the residence address nor the place of employment of the defendant is known then to the defendant at any other known address.

(e) **Content of notice.** The notice required by subdivision (d) of this section shall be in substantially the following form and may be included in the restraining notice:

NOTICE TO JUDGMENT DEBTOR

Money or property belonging to you may have been taken or held in order to satisfy a judgment which has been entered against you. Read this carefully.

YOU MAY BE ABLE TO GET YOUR MONEY BACK

State and federal laws prevent certain money or property from being taken to satisfy judgments or orders. Such money or property is said to be "exempt". The following is a partial list of money which may be exempt:

1. Supplemental security income, (SSI);
2. Social security;
3. Public assistance (welfare);
4. Spousal support, maintenance (alimony) or child support;
5. Unemployment benefits;
6. Disability benefits;
7. Workers' compensation benefits;
8. Public or private pensions;
9. Veterans benefits;
10. Ninety percent of your wages or salary earned in the last sixty days;
11. Twenty-five hundred dollars [**$2850**] of any bank account containing statutorily exempt payments that were deposited electronically or by direct deposit within the last forty-five days, including, but not limited to, your social security, supplemental security income, veterans benefits, public assistance, workers' compensation, unemployment insurance, public or private pensions, railroad retirement benefits, black lung benefits, or child support payments;
12. Railroad retirement; and
13. Black lung benefits.

If you think that any of your money that has been taken or held is exempt, you must act promptly because the money may be applied to the judgment.... If you claim that any of your money that has been taken or held is exempt, you may contact the person sending this notice.
Also, YOU MAY CONSULT AN ATTORNEY, INCLUDING ANY FREE LEGAL SERVICES ORGANIZATION IF YOU QUALIFY. You can also go to court without an attorney to get your money back. Bring this notice with you when you go. You are allowed to try to prove to a judge that your money is exempt from collection under New York civil practice law and rules, sections fifty-two hundred twenty-two-a, fifty-two hundred thirty-nine and fifty-two hundred forty. If you do not have a lawyer, the clerk of the court may give you forms to help you prove your account contains exempt money that the creditor cannot collect. The law (New York civil practice law and rules, article four and sections fifty-

two hundred thirty-nine and fifty-two hundred forty) provides a procedure for determination of a claim to an exemption.

* * *

(g) Restraining notice in the form of magnetic tape or other electronic means. Where such person consents thereto in writing, a restraining notice in the form of magnetic tape or other electronic means, as defined in subdivision (f) of rule twenty-one hundred three of this chapter, may be served upon a person other than the judgment debtor.... A restraining notice in such form shall contain all of the information required to be specified in a restraining notice under subdivision (a), except for the original signature or copy of the original signature of the clerk or attorney who issued the restraining notice. The provisions of this subdivision notwithstanding, the notice required by subdivisions (d) and (e) shall be given to the judgment debtor ... in the written form set forth therein.

(h) Effect of restraint on judgment debtor's banking institution account into which statutorily exempt payments are made electronically or by direct deposit. Notwithstanding the provisions of subdivision (b) of this section, if direct deposit or electronic payments reasonably identifiable as statutorily exempt payments as defined in paragraph two of subdivision (*l*) of section fifty-two hundred five of this article were made to the judgment debtor's account during the forty-five day period preceding the date that the restraining notice was served on the banking institution, then the banking institution shall not restrain two thousand five hundred dollars [**$2850**] in the judgment debtor's account. If the account contains an amount equal to or less than two thousand five hundred dollars [**$2850**], the account shall not be restrained and the restraining notice shall be deemed void....

(i) Effect of restraint on judgment debtor's banking institution account. A restraining notice issued pursuant to this section shall not apply to an amount equal to or less than the greater of two hundred forty times the federal minimum hourly wage prescribed in the Fair Labor Standards Act of 1938 or two hundred forty times the state minimum hourly wage prescribed in section six hundred fifty-two of the labor law as in effect at the time the earnings are payable (as published on the websites of the United States department of labor and the state department of labor) except such part thereof as a court determines to be unnecessary for the reasonable requirements of the judgment debtor and his or her dependents. This amount shall be equal to ... seventeen hundred forty dollars on July twenty-fourth, two thousand nine, and shall rise thereafter in tandem with the minimum wage.... Where a judgment debtor's account contains an amount equal to or less than [this amount] the account shall not be restrained and the restraining notice shall be deemed void, except as to those funds that a court determines to be unnecessary for the reasonable requirements of the judgment debtor and his or her dependents * * *

§5222-a. Service of notices and forms and procedure for claim of exemption.

(a) Applicability. Any person authorized under subdivision (a) of section fifty-two hundred twenty-two of this article issuing a restraining notice affecting a natural person's account at a banking institution pursuant to such subdivision must comply with this section, in addition to the general provisions set forth in such section. Any sheriff levying against a natural person's account at a banking institution pursuant to section fifty-two hundred thirty-two of this article must comply with this section, in addition to the general provisions set forth in section fifty-two hundred thirty-two of this article....

(b) Service of exemption notice and exemption claim form.

1. Service with restraining notice upon banking institution. The person issuing the restraining notice pursuant to subdivision (a) of section fifty-two hundred twenty-two of this article shall provide the banking institution with the restraining notice, a copy of the restraining notice, an exemption notice and two exemption claim forms with sections titled "ADDRESS A" and "ADDRESS B" completed. The exemption notice and exemption claim forms shall be in the forms set forth in paragraph four of this subdivision. The notice and the forms shall be served on the banking institution together with the restraining notice and copy of the restraining notice. Service must be accomplished in accordance with subdivision (a) or (g) of section fifty-two hundred twenty-two of this article. Failure to serve the notice and forms together with the restraining notice renders the restraining notice void, and the banking institution shall not restrain the account.

2. Service of execution by levy upon a garnishee banking institution. When serving an execution pursuant to subdivision (a) of section fifty-two hundred thirty-two of this article, the sheriff shall provide the banking institution with an exemption notice and two exemption claim forms, which shall be in the forms set forth in paragraph four of this subdivision. The sheriff shall serve both the exemption notice and the exemption claim forms on the banking institution together with the execution notice. Service must be accomplished in accordance with subdivision (a) of section fifty-two hundred thirty-two of this article. Failure to serve the notice and forms renders the execution void, and the banking institution shall not levy upon the account.

3. Service upon judgment debtor. Within two business days after receipt of the restraining notice or execution, exemption notice and exemption claim

forms, the banking institution shall serve upon the judgment debtor the copy of the restraining notice, the exemption notice and two exemption claim forms. The banking institution shall serve the notice and forms by first class mail to the last known address of the judgment debtor. The inadvertent failure by a depository institution to provide the notice required by this subdivision shall not give rise to liability on the part of the depository institution.

4. Content of exemption notice and exemption claim form. a. The exemption notice shall be in the following form:

"EXEMPTION NOTICE as required by New York Law
YOUR BANK ACCOUNT IS RESTRAINED OR "FROZEN"

The attached Restraining Notice or notice of Levy by Execution has been issued against your bank account. You are receiving this notice because a creditor has obtained a money judgment against you, and one or more of your bank accounts has been restrained to pay the judgment. A money judgment is a court's decision that you owe money to a creditor. You should be aware that FUTURE DEPOSITS into your account(s) might also be restrained if you do not respond to this notice. You may be able to "vacate" (remove) the judgment. If the judgment is vacated, your bank account will be released. Consult an attorney (including free legal services) or visit the court clerk for more information about how to do this.

Under state and federal law, certain types of funds cannot be taken from your bank account to pay a judgment. Such money is said to be "exempt."

DOES YOUR BANK ACCOUNT CONTAIN ANY
OF THE FOLLOWING TYPES OF FUNDS?

1. Social security;
2. Social security disability (SSD);
3. Supplemental security income (SSI);
4. Public assistance (welfare);
5. Income earned while receiving SSI or public assistance;
6. Veterans benefits;
7. Unemployment insurance;
8. Payments from pensions and retirement accounts;
9. Disability benefits;
10. Income earned in the last 60 days (90% of which is exempt);
11. Workers' compensation benefits;

12. Child support;
13. Spousal support or maintenance (alimony);
14. Railroad retirement; and/or
15. Black lung benefits.

If YES, you can claim that your money is exempt and cannot be taken. To make the claim, you must

(a) complete the EXEMPTION CLAIM FORM attached;
(b) deliver or mail the form to the bank with the restrained or "frozen" account; and
(c) deliver or mail the form to the creditor or its attorney at the address listed on the form.

You must send the forms within 20 DAYS of the postmarked date on the envelope holding this notice. You may be able to get your account released faster if you send to the creditor or its attorney written proof that your money is exempt. Proof can include an award letter from the government, an annual statement from your pension, pay stubs, copies of checks, bank records showing the last two months of account activity, or other papers showing that the money in your bank account is exempt. If you send the creditor's attorney proof that the money in your account is exempt, the attorney must release that money within seven days. You do not need an attorney to make an exemption claim using the form."

b. The exemption claim form shall be in the following form:

NAME OF COURT, NAME OF COUNTY

————————————————————x

PLAINTIFF/PETITIONER/CLAIMANT V. DEFENDANT/RESPONDENT	INDEX NO. EXEMPTION CLAIM FORM

————————————————————x

NAME AND ADDRESS OF JUDGMENT CREDITOR OR ATTORNEY (To be completed by judgment creditor or attorney) ADDRESS A____________________ ____________________	NAME AND ADDRESS OF FINANCIAL INSTITUTION (To be completed by judgment creditor or attorney) ADDRESS B____________________ ____________________

Directions: To claim that some or all of the funds in your account are exempt, complete both copies of this form, and make one copy for yourself. Mail or deliver one form to ADDRESS A and one form to ADDRESS B within twenty days of the date on the envelope holding this notice. **If you have any documents, such as an award letter, an annual statement from your pension, paystubs, copies of checks or bank records showing the last two months of account activity, include copies of the documents with this form. Your account may be released more quickly.

I state that my account contains the following type(s) of funds (check all that apply):

____ Social security

____ Social security disability (SSD)

____ Supplemental security income (SSI)

____ Public assistance

____ Wages while receiving SSI or public assistance

____ Veterans benefits

____ Unemployment insurance

____ Payments from pensions and retirement accounts

____ Income earned in the last 60 days (90% of which is exempt)

____ Child support

____ Spousal support or maintenance (alimony)

____ Workers' compensation

____ Railroad retirement or black lung benefits

____ Other (describe exemption): ______________________________

I request that any correspondence to me regarding my claim be sent to the following address:

____

(FILL IN YOUR COMPLETE ADDRESS)

I certify under penalty of perjury that the statement above is true to the best of my knowledge and belief.

____________________ ____

DATE SIGNATURE OF JUDGMENT DEBTOR

(c) Claim of exemption.

1. To claim an exemption pursuant to the procedures in this section, the judgment debtor shall complete the exemption claim forms, sign them under penalty of perjury, and serve them within twenty days of the date postmarked on the correspondence containing the notice and forms. The judgment debtor shall serve one completed exemption claim form on the banking institution and the other on the attorney for the judgment creditor. In the event that there is no attorney for the judgment creditor, then the exemption claim form must be served directly on the judgment creditor. The judgment debtor may serve the exemption claim forms in person or by first-class mail.

2. Where the banking institution receives an exemption claim form, it shall notify the judgment creditor forthwith of the date on which the funds will be released pursuant to paragraph three of this subdivision.

3. The banking institution shall release all funds in the judgment debtor's account eight days after the date postmarked on the envelope containing the executed exemption claim form mailed to the banking institution or the date of personal delivery of the executed exemption claim form to the banking institution, and the restraint shall be deemed void, except where the judgment creditor interposes an objection to the exemption within that time.

4. Where the executed exemption claim form sent to the judgment creditor is accompanied by information demonstrating that all funds in the account are exempt, the judgment creditor shall, within seven days of the postmark on the envelope containing the exemption claim form and accompanying information, instruct the banking institution to release the account, and the restraint shall be deemed void. Where the account contains some funds from exempt sources, and other funds from unknown sources, the judgment creditor shall apply the lowest intermediate balance principle of accounting and, within seven days of the postmark on the envelope containing the exemption claim form and accompanying information, shall instruct the banking institution to release the exempt money in the account.... Information demonstrating that funds are exempt includes, but is not limited to, originals or copies of benefit award letters, checks, check stubs or any other document that discloses the source of the judgment debtor's income, and bank records showing the last two months of account activity. If the judgment creditor fails to act in accordance with this subdivision, the judgment creditor shall be deemed to have acted in bad faith and the judgment debtor may seek a court award of the damages, costs, fees and penalties provided for in subdivision (g) of this section.

5. If no claim of exemption is received by the banking institution within twenty-five days after the notice and forms are mailed to the judgment debtor,

the funds remain subject to the restraining notice or execution. Failure of the judgment debtor to deliver the executed exemption claim form does not constitute a waiver of any right to an exemption.

(d) Objection to exemption claim and request for hearing. A judgment creditor may object to the claim of exemption by moving for an order pursuant to section fifty-two hundred forty of this article. The judgment creditor must serve the banking institution and the judgment debtor with its motion papers within eight days after the date postmarked on the envelope containing the executed exemption claim form or the date of personal delivery of the executed exemption claim form to the banking institution, and the provisions of paragraph one of subdivision (b) of rule twenty-one hundred three of this chapter shall not enlarge the judgment creditor's time to move pursuant to this section. The judgment debtor shall be served at the address provided on the exemption claim form. The affirmation or affidavit in support of the motion shall demonstrate a reasonable belief that such judgment debtor's account contains funds that are not exempt from execution and the amount of such nonexempt funds. The executed exemption claim form shall be attached to the affirmation or affidavit. The affirmation or affidavit shall not be conclusory, but is required to show the factual basis upon which the reasonable belief is based. The hearing to decide the motion shall be noticed for seven days after service of the moving papers. The executed exemption claim form shall be prima facie evidence at such hearing that the funds in the account are exempt funds. The burden of proof shall be upon the judgment creditor to establish the amount of funds that are not exempt. The court shall, within five days of the hearing, issue an order stating whether or not funds in the account are exempt and ordering the appropriate relief. The judgment creditor or its attorney must serve the order on the banking institution and the judgment debtor no later than two business days after the court issues the order.

(e) Duties of banking institution if objection is made to exemption claim. Upon receipt of a written objection pursuant to subdivision (d) of this section from the judgment creditor or its attorney within the specified eight-day period, the banking institution shall retain the funds claimed to be exempt for twenty-one days unless otherwise ordered by the court. If the period of twenty-one days expires and the banking institution has not been otherwise ordered by the court, the banking institution shall release the funds to the judgment debtor.

(f) Release of funds. At any time during the procedure specified in this section, the judgment debtor or the judgment creditor may, by a writing dated after the service of the restraining notice, direct the banking institution to release the funds in question to the other party. Upon receipt of a release, the banking institution shall release the funds as directed.

(g) **Proceedings; bad faith claims.** Where the judgment creditor objects to a claim of exemption pursuant to subdivision (d) of this section and the court finds that the judgment creditor disputed the claim of exemption in bad faith, as provided in paragraph four of subdivision (c) of this section, the judgment debtor shall be awarded costs, reasonable attorney fees, actual damages and an amount not to exceed one thousand dollars.

* * *

§ 5223. Disclosure. At any time before a judgment is satisfied or vacated, the judgment creditor may compel disclosure of all matter relevant to the satisfaction of the judgment, by serving upon any person a subpoena, which shall specify all of the parties to the action, the date of the judgment, the court in which it was entered, the amount of the judgment and the amount then due thereon, and shall state that false swearing or failure to comply with the subpoena is punishable as a contempt of court.

§ 5224. Subpoena; procedure.

(a) **Kinds and service of subpoena.** Any or all of the following kinds of subpoenas may be served:

1. a subpoena requiring attendance for the taking of a deposition upon oral or written questions at a time and place named therein; or
2. a subpoena duces tecum requiring the production of books and papers for examination at a time and place named therein; or
3. an information subpoena, accompanied by a copy and original of written questions and a prepaid, addressed return envelope. Service of an information subpoena may be made by registered or certified mail, return receipt requested. Answers shall be made in writing under oath by the person upon whom served, if an individual, or by an officer, director, agent or employee having the information, if a corporation, partnership or sole proprietorship. Each question shall be answered separately and fully and each answer shall refer to the question to which it responds. Answers shall be returned together with the original of the questions within seven days after receipt. Where the person serving the subpoena is a judgment creditor ... the following additional rules shall apply:

> (i) information subpoenas, served on an individual or entity other than the judgment debtor, may be served on an individual, corporation, partnership or sole proprietorship only if the judgment creditor or the judgment creditor's attorney has a reasonable belief that the party receiving the subpoena has in their possession information about the debtor that will assist the creditor in collecting his or her judgment.

Any information subpoena served pursuant to this subparagraph shall contain a certification signed by the judgment creditor or his or her attorney stating the following: I HEREBY CERTIFY THAT THIS INFORMATION SUBPOENA COMPLIES WITH RULE 5224 OF THE CIVIL PRACTICE LAW AND RULES AND SECTION 601 OF THE GENERAL BUSINESS LAW THAT I HAVE A REASONABLE BELIEF THAT THE PARTY RECEIVING THIS SUBPOENA HAS IN THEIR POSSESSION INFORMATION ABOUT THE DEBTOR THAT WILL ASSIST THE CREDITOR IN COLLECTING THE JUDGMENT. By signing the certification, the judgment creditor or attorney certifies that, to the best of that person's knowledge, information and belief, formed after an inquiry reasonable under the circumstances, that the individual or entity receiving the subpoena has relevant information about the debtor.

(ii) if an information subpoena, served on an individual or entity other than the judgment debtor, does not contain the certification provided for in subparagraph (i) of this paragraph, such subpoena shall be deemed null and void.

* * *

4. an information subpoena in the form of magnetic tape or other electronic means. Where the person to be served consents thereto in writing, an information subpoena in the form of magnetic tape or electronic means, as defined in subdivision (f) of rule twenty-one hundred three of this chapter, may be served upon the individual, or if a corporation, partnership, limited liability company, or sole proprietorship, upon the officer, director, agent or employee having the information. Answers shall be provided within seven days.

(a-1) Scope of subpoena duces tecum. A subpoena duces tecum authorized by this rule and served on a judgment debtor, or on any individual while in the state, or on a corporation, partnership, limited liability company or sole proprietorship doing business, licensed, qualified, or otherwise entitled to do business in the state, shall subject the person or other entity or business served to the full disclosure prescribed by section fifty-two hundred twenty-three of this article whether the materials sought are in the possession, custody or control of the subpoenaed person, business or other entity within or without the state. Section fifty-two hundred twenty-nine of this article shall also apply to disclosure under this rule.

(b) Fees. A judgment debtor served with a subpoena under this section and any other person served with an information subpoena shall not be entitled to any fee. Any other person served with a subpoena requiring attendance or the production of books and papers shall be paid or tendered in advance authorized traveling expenses and one day's witness fee.

(c) Time and place of examination. A deposition on oral or written questions or an examination of books and papers may proceed upon not less than ten days' notice to the person subpoenaed, unless the court orders shorter notice, before any person authorized by subdivision (a) of rule 3113. An examination shall be held during business hours and, if taken within the state, at a place specified in rule 3110. Upon consent of the witness, an examination may be held at any other place within the state and before any officer authorized to administer an oath.

* * *

(f) Subsequent examination. Leave of court is required to compel a judgment debtor to appear for the taking of his deposition or to compel the production by him of books and papers within one year after the conclusion of a previous examination of him with respect to the same judgment.

§5225. Payment or delivery of property of judgment debtor.

(a) Property in the possession of judgment debtor. Upon motion of the judgment creditor, upon notice to the judgment debtor, where it is shown that the judgment debtor is in possession or custody of money or other personal property in which he has an interest, the court shall order that the judgment debtor pay the money, or so much of it as is sufficient to satisfy the judgment, to the judgment creditor and, if the amount to be so paid is insufficient to satisfy the judgment, to deliver any other personal property, or so much of it as is of sufficient value to satisfy the judgment, to a designated sheriff. Notice of the motion shall be served on the judgment debtor in the same manner as a summons or by registered or certified mail, return receipt requested.

(b) Property not in the possession of judgment debtor. Upon a special proceeding commenced by the judgment creditor, against a person in possession or custody of money or other personal property in which the judgment debtor has an interest, or against a person who is a transferee of money or other personal property from the judgment debtor, where it is shown that the judgment debtor is entitled to the possession of such property or that the judgment creditor's rights to the property are superior to those of the transferee, the court shall require such person to pay the money, or so much of it as is sufficient to satisfy the judgment, to the judgment creditor and, if the amount to be so paid is insufficient to satisfy the judgment, to deliver any other personal property, or so much of it as is of sufficient value to satisfy the judgment, to a designated sheriff. Costs of the proceeding shall not be awarded against a person who did not dispute the judgment debtor's interest or right to possession. Notice of the proceeding shall also be served upon the judgment debtor in the same manner as a summons or by registered or certified mail, return receipt requested. The court may permit the judgment debtor to intervene in the proceeding. The court may permit any adverse claimant to intervene in the proceeding and may determine his rights in accordance with section 5239.

(c) **Documents to effect payment or delivery.** The court may order any person to execute and deliver any document necessary to effect payment or delivery.

§5226. Installment payment order. Upon motion of the judgment creditor, upon notice to the judgment debtor, where it is shown that the judgment debtor is receiving or will receive money from any source, or is attempting to impede the judgment creditor by rendering services without adequate compensation, the court shall order that the judgment debtor make specified installment payments to the judgment creditor. Notice of the motion shall be served on the judgment debtor in the same manner as a summons or by registered or certified mail, return receipt requested. In fixing the amount of the payments, the court shall take into consideration the reasonable requirements of the judgment debtor and his dependents, any payments required to be made by him or deducted from the money he would otherwise receive in satisfaction of other judgments and wage assignments, the amount due on the judgment, and the amount being or to be received, or, if the judgment debtor is attempting to impede the judgment creditor by rendering services without adequate compensation, the reasonable value of the services rendered.

§5227. Payment of debts owed to judgment debtor. Upon a special proceeding commenced by the judgment creditor, against any person who it is shown is or will become indebted to the judgment debtor, the court may require such person to pay to the judgment creditor the debt upon maturity, or so much of it as is sufficient to satisfy the judgment, and to execute and deliver any document necessary to effect payment; or it may direct that a judgment be entered against such person in favor of the judgment creditor. Costs of the proceeding shall not be awarded against a person who did not dispute the indebtedness. Notice of the proceeding shall also be served upon the judgment debtor in the same manner as a summons or by registered or certified mail, return receipt requested. The court may permit the judgment debtor to intervene in the proceeding. The court may permit any adverse claimant to intervene in the proceeding and may determine his rights in accordance with section 5239.

§5228. Receivers. (a) Appointment of receiver. Upon motion of a judgment creditor, upon such notice as the court may require, the court may appoint a receiver who may be authorized to administer, collect, improve, lease, repair or sell any real or personal property in which the judgment debtor has an interest or to do any other acts designed to satisfy the judgment. As far as practicable, the court shall require that notice be given to the judgment debtor and to any other judgment creditors of the judgment debtor. The order of appointment shall specify the property to be received, the duties of the receiver and the manner in which they are to be performed. A receiver shall have no power to employ counsel unless expressly so authorized by order of the court. A receiver shall be entitled to necessary expenses and to such commissions, not exceeding five percent of the sums received and disbursed by him, as the court which appointed him allows, but if a judgment creditor is appointed receiver, he shall not be entitled to compensation. If a receiver has been appointed, a court making an order directing payment, or delivery, of property shall direct that payment, or delivery, be made to the receiver rather than to a sheriff. Sections 6402, 6403, 6404 and 6405 are applicable to receivers appointed under this subdivision.

§5229. Enforcement before judgment entered. In any court, before a judgment is entered, upon motion of the party in whose favor a verdict or decision has been rendered, the trial judge may order examination of the adverse party and order him restrained with the same effect as if a restraining notice had been served upon him after judgment.

§5230. Executions.

(a) Form. An execution shall specify the date that the judgment … was entered, the court in which it was entered, the amount of the judgment … and the amount due thereon and it shall specify the names of the parties in whose favor and against whom the judgment … was entered. An execution shall direct that only the property in which a named judgment debtor … who is not deceased has an interest, or the debts owed to the named judgment debtor … be levied upon or sold thereunder and shall specify the last known address of that judgment debtor.… … [A]n execution notice shall state that, pursuant to subdivision (*l*) of section fifty-two hundred five of this article, two thousand five hundred dollars [**$2850**] of an account containing direct deposit or electronic payments reasonably identifiable as statutorily exempt payments, as defined in paragraph two of subdivision (*l*) of section fifty-two hundred five of this article, is exempt from execution and that the garnishee cannot levy upon or restrain two thousand five hundred dollars [**$2850**] in such an account.… [A]n execution notice shall likewise state that pursuant to subdivision (i) of section fifty-two hundred twenty-two of this article, an execution shall not apply to an amount equal to or less than ninety percent of the greater of two hundred forty times the federal minimum hourly wage prescribed in the Fair Labor Standards Act of 1938 or two hundred forty times the state minimum hourly wage prescribed in section six hundred fifty-two of the labor law as in effect at the time the earnings are payable, except such part as a court determines to be unnecessary for the reasonable requirements of the judgment debtor and his or her dependents. Where the judgment or order was entered in a court other than the supreme, county or a family court, the execution shall also specify the date on which a transcript of the judgment or order was filed with the clerk of the county in which the judgment was entered....

(b) Issuance. At any time before a judgment ... is satisfied or vacated, an execution may be issued from the supreme court, county court ... in the county in which the judgment was first docketed, by the clerk of the court or the attorney for the judgment creditor as officer of the court, to the sheriffs of one or more counties of the state, directing each of them to satisfy the judgment ... out of the real and personal property of the judgment debtor ... and the debts due to him or her....

(c) Return. An execution shall be returned to the clerk of the court from which it was issued ... within sixty days after issuance unless the execution has been served in accordance with section 5231 or subdivision (a) of section 5232. The time may be extended in writing for a period of not more than sixty additional days by the attorney for the judgment creditor.... Further like extensions may be given by the attorney for the judgment creditor ... unless another execution against the same judgment debtor ... has been delivered to the same enforcement officer and has not been returned.

(d) Records of sheriff.... Each sheriff ... shall keep a record of executions delivered showing the names of the parties and the judgment debtor ... ; the dates of issue and return; the date and time of delivery, which shall be endorsed upon the execution; the amount due at the time the execution was delivered; and the amount of the judgment ... and of the sheriff's fees unpaid, if any, at the time of the return.

* * *

§5231. Income execution.

(a) Form. An income execution shall specify, in addition to the requirements of subdivision (a) of section 5230, the name and address of the person or entity from whom the judgment debtor is receiving or will receive money; the amount of money, the frequency of its payment and the amount of the installments to be collected therefrom; and shall contain a notice to the judgment debtor that he or she shall commence payment of the installments specified to the sheriff forthwith and that, upon his or her default, the execution will be served upon the person or entity from whom he or she is receiving or will receive money.

(b) Issuance. Where a judgment debtor is receiving or will receive money from any source, an income execution for installments therefrom of not more than ten percent thereof may be issued and delivered to the sheriff of the county in which the judgment debtor resides or, where the judgment debtor is a non-resident, the county in which he is employed; provided, however, that (i) no amount shall be withheld from the judgment debtor's earnings pursuant to an income execution for any week unless the disposable earnings of the judgment debtor for that week exceed the greater of thirty times the federal minimum hourly wage prescribed in the Fair Labor Standards Act of 1938 or thirty times the state minimum hourly wage prescribed in section six hundred fifty-two of the labor law as in effect at the time the earnings are payable; (ii) the amount withheld from the judgment debtor's earnings pursuant to an income execution for any week shall not exceed twenty-five percent of the disposable earnings of the judgment debtor for that week, or, the amount by which the disposable earnings of the judgment debtor for that week exceed [the relevant minimum wage figure from subsection (i)], whichever is less;....

(c) Definition of earnings and disposable earnings. (i) As used herein earnings means compensation paid or payable for personal services, whether denominated as wages, salary, commission, bonus, or otherwise, and includes periodic payments pursuant to a pension or retirement program.

(ii) As used herein disposable earnings means that part of the earnings of any individual remaining after the deduction from those earnings of any amounts required by law to be withheld.

(d) Service upon debtor; first service by sheriff. Within twenty days after an income execution is delivered to the sheriff, the sheriff shall serve a copy of it upon the judgment debtor, in the same manner as a summons or, in lieu thereof, by certified mail return receipt requested provided an additional copy is sent by regular mail to the debtor. If service is by mail as herein provided, the person effecting service shall retain the receipt together with a post office certificate of mailing as proof of such service.

(e) Levy upon default or failure to serve debtor; second service by sheriff. If a judgment debtor fails to pay installments pursuant to an income execution served upon him or her for a period of twenty days, or if the sheriff is unable to serve an income execution upon the judgment debtor within twenty days after the execution is delivered to the sheriff, the sheriff shall levy upon the money that the judgment debtor is receiving or will receive by serving a copy of the income execution, indorsed to indicate the extent to which paid installments have satisfied the judgment, upon the person or entity from whom the judgment debtor is receiving or will receive money. The income execution shall be served personally within any county in which the person or entity from whom the judgment debtor is receiving or will receive money has an office or place of business in the same manner as a summons, or by certified mail return receipt requested, except that such service shall not be made by delivery to a person authorized to receive service of summons solely by a designation filed pursuant to a provision of law other than rule 318.

(f) Withholding of installments. A person served with an income execution shall withhold from money then or thereafter due to the judgment debtor installments as provided therein and pay them over to the sheriff. If such person shall fail to so pay the sheriff, the judgment creditor may commence a proceeding against him for accrued installments. If the money due to the judgment debtor consists of salary or wages and his employment is terminated by resignation or dismissal at any time after service of the execution, the levy shall thereafter be ineffective, and the execution shall be returned, unless the debtor is reinstated or re-employed within ninety days after such termination.

(g) Statement on income execution. Any income execution delivered to the sheriff on or after the effective date of this act shall contain the following statement:

> THIS INCOME EXECUTION DIRECTS THE WITHHOLDING OF UP TO TEN PERCENT OF THE JUDGMENT DEBTOR'S GROSS INCOME. IN CERTAIN CASES, HOWEVER, STATE OR FEDERAL LAW DOES NOT PERMIT THE WITHHOLDING OF THAT MUCH OF THE JUDGMENT DEBTOR'S GROSS INCOME. THE JUDGMENT DEBTOR IS REFERRED TO NEW YORK CIVIL PRACTICE LAW AND RULES §5231 AND 15 UNITED STATES CODE §1671 ET SEQ.
>
> I. LIMITATIONS ON THE AMOUNT THAT CAN BE WITHHELD.
>
> A. AN INCOME EXECUTION FOR INSTALLMENTS FROM A JUDGMENT DEBTOR'S GROSS INCOME CANNOT EXCEED TEN PERCENT (10%) OF THE JUDGMENT DEBTOR'S GROSS INCOME.
>
> B. IF A JUDGMENT DEBTOR'S WEEKLY DISPOSABLE EARNINGS ARE LESS THAN THIRTY (30) TIMES THE CURRENT FEDERAL MINIMUM WAGE (, PER HOUR), OR ( ), NO DEDUCTION

CAN BE MADE FROM THE JUDGMENT DEBTOR'S EARNINGS UNDER THIS INCOME EXECUTION.
C. A JUDGMENT DEBTOR'S WEEKLY DISPOSABLE EARNINGS CANNOT BE REDUCED BELOW THE AMOUNT ARRIVED AT BY MULTIPLYING THIRTY (30) TIMES THE CURRENT FEDERAL MINIMUM WAGE (, PER HOUR), OR ( ), UNDER THIS INCOME EXECUTION.
D. IF DEDUCTIONS ARE BEING MADE FROM A JUDGMENT DEBTOR'S EARNINGS UNDER ANY ORDERS FOR ALIMONY, SUPPORT OR MAINTENANCE FOR FAMILY MEMBERS OR FORMER SPOUSES, AND THOSE DEDUCTIONS EQUAL OR EXCEED TWENTY-FIVE PERCENT (25%) OF THE JUDGMENT DEBTOR'S DISPOSABLE EARNINGS, NO DEDUCTION CAN BE MADE FROM THE JUDGMENT DEBTOR'S EARNINGS UNDER THIS INCOME EXECUTION.
E. IF DEDUCTIONS ARE BEING MADE FROM A JUDGMENT DEBTOR'S EARNINGS UNDER ANY ORDERS FOR ALIMONY, SUPPORT OR MAINTENANCE FOR FAMILY MEMBERS OR FORMER SPOUSES, AND THOSE DEDUCTIONS ARE LESS THAN TWENTY-FIVE PERCENT (25%) OF THE JUDGMENT DEBTOR'S DISPOSABLE EARNINGS, DEDUCTIONS MAY BE MADE FROM THE JUDGMENT DEBTOR'S EARNINGS UNDER THIS INCOME EXECUTION. HOWEVER, THE AMOUNT ARRIVED AT BY ADDING THE DEDUCTIONS FROM EARNINGS MADE UNDER THIS EXECUTION TO THE DEDUCTIONS MADE FROM EARNINGS UNDER ANY ORDERS FOR ALIMONY, SUPPORT OR MAINTENANCE FOR FAMILY MEMBERS OR FORMER SPOUSES CANNOT EXCEED TWENTY-FIVE PERCENT (25%) OF THE JUDGMENT DEBTOR'S DISPOSABLE EARNINGS.
NOTE: NOTHING IN THIS NOTICE LIMITS THE PROPORTION OR AMOUNT WHICH MAY BE DEDUCTED UNDER ANY ORDER FOR ALIMONY, SUPPORT OR MAINTENANCE FOR FAMILY MEMBERS OR FORMER SPOUSES.

II. EXPLANATION OF LIMITATIONS

DEFINITIONS: DISPOSABLE EARNINGS DISPOSABLE EARNINGS ARE THAT PART OF AN INDIVIDUAL'S EARNINGS LEFT AFTER DEDUCTING THOSE AMOUNTS THAT ARE REQUIRED BY LAW TO BE WITHHELD (FOR EXAMPLE, TAXES, SOCIAL SECURITY, AND UNEMPLOYMENT INSURANCE, BUT NOT DEDUCTIONS FOR UNION DUES, INSURANCE PLANS,

ETC.). GROSS INCOME GROSS INCOME IS SALARY, WAGES OR OTHER INCOME, INCLUDING ANY AND ALL OVERTIME EARNINGS, COMMISSIONS, AND INCOME FROM TRUSTS, BEFORE ANY DEDUCTIONS ARE MADE FROM SUCH INCOME.

ILLUSTRATIONS REGARDING EARNINGS:

IF DISPOSABLE EARNINGS IS:	AMOUNT TO PAY OR DEDUCT FROM EARNINGS UNDER THIS INCOME EXECUTION IS:
(a) 30 TIMES FEDERAL MINIMUM WAGE ( ) OR LESS	NO PAYMENT OR DEDUCTION ALLOWED
(b) MORE THAN 30 TIMES FEDERAL MINIMUM WAGE ( ) AND LESS THAN 40 TIMES FEDERAL MINIMUM WAGE	THE LESSER OF: THE EXCESS OVER 30 TIMES THE FEDERAL MINIMUM WAGE ( ) IN DISPOSABLE EARNINGS, or 10% OF GROSS EARNINGS
(c) 40 TIMES THE FEDERAL MINIMUM WAGE ( ) OR MORE	THE LESSER OF: 25% OF DISPOSABLE EARNINGS OR 10% OF GROSS EARNINGS.

III. NOTICE: YOU MAY BE ABLE TO CHALLENGE THIS INCOME EXECUTION THROUGH THE PROCEDURES PROVIDED IN CPLR §5231 (i) AND CPLR §5240 IF YOU THINK THAT THE AMOUNT OF YOUR INCOME BEING DEDUCTED UNDER THIS INCOME EXECUTION EXCEEDS THE AMOUNT PERMITTED BY STATE OR FEDERAL LAW, YOU SHOULD ACT PROMPTLY BECAUSE THE MONEY WILL BE APPLIED TO THE JUDGMENT. IF YOU CLAIM THAT THE AMOUNT OF YOUR INCOME BEING DEDUCTED UNDER THIS INCOME EXECUTION EXCEEDS THE AMOUNT PERMITTED BY STATE OR FEDERAL LAW, YOU SHOULD CONTACT YOUR EMPLOYER OR OTHER PERSON PAYING YOUR INCOME. FURTHER, YOU MAY CONSULT AN ATTORNEY, INCLUDING LEGAL AID IF YOU QUALIFY. NEW YORK STATE LAW PROVIDES TWO PROCEDURES THROUGH WHICH AN INCOME EXECUTION CAN BE CHALLENGED:
CPLR §5231(i) MODIFICATION. AT ANY TIME, THE JUDGMENT DEBTOR MAY MAKE A MOTION TO A COURT FOR AN ORDER MODIFYING AN INCOME EXECUTION. CPLR §5240 MODIFICATION OR PROTECTIVE ORDER: SUPERVISION OF ENFORCE-

MENT. AT ANY TIME, THE JUDGMENT DEBTOR MAY MAKE A MOTION TO A COURT FOR AN ORDER DENYING, LIMITING, CONDITIONING, REGULATING, EXTENDING OR MODIFYING THE USE OF ANY POST-JUDGMENT ENFORCEMENT PROCEDURE, INCLUDING THE USE OF INCOME EXECUTIONS.

* * *

(j) **Priority; delivery to another sheriff.** Two or more income executions issued against the same judgment debtor, specifying the same person or entity from whom the money is received and delivered to the same or different enforcement officers shall be satisfied out of that money in the order in which the executions are delivered to an officer authorized to levy in [the relevant location]....

(k) **Accounting by sheriff.** It shall be the duty of the sheriff to whom such income execution shall be delivered, from time to time and at least once every ninety days from the time a levy shall be made thereunder, to account for and pay over to the person entitled thereto all monies collected thereon, less his lawful fees and expenses for collecting the same.

§ 5232. Levy upon personal property.

(a) **Levy by service of execution.** The sheriff ... shall levy upon any interest of the judgment debtor ... in personal property not capable of delivery, or upon any debt owed to the judgment debtor..., by serving a copy of the execution upon the garnishee, in the same manner as a summons.... A levy by service of the execution is effective only if, at the time of service, the person served owes a debt to the judgment debtor ... or he or she is in the possession or custody of property not capable of delivery in which he or she knows or has reason to believe the judgment debtor ... has an interest.... All property not capable of delivery in which the judgment debtor ... is known or believed to have an interest then in or thereafter coming into the possession or custody of such a person, including any specified in the notice, and all debts of such a person, including any specified in the notice, then due or thereafter coming due to the judgment debtor ... shall be subject to the levy. The person served with the execution shall forthwith transfer all such property, and pay all such debts upon maturity, to the sheriff ... and execute any document necessary to effect the transfer or payment. After such transfer or payment, property coming into the possession or custody of the garnishee, or debt incurred by him, or her shall not be subject to the levy. Until such transfer or payment is made, or until the expiration of ninety days after the service of the execution upon him or her, or of such further time as is provided by any order of the court served upon him or her, whichever event first occurs, the garnishee is forbidden to make or suffer any sale, assignment or transfer of, or any interference with, any such property, or pay over or otherwise dispose of any such debt, to any person other than the sheriff ... except upon direction of the sheriff ... or pursuant to an order of the court. At the expiration of ninety days after a levy is made by service of the execution, or of such further time as the court, upon motion of the judgment creditor ... has provided, the levy shall be void....

(b) Levy by seizure. The sheriff ... shall levy upon any interest of the judgment debtor in personal property capable of delivery by taking the property into custody.... The sheriff ... shall forthwith serve a copy of the execution in the manner prescribed by subdivision (a) upon the person from whose possession or custody the property was taken.

(c) Notice to judgment debtor.... Where an execution does not state that a notice in the form presented by subdivision (e) of section fifty-two hundred twenty-two of this chapter has been duly served upon the judgment debtor ... within a year, the sheriff ... shall, not later than four days after service of the execution upon any garnishee, mail by first class mail, or personally deliver, to each judgment debtor ... who is a natural person, a copy of the execution together with such notice. The sheriff ... shall specify on the notice to judgment debtor ... the name and address of the judgment creditor or the judgment creditor's attorney.... The notice shall be mailed to the judgment debtor ... at his or her residence address; and in the event such mailing is returned as undeliverable by the post office, or if the residence address of the judgment debtor ... is unknown, then to the judgment debtor ... in care of the place of employment of the judgment debtor ... if known, in an envelope bearing the legend "personal and confidential" and not indicating on the outside thereof, by the return address or otherwise, that the communication is from a sheriff ... or concerns a debt; or if neither the residence nor the place of employment of the judgment debtor ... is known, then to the judgment debtor ... at any other known address.

* * *

(e) Notwithstanding the provisions of subdivision (a) of this section, if direct deposit or electronic payments reasonably identifiable as statutorily exempt payments as defined in paragraph two of subdivision (*l*) of section fifty-two hundred five of this article were made to the judgment debtor's account during the forty-five day period preceding the date that the execution notice was served on the garnishee banking institution, then a garnishee banking institution shall not execute, levy, attach, garnish or otherwise restrain or encumber two thousand five hundred dollars [**$2850**] in the judgment debtor's account. Notwithstanding the provisions of subdivision (a) of this section, an execution shall not apply to an amount equal to or less than the greater of two hundred forty times the federal minimum hourly wage prescribed in the Fair Labor Standards Act of 1938 or two hundred forty times the state minimum hourly wage prescribed in section six hundred fifty-two of the labor law as in effect at the time the earnings are payable (as published on the websites of the United States department of labor and the state department of labor) except such part thereof as a court determines to be unnecessary for the reasonable requirements of the judgment debtor and his or her dependents. This amount shall be equal to ... seventeen hundred forty dollars on July twenty-fourth, two thousand nine, and shall rise thereafter in tandem with the minimum wage....

* * *

(g) Where a levy by execution pursuant to this section is made against a natural person's account at a banking institution, the sheriff ... shall serve the banking institution with the exemption notice and two exemption claim forms prescribed in subdivision (b) of section fifty-two hundred twenty-two-a of this article. The notice and forms must be served upon the banking institution simultaneously with the execution and section fifty-two hundred twenty-two-a of this article shall apply, and all procedures stated therein must be followed. The banking institution shall not transfer the funds in the account to the sheriff ... for at least twenty-seven days. If, after thirty days, the banking institution has not received an exemption claim form from the judgment debtor, or a court order directing otherwise, it may thereafter transfer the funds to the sheriff....

* * *

§5233. Sale of personal property.

(a) Public auction. The interest of the judgment debtor in personal property obtained by a sheriff pursuant to execution or order, other than legal tender of the United States, shall be sold by the sheriff at public auction at such time and place and as a unit or in such lots, or combination thereof, as in his judgment will bring the highest price, but no sale may be made to that sheriff or to his deputy or undersheriff. The property shall be present and within the view of those attending the sale unless otherwise ordered by the court.

(b) Public notice. A printed notice of the time and place of the sale shall be posted at least six days before the sale in three public places in the town or city in which the sale is to be held, provided however, in the city of New York, in lieu of posting such notice may be advertised in the auction columns of any morning newspaper published daily and Sunday in such city an edition of which appears on the newsstands the previous night and has a circulation of not less than three hundred thousand. An omission to so post or advertise notice, or the defacing or removal of a posted notice, does not affect the title of a purchaser without notice of the omission or offense.

(c) **Order for immediate sale or disposition.** The court may direct immediate sale or other disposition of property with or without notice if the urgency of the case requires.

* * *

§5235. Levy upon real property. After the expiration of ten years after the filing of the judgment-roll, the sheriff shall levy upon any interest of the judgment debtor in real property, pursuant to an execution other than one issued upon a judgment for any part of a mortgage debt upon the property, by filing with the clerk of the county in which the property is located a notice of levy describing the judgment, the execution and the property. The clerk shall record and index the notice against the name of the judgment debtor, or against the property, in the same books, and in the same manner as a notice of the pendency of an action.

§5236. Sale of real property.

(a) **Time of sale; public auction.** Between the fifty-sixth and the sixty-third day after the first publication of a copy of the notice of sale, unless the time is extended by order or the sale postponed by the sheriff, the interest of the judgment debtor in real property which has been levied upon under an execution delivered to the sheriff or which was subject to the lien of the judgment at the time of such delivery shall be sold by the sheriff pursuant to the execution at public auction at such time and place within the county where the real property is situated and as a unit or in such parcels, or combination thereof, as in his judgment will bring the highest price, but no sale may be made to that sheriff or to his deputy or undersheriff. If the property is situated in more than one county, it may be sold in a county in which any part is situated, unless the court orders otherwise.

* * *

(c) **Notice of sale.** A printed notice of the time and place of the sale containing a description of the property to be sold shall be posted at least fifty-six days before the sale in three public places in the town or city in which the property is located, and, if the sale is to be held in another town or city, in three public places therein. Service by the sheriff of a copy of said notice on the judgment debtor shall be made as provided in section 308. A list containing the name and address of the judgment debtor and of every judgment creditor whose judgment was a lien on the real property to be sold and of every person who had of record any interest in or lien on such property forty-five days prior to the day fixed for the sale shall be furnished the sheriff by the judgment creditor, and each person on the list shall be served by the sheriff with a copy of the notice by personal delivery or by registered or certified mail, return receipt requested, at least thirty days prior to the day fixed for the sale. A copy of the notice shall be published at least once in each of four periods of fourteen successive days, the first of which periods may be measured from any day between the fifty-sixth and sixty-third days, preceding the time fixed for the sale in a newspaper published in the county in which the property is located or, if there is none, in a newspaper published in an adjoining county. An omission to give any notice required by this or the following subdivision, or the defacing or removal of a notice posted pursuant to either, does not affect the title of a purchaser without notice of the omission or offense.

* * *

(e) **Effect of notice as against judgment creditors.** A judgment creditor duly notified pursuant to subdivisions (c) or (d) who fails to deliver an execution to the sheriff prior to the sale shall have no further lien on the property and, except as against the judgment debtor, no further interest in the proceeds of the sale.

(f) **Conveyance; proof of notice.** Within ten days after the sale, the sheriff shall execute and deliver to the purchaser proofs of publication, service and posting of the notice of sale, and a deed which shall convey the right, title and interest sold. Such proofs may be filed and recorded in the office of the clerk of the county where the property is located.

* * *

§ 5239. Proceeding to determine adverse claims. Prior to the application of property or debt by a sheriff or receiver to the satisfaction of a judgment, any interested person may commence a special proceeding against the judgment creditor or other person with whom a dispute exists to determine rights in the property or debt. Service of process in such a proceeding shall be made by service of a notice of petition upon the respondent, the sheriff or receiver, and such other person as the court directs, in the same manner as a notice of motion. The proceeding may be commenced in the county where the property was levied upon, or in a court or county specified in subdivision (a) of section 5221. The court may vacate the execution or order, void the levy, direct the disposition of the property or debt, or direct that damages be awarded. Where there appear to be disputed questions of fact, the court shall order a separate trial, indicating the person who shall have possession of the property pending a decision and the undertaking, if any, which such person shall give. If the court determines that any claim asserted was fraudulent, it may require the claimant to pay to any party adversely affected thereby the reasonable expenses incurred by such party in the proceeding, including reasonable attorneys' fees, and any other damages suffered by reason of the claim. The court may permit any interested person to intervene in the proceeding.

* * *

§5251. Disobedience of subpoena, restraining notice or order; false swearing; destroying notice of sale. Refusal or willful neglect of any person to obey a subpoena or restraining notice issued, or order granted, pursuant to this title; false swearing upon an examination or in answering written questions; and willful defacing or removal of a posted notice of sale before the time fixed for the sale, shall each be punishable as a contempt of court.

* * *

§5253. Cost of living adjustment for personal and real property exempt from application to the satisfaction of money judgments....

(a) Beginning on April first, two thousand twelve, and at each three-year interval ending on April first thereafter, the dollar amount of the exemption provided in sections fifty-two hundred five and fifty-two hundred six of this article and sections two hundred eighty-two and two hundred eighty-three of the debtor and creditor law shall be adjusted as provided in subdivision (b) of this section.

(b) The superintendent of financial services shall determine the amount of the adjustment based on the change in the consumer price index for all urban consumers, New York-Northern New Jersey-Long Island, NY-NJ-CT-PA, published by the U.S. department of labor, bureau of labor statistics, for the most recent three-year period ending on December thirty-first preceding the adjustment, with each adjusted amount rounded to the nearest twenty-five dollars.

(c) Beginning on April first, two thousand twelve, and at each three-year interval ending on April first thereafter, the superintendent of financial services shall publish the current dollar amount of the applicable exemption provided in this article, together with the date of the next scheduled adjustment. * * *

Appendix B

California Code of Civil Procedure (CCP)

Title 9. Enforcement of Judgments

Division 1. Definitions and General Provisions 680.010–694.090

* * *

Chapter 7. Levying Officers 687.010–687.050

687.010.

(a) The judgment creditor shall give the levying officer instructions in writing.... The instructions shall contain the information needed or requested by the levying officer to comply with this title, including, but not limited to, all of the following:

(1) An adequate description of any property to be levied upon.

(2) A statement whether the property is a dwelling.

(3) If the property is a dwelling, whether it is real or personal property.

(4) The name of the judgment debtor. If the judgment debtor is other than a natural person, the type of legal entity shall be stated.

* * *

687.030.

Except as otherwise provided by statute, where the method of levy upon property requires that the property be taken into custody or where the levying officer is otherwise directed to take property into custody, the levying officer may do so by any of the following methods:

(a) Removing the property to a place of safekeeping.

(b) Installing a keeper.

(c) Otherwise obtaining possession or control of the property.

* * *

Division 2. Enforcement of Money Judgments 695.010–709.030

Chapter 1. General Provisions 695.010–695.221

Article 1. Property Subject to Enforcement of Money Judgment 695.010–695.070

695.010.

(a) Except as otherwise provided by law, all property of the judgment debtor is subject to enforcement of a money judgment.

* * *

695.030.

(a) Except as otherwise provided by statute, property of the judgment debtor that is not assignable or transferable is not subject to enforcement of a money judgment.

(b) The following property is subject to enforcement of a money judgment:

(1) An interest in a trust, to the extent provided by law.

(2) A cause of action for money or property that is the subject of a pending action or special proceeding.

* * *

695.060.

Except as provided in Section 708.630, a license issued by a public entity to engage in any business, profession, or activity is not subject to enforcement of a money judgment.

* * *

Chapter 2. Liens 697.010–697.920

* * *

Article 2. Judgment Lien on Real Property 697.310–697.410

697.310.

(a) Except as otherwise provided by statute, a judgment lien on real property is created under this section by recording an abstract of a money judgment with the county recorder.

(b) Unless the money judgment is satisfied or the judgment lien is released, subject to Section 683.180 (renewal of judgment), a judgment lien created under this section continues until 10 years from the date of entry of the judgment.

* * *

697.340.

Except as provided in Section 704.950: (a) A judgment lien on real property attaches to all interests in real property in the county where the lien is created (whether present or future, vested or contingent, legal or equitable) that are subject to enforcement of the money judgment against the judgment debtor ... at the time the lien was created, but does not reach rental payments, a leasehold estate with an unexpired term of less than two years, the interest of a beneficiary under a trust, or real property that is subject to an attachment lien in favor of the creditor and was transferred before judgment.

(b) If any interest in real property in the county on which a judgment lien could be created under subdivision (a) is acquired after the judgment lien was created, the judgment lien attaches to such interest at the time it is acquired.

* * *

Article 3. Judgment Lien on Personal Property 697.510–697.670

697.510.

(a) A judgment lien on personal property described in Section 697.530 is created by filing a notice of judgment lien in the office of the Secretary of State pursuant to this article.... .

(b) Except as otherwise provided in subdivision (c), (e), or (g), the judgment lien continues for five years from the date of filing.

(c) The effectiveness of a filed judgment lien lapses on the expiration of the period described in subdivision (b) unless, before the lapse, a continuation statement is filed pursuant to subdivision (d). Upon lapse, the judgment lien created by the filing of a notice pursuant to subdivision (a) ceases to be effective.

(d) A continuation statement may be filed only within the six-month period prior to the expiration of the five-year period specified in subdivision (b).

(e) A continuation statement that is not filed within the six-month period prescribed by subdivision (d) is ineffective. Upon timely filing of a continuation statement, the effectiveness of the initial notice of judgment lien continues for a period of five years commencing on the day on which the notice of judgment lien would have become ineffective in the absence of the filing. Upon the expiration of the five-year period, the notice of judgment lien lapses in the same manner as provided in subdivision (c), unless, before the lapse, another continuation statement is filed pursuant to subdivision (d). Succeeding continuation statements may be filed in the same manner to continue the effectiveness of the initial notice of judgment lien.

* * *

(*l*) The provisions of Sections 9522 and 9523 of the Commercial Code shall apply to a notice of judgment lien to the same extent as to a filed financing statement.

(m) Terms for which definitions are not set forth in Division 1 (commencing with Section 680.010) have the definitions set forth in the Commercial Code.

697.520.

A judgment lien on personal property may be created pursuant to this article as an alternative or in addition to a lien created by levy under a writ of execution pursuant to Chapter 3 (commencing with Section 699.010) or by use of an enforcement procedure provided by Chapter 6 (commencing with Section 708.010).

697.530.

(a) A judgment lien on personal property is a lien on all interests in the following personal property that are subject to enforcement of the money judgment against the judgment debtor pursuant to Article 1 (commencing with Section 695.010) of Chapter 1 at the time when the lien is created if the personal property is, at that time, any of the following:

(1) Accounts receivable, and the judgment debtor is located in this state.

(2) Tangible chattel paper, as defined in paragraph (79) of subdivision (a) of Section 9102 of the Commercial Code, and the judgment debtor is located in this state.

(3) Equipment, located within this state.

(4) Farm products, located within this state.

(5) Inventory, located within this state.

(6) Negotiable documents of title, located within this state.

(b) If any interest in personal property on which a judgment lien could be created under subdivision (a) is acquired after the judgment lien was created, the judgment lien attaches to the interest at the time it is acquired.

(c) To the extent provided by Section 697.620, a judgment lien on personal property continues on the proceeds received upon the sale, collection, or other disposition of the property subject to the judgment lien.

(d) Notwithstanding any other provision of this section, the judgment lien does not attach to:

(1) A vehicle or vessel required to be registered with the Department of Motor Vehicles or a mobilehome or commercial coach required to be registered pursuant to the Health and Safety Code.

(2) As-extracted collateral, as defined in paragraph (6) of subdivision (a) of Section 9102 of the Commercial Code, and timber to be cut.

(3) The inventory of a retail merchant held for sale except to the extent that the inventory of the retail merchant consists of durable goods having a unit retail value of at least five hundred dollars ($500). * * *

* * *

697.560.

At the time of filing the notice of judgment lien on personal property or promptly thereafter, the judgment creditor shall serve a copy of the notice of judgment lien on the judgment debtor. Service shall be made personally or by mail. The failure to comply with this requirement does not affect the validity of the judgment lien.

697.570.

Upon presentation of a notice of judgment lien on personal property for filing and tender of the filing fee to the office of the Secretary of State, the notice of judgment lien shall be filed, marked, and indexed in the same manner as a financing statement. The fee for filing in the office of the Secretary of State is the same as the fee for filing a financing statement in the standard form. A notice shall not be filed if it is presented for filing more than 10 days after the date of the notice. * * *

697.590–620 [*reproducing priority and proceeds rules in Article 9 of the UCC, with minor modifications*].

Article 4. Execution Lien 697.710–697.750

697.710.

A levy on property under a writ of execution creates an execution lien on the property from the time of levy until the expiration of two years after the date of issuance of the writ unless the judgment is sooner satisfied.

697.720.

Subject to Section 701.630, if an interest in real property subject to an execution lien is transferred or encumbered, the interest transferred or encumbered remains subject to the lien after the transfer or encumbrance.

697.730.

(a) Subject to Section 701.630 and except as provided in subdivision (b), if tangible personal property subject to an execution lien is in the custody of a levying officer and is transferred or encumbered, the property remains subject to the lien after the transfer or encumbrance. * * *

697.740.

Except as provided in Sections 9617 and 9622 of the Commercial Code and in Section 701.630, if personal property subject to an execution lien is not in the custody of a levying officer and the property is transferred or encumbered, the property remains subject to the lien after the transfer or encumbrance except where the transfer or encumbrance is made to one of the following persons:

(a) A person who acquires an interest in the property under the law of this state for reasonably equivalent value without knowledge of the lien. For purposes of this subdivision, value is given for a transfer or encumbrance if, in exchange for the transfer or encumbrance, property is transferred or an antecedent debt is secured or satisfied.

(b) A buyer in ordinary course of business (as defined in Section 1201 of the Commercial Code) * * *

Chapter 3. Execution 699.010–701.830

Article 1. General Provisions 699.010–699.090

* * *

699.030.

If personal property sought to be levied upon is located in a private place of the judgment debtor:

(a) The levying officer making the levy shall demand delivery of the property by the judgment debtor and shall advise the judgment debtor that the judgment debtor may be liable for costs and attorney's fees incurred in any further proceedings to obtain delivery of the property. If the judgment debtor does not deliver the property, the levying officer shall make no further effort to obtain custody of the property and shall promptly notify the judgment creditor of the failure to obtain custody of the property.

(b) The judgment creditor may apply to the court ex parte, or on noticed motion if the court so directs or a court rule so requires, for an order directing the levying officer to seize the property in the private place. The application may be made whether or not a writ has been issued and whether or not demand has been made pursuant to subdivision (a). The application for the order shall describe with particularity both the property sought to be levied upon, and the place where it is to be found, according to the best knowledge, information, and belief of the judgment creditor. The court may not issue the order unless the judgment creditor establishes that there is probable cause to believe that property sought to be levied upon is located in the place described. The levying officer making the levy, at the time delivery of the property pursuant to the order is demanded, shall announce his or her identity, purpose, and authority. If the property is not voluntarily delivered, the levying officer may cause the building or enclosure where the property is believed to be located to be broken open in such manner as the levying officer reasonably believes will cause the least damage, but if the levying officer reasonably believes that entry and seizure of the property will involve a substantial risk of death or serious bodily harm to any person, the levying officer shall refrain from entering and shall promptly make a return to the court setting forth the reasons for believing that the risk exists. In such a case, the court shall make such orders as may be appropriate.

699.040.

(a) If a writ of execution is issued, the judgment creditor may apply to the court ex parte, or on noticed motion if the court so directs or a court rule so requires, for an order directing the judgment debtor to transfer to the levying officer either or both of the following:

(1) Possession of the property sought to be levied upon if the property is sought to be levied upon by taking it into custody.

(2) Possession of documentary evidence of title to property of or a debt owed to the judgment debtor that is sought to be levied upon. An order pursuant to this paragraph may be served when the property or debt is levied upon or thereafter.

(b) The court may issue an order pursuant to this section upon a showing of need for the order.

(c) The order shall be personally served on the judgment debtor and shall contain a notice to the judgment debtor that failure to comply with the order may subject the judgment debtor to arrest and punishment for contempt of court.

* * *

699.080.

(a) A registered process server may levy under a writ of execution on the following types of property:

(1) Real property, pursuant to Section 700.015.

(2) Growing crops, timber to be cut, or minerals or the like including oil and gas, to be extracted or accounts receivable resulting from the sale thereof at the wellhead or minehead, pursuant to Section 700.020.

(3) Personal property in the custody of a levying officer, pursuant to Section 700.050.

(4) Personal property used as a dwelling, pursuant to subdivision (a) of Section 700.080.

(5) Deposit accounts, pursuant to Section 700.140.

(6) Property in a safe-deposit box, pursuant to Section 700.150.

(7) Accounts receivable or general intangibles, pursuant to Section 700.170.

(8) Final money judgments, pursuant to Section 700.190.

(9) Interest of a judgment debtor in personal property in the estate of a decedent, pursuant to Section 700.200.

* * *

Article 2. Writ of Execution and Notice of Levy 699.510–699.560

699.510.

(a) Subject to subdivision (b), after entry of a money judgment, a writ of execution shall be issued by the clerk of the court, upon application of the judgment creditor, and shall be directed to the levying officer in the county where the levy is to be made and to any registered process server.... A separate writ shall be issued for each county where a levy is to be made. Writs may be issued successively until the money judgment is satisfied, except that a new writ may not be issued for a county until the expiration of 180 days after the issuance of a prior writ for that county unless the prior writ is first returned.

* * *

699.530.

(a) Upon delivery of the writ of execution to the levying officer to whom the writ is directed, together with the written instructions of the judgment creditor, the levying officer shall execute the writ in the manner prescribed by law.

(b) The levying officer may not levy upon any property under the writ after the expiration of 180 days from the date the writ was issued.

699.540.

The notice of levy required by Article 4 (commencing with Section 700.010) shall inform the person notified of all of the following:

(a) The capacity in which the person is notified.

(b) The property that is levied upon.

(c) The person's rights under the levy, including the right to claim an exemption pursuant to Chapter 4 (commencing with Section 703.010) and the right to make a third-party claim pursuant to Division 4 (commencing with Section 720.010).

(d) The person's duties under the levy.

(e) All names listed in the writ of execution pursuant to an affidavit of identity, as defined in Section 680.135, if any.

* * *

699.560.

(a) Except as provided in subdivisions (b) and (c), the writ expires and the levying officer to whom the writ of execution is delivered shall return the writ to the court, or store the writ as provided in Section 263.6, and file a return with the court reporting the levying officer's actions and an accounting of amounts collected, and costs incurred, at the earliest of the following times:

(1) Two years from the date of issuance of the writ, unless paragraph (1) of subdivision (a) of Section 706.022 is applicable.

(2) Promptly after all of the duties under the writ are performed.

(3) When return is requested in writing by the judgment creditor.

(4) If no levy takes place under the writ within 180 days after its issuance, promptly after the expiration of the 180-day period.

(5) Upon expiration of the time for enforcement of the money judgment.

* * *

(d) If a levy has been made under the Wage Garnishment Law (Chapter 5 (commencing with Section 706.010)), and the earnings withholding order remains in effect, the writ of execution shall be returned as provided in subdivision (a) and a supplemental return shall be made as provided in Section 706.033. * * *

Article 3. Property Subject to Execution 699.710–699.720

699.710.

Except as otherwise provided by law, all property that is subject to enforcement of a money judgment pursuant to Article 1 (commencing with Section 695.010) of Chapter 1 is subject to levy under a writ of execution to satisfy a money judgment.

699.720.

(a) The following types of property are not subject to execution:

(1) An alcoholic beverage license that is transferable under Article 5 (commencing with Section 24070) of Chapter 6 of Division 9 of the Business and Professions Code.

(2) The interest of a partner in a partnership or member in a limited liability company if the partnership or the limited liability company is not a judgment debtor.

(3) A cause of action that is the subject of a pending action or special proceeding.

(4) A judgment in favor of the judgment debtor prior to the expiration of the time for appeal from the judgment or, if an appeal is filed, prior to the final determination of the appeal.

(5) A debt (other than earnings) owing and unpaid by a public entity.

(6) The loan value of an unmatured life insurance, endowment, or annuity policy.

(7) A franchise granted by a public entity and all the rights and privileges of the franchise.

(8) The interest of a trust beneficiary.

(9) A contingent remainder, executory interest, or other interest in property that is not vested.

(10) Property in a guardianship or conservatorship estate.

(b) Nothing in subdivision (a) affects or limits the right of the judgment creditor to apply property to the satisfaction of a money judgment pursuant to any applicable procedure other than execution.

Article 4. Methods of Levy 700.010–700.200

700.010.

(a) At the time of levy pursuant to this article or promptly thereafter, the levying officer shall serve a copy of the following on the judgment debtor:

(1) The writ of execution.

(2) A notice of levy.

(3) If the judgment debtor is a natural person, a copy of the form listing exemptions prepared by the Judicial Council pursuant to subdivision (c) of Section 681.030, the list of exemption amounts published pursuant to subdivision (e) of Section 703.150, a copy of the form that the judgment debtor may use to make a claim of exemption pursuant to Section 703.520, and a copy of the form the judgment debtor may use to provide a financial statement pursuant to Section 703.530.

* * *

(b) Service under this section shall be made personally or by mail.

700.015.

(a) To levy upon real property, the levying officer shall record with the recorder of the county where the real property is located a copy of the writ of execution and a notice of levy that describes the property levied upon and states that the judgment debtor's interest in the described property has been levied upon. If the judgment debtor's interest in the real property stands upon the records of the county in the name of a person other than the judgment debtor, the notice of levy shall identify the third person and the recorder shall index the copy of the writ and notice of levy in the names of both the judgment debtor and the third person.

* * *

700.030.

Unless another method of levy is provided by this article, to levy upon tangible personal property in the possession or under the control of the judgment debtor, the levying officer shall take the property into custody.

700.040.

(a) Unless another method of levy is provided by this article, to levy upon tangible personal property in the possession or under the control of a third person, the levying officer shall personally serve a copy of the writ of execution and a notice of levy on the third person.

* * *

700.070.

To levy upon tangible personal property of a going business in the possession or under the control of the judgment debtor, the levying officer shall comply with Section 700.030, except to the extent that the judgment creditor instructs that levy be made in the following manner:

(a) The levying officer shall place a keeper in charge of the business for the period requested by the judgment creditor. During the period, the business may continue to operate in the ordinary course of business provided that all sales are final and are for cash or its equivalent. For the purpose of this subdivision, a check is the equivalent of cash. The levying officer is not liable for accepting payment in the form of a cash equivalent. The keeper shall take custody of the proceeds from all sales unless otherwise directed by the judgment creditor.

(b) The levying officer shall take the tangible personal property into exclusive custody at the earliest of the following times:

(1) At any time the judgment debtor objects to placement of a keeper in charge of the business.

(2) At any time when requested by the judgment creditor.

(3) At the end of 10 days from the time the keeper is placed in charge of the business.

(c) Where a keeper is placed in a business for the purpose of taking into custody tangible personal property consisting solely of money or equivalent proceeds of sales, the provisions of subdivision (b) shall not apply, and the levying officer shall take such property into exclusive custody at the end of each daily keeper period.

* * *

700.130.

To levy upon a security, the levying officer shall comply with Section 8112 of the Commercial Code. The legal process referred to in Section 8112 of the Commercial Code means the legal process required by the state in which the chief executive office of the issuer of the security is located and, where that state is California, means personal service by the levying officer of a copy of the writ of execution and notice of levy on the person who is to be served.

700.140.

(a) Subject to Sections 684.115 and 700.160, to levy upon a deposit account, the levying officer shall personally serve a copy of the writ of execution and a notice of levy on the financial institution with which the deposit account is maintained.

(b) The execution lien that arises upon service of a writ of execution and notice of levy reaches only amounts in a deposit account at the time of service on the financial institution, including the amount of any deposit not yet finally collected unless the deposit is returned unpaid to the financial institution.

* * *

(d) The financial institution shall not honor a withdrawal request or a check or other order for the payment of money from the deposit account if presentment of the withdrawal request or item to the financial institution occurs during the time the execution lien is in effect unless, following the withdrawal or payment, sufficient funds are available to cover the levy. For these purposes, a withdrawal from the deposit account to cover the financial institution's standard fee or charge for processing the levy shall not be considered a payment of money from the account in violation of this subdivision. * * *

700.150.

(a) Subject to Section 700.160, to levy upon property in a safe-deposit box, the levying officer shall personally serve a copy of the writ of execution and a notice of levy on the financial institution with which the safe-deposit box is maintained.

* * *

700.170.

(a) Unless another method of levy is provided by this article, to levy upon an account receivable or general intangible, the levying officer shall personally serve a copy of the writ of execution and a notice of levy on the account debtor. * * *

700.190.

(a) As used in this section, "final money judgment" means a money judgment after the time for appeal from the judgment has expired or, if an appeal is filed, after the appeal has been finally determined.

(b) To levy upon a final money judgment, the levying officer shall file a copy of the writ of execution and a notice of levy with the clerk of the court that entered the final money judgment. The court clerk shall endorse upon the judgment a statement of the existence of the execution lien and the time it was created. If an abstract of the judgment is issued, it shall include a statement of the execution lien in favor of the judgment creditor.

(c) At the time of levy or promptly thereafter, the levying officer shall serve a copy of the writ of execution and a notice of levy on the judgment debtor obligated to pay the final money judgment levied upon. Service shall be made personally or by mail.

* * *

Article 5. Duties and Liabilities of Third Persons After Levy 701.010–701.070

701.010.

(a) Except as otherwise provided by statute, when a levy is made by service of a copy of the writ of execution and a notice of levy on a third person, the third person at the time of levy or promptly thereafter shall comply with this section.

(b) Unless the third person has good cause for failure or refusal to do so:

(1) The third person shall deliver to the levying officer any of the property levied upon that is in the possession or under the control of the

third person at the time of levy unless the third person claims the right to possession of the property.

(2) To the extent that the third person does not deny an obligation levied upon, or claim a priority over the judgment creditor's lien, the third person shall pay to the levying officer both of the following:

(A) The amount of the obligation levied upon that is due and payable to the judgment debtor at the time of levy.

(B) Amounts that become due and payable to the judgment debtor on the obligation levied upon during the period of the execution lien.

(3) If the third person makes a delivery or payment to the levying officer pursuant to this section, the third person shall execute and deliver any documents necessary to effect the transfer of the property.

(c) For the purposes of this section, "good cause" includes, but is not limited to, a showing that the third person did not know or have reason to know of the levy from all the facts and circumstances known to the third person.

701.020.

(a) If a third person is required by this article to deliver property to the levying officer or to make payments to the levying officer and the third person fails or refuses without good cause to do so, the third person is liable to the judgment creditor for whichever of the following is the lesser amount:

(1) The value of the judgment debtor's interest in the property or the amount of the payments required to be made.

(2) The amount required to satisfy the judgment pursuant to which the levy is made.

(b) The third person's liability continues until the earliest of the following times:

(1) The time when the property levied upon is delivered to the levying officer or the payments are made to the levying officer.

(2) The time when the property levied upon is released pursuant to Section 699. 060.

(3) The time when the judgment is satisfied or discharged.

(c) If the third person's liability is established, the court that determines the liability may, in its discretion, require the third person to pay the costs and reasonable attorney's fees incurred by the judgment creditor in establishing the liability.

* * *

701.050.

After service of a copy of the writ of execution and a notice of levy on an account debtor obligated on an account receivable, chattel paper, or general intangible:

(a) If the account debtor has been making payments or is required to make payments to the judgment debtor, the account debtor shall make payments to the levying officer as they become due unless otherwise directed by court order or by the levying officer. Payments made to the judgment debtor after the account debtor has received notice of the levy do not discharge the obligation of the account debtor to make payments as required by this subdivision.

* * *

Article 6. Sale and Collection 701.510–701.680

701.510.

Subject to Sections 687.020 and 701.520, the levying officer shall sell all property that has been levied upon....

701.520.

(a) Except as provided in this section, any [liquid] property that has been levied upon shall be collected rather than sold....

* * *

701.570.

(a) A sale of property shall be held at the date, time, and place specified in the notice of sale, which shall be in the county where the property or a part thereof is situated and between the hours of nine in the morning and five in the afternoon. Subject to subdivision (d), real property consisting of one parcel, or of two or more contiguous parcels, situated in two or more counties may be sold in one county as instructed by the judgment creditor.

(b) The sale shall be made at auction to the highest bidder.

(c) If personal property capable of manual delivery is to be sold, it shall be within the view of those who attend the sale unless, upon application of the judgment creditor or the judgment debtor, the court orders otherwise.

(d) Property shall be sold separately or in such groups or lots as are likely to bring the highest price. The judgment debtor may request that the property be sold separately or together and may request that the property be sold in a particular order. If the judgment debtor is not present at the sale, the request may be made in writing and delivered to the levying officer prior to the sale. The levying officer shall honor the request if, in the opinion of the levying officer, the requested manner of sale is likely to yield an amount at least equal to any other manner of sale or the amount required to satisfy the money judgment. The levying officer is not liable for a decision made in good faith under this subdivision.

(e) After sufficient property has been sold to yield the amount required to satisfy the money judgment, no more shall be sold.

* * *

701.590.

(a) Except as otherwise provided in this section, the purchaser at a sale shall pay in cash or by certified check or cashier's check.

(b) The judgment creditor may bid by giving the levying officer a written receipt crediting all or part of the amount required to satisfy the judgment, except that the levying officer's costs remaining unsatisfied and the amount of preferred labor claims, exempt proceeds, and any other claim that is required by statute to be satisfied, shall be paid in cash or by certified check or cashier's check.

* * *

Chapter 4. Exemptions 703.010–704.995

Article 1. General Provisions 703.010–703.150

* * *

703.020.

(a) The exemptions provided by this chapter apply only to property of a natural person.

* * *

703.030.

(a) An exemption for property that is described in this chapter or in any other statute as exempt may be claimed within the time and in the manner prescribed in the applicable enforcement procedure. If the exemption is not so claimed, the exemption is waived and the property is subject to enforcement of a money judgment.

(b) Except as otherwise specifically provided by statute, property that is described in this chapter or in any other statute as exempt without making a claim is not subject to any procedure for enforcement of a money judgment.

(c) Nothing in this section limits the authority of the court pursuant to Section 473 to relieve a person upon such terms as may be just from failure to claim an exemption within the time and in the manner prescribed in the applicable enforcement procedure.

* * *

703.080.

(a) Subject to any limitation provided in the particular exemption, a fund that is exempt remains exempt to the extent that it can be traced into deposit accounts or in the form of cash or its equivalent.

(b) The exemption claimant has the burden of tracing an exempt fund.

(c) The tracing of exempt funds in a deposit account shall be by application of the lowest intermediate balance principle unless the exemption claimant or the judgment creditor shows that some other method of tracing would better serve the interests of justice and equity under the circumstances of the case.

* * *

703.150.

(a) On April 1, 2004, and at each three-year interval ending on April 1 thereafter, the dollar amounts of exemptions provided in subdivision (b) of Section 703.140 in effect immediately before that date shall be adjusted as provided in subdivision (d).

(b) On April 1, 2007, and at each three-year interval ending on April 1 thereafter, the dollar amounts of exemptions provided in Article 3 (commencing with Section 704.010) in effect immediately before that date shall be adjusted as provided in subdivision (d).

(c) On April 1, 2013, and at each three-year interval ending on April 1 thereafter, the Judicial Council shall submit to the Legislature the amount by which the dollar amounts of exemptions provided in subdivision (a) of Section 704.730 in effect immediately before that date may be increased as provided in subdivision (d). Those increases shall not take effect unless they are approved by the Legislature.

(d) The Judicial Council shall determine the amount of the adjustment based on the change in the annual California Consumer Price Index for All Urban Consumers, published by the Department of Industrial Relations, Division of Labor Statistics, for the most recent three-year period ending on December 31 preceding the adjustment, with each adjusted amount rounded to the nearest twenty-five dollars ($25).

(e) Beginning April 1, 2004, the Judicial Council shall publish a list of the current dollar amounts of exemptions provided in subdivision (b) of Section 703.140 and in Article 3 (commencing with Section 704.010), together with the date of the next scheduled adjustment. In any year that the Legislature votes to increase the exemptions provided in subdivision (a) of Section 704.730, the Judicial Council shall publish a list of current dollar amounts of exemptions.

(f) Adjustments made under subdivision (a) do not apply with respect to cases commenced before the date of the adjustment, subject to any contrary rule applicable under the federal Bankruptcy Code. The applicability of adjustments made under subdivisions (b) and (c) is governed by Section 703.050.

Article 2. Procedure for Claiming Exemptions After Levy 703.510–703.610

703.510.

(a) Except as otherwise provided by statute, property that has been levied upon may be claimed to be exempt as provided in this article.

(b) If property that is exempt without making a claim is levied upon, it may be released pursuant to the exemption procedure provided in this article.

703.520.

(a) The claimant may make a claim of exemption by filing with the levying officer a claim of exemption together with a copy thereof. The claim shall be made within 10 days after the date the notice of levy on the property claimed to be exempt was served on the judgment debtor.

(b) The claim of exemption shall be executed under oath and shall include all of the following:

(1) The name of the claimant and the mailing address where service of a notice of opposition to the claim may be made upon the claimant.

(2) The name and last known address of the judgment debtor if the claimant is not the judgment debtor.

(3) A description of the property claimed to be exempt. If an exemption is claimed pursuant to Section 704.010 or 704.060, the claimant shall describe all other property of the same type (including exempt pro-

ceeds of property of the same type) owned by the judgment debtor alone or in combination with others on the date of levy and identify the property, whether or not levied upon, to which the exemption is to be applied. If an exemption is claimed pursuant to subdivision (b) of Section 704.100, the claimant shall state the nature and amount of all other property of the same type owned by the judgment debtor or the spouse of the judgment debtor alone or in combination with others on the date of levy.

(4) A financial statement if required by Section 703.530.

(5) A citation of the provision of this chapter or other statute upon which the claim is based.

(6) A statement of the facts necessary to support the claim.

703.530.

(a) If property is claimed as exempt pursuant to a provision exempting property to the extent necessary for the support of the judgment debtor and the spouse and dependents of the judgment debtor, the claim of exemption shall include a financial statement.

(b) The financial statement shall include all of the following information:

(1) The name of the spouse of the judgment debtor.

(2) The name, age, and relationship of all persons dependent upon the judgment debtor or the spouse of the judgment debtor for support.

(3) All sources and the amounts of earnings and other income of the judgment debtor and the spouse and dependents of the judgment debtor.

(4) A list of the assets of the judgment debtor and the spouse and dependents of the judgment debtor and the value of such assets.

(5) All outstanding obligations of the judgment debtor and the spouse and dependents of the judgment debtor.

(c) The financial statement shall be executed under oath by the judgment debtor and, unless the spouses are living separate and apart, by the spouse of the judgment debtor.

703.540.

Promptly after the filing of the claim of exemption, the levying officer shall serve both of the following on the judgment creditor personally or by mail:

(a) A copy of the claim of exemption.

(b) A notice of claim of exemption stating that the claim of exemption has been made and that the levying officer will release the property unless, within the time allowed as specified in the notice, both of the following are filed with the levying officer:

(1) A copy of the notice of opposition to the claim of exemption.

(2) A copy of the notice of motion for an order determining the claim of exemption.

703.550.

Within 10 days after service of the notice of claim of exemption, a judgment creditor who opposes the claim of exemption shall file with the court a notice of opposition to the claim of exemption and a notice of motion for an order determining the claim of exemption and shall file with the levying officer a copy of the notice of opposition and a copy of the notice of motion. Upon the filing of the copies of the notice of opposition and notice of motion, the levying officer shall promptly file the claim of exemption with the court. If copies of the notice of opposition and notice of motion are not filed with the levying officer within the time allowed, the levying officer shall immediately release the property to the extent it is claimed to be exempt.

703.560.

The notice of opposition to the claim of exemption shall be executed under oath and shall include both of the following:

(a) An allegation either (1) that the property is not exempt under the provision of this chapter or other statute relied upon or (2) that the equity in the property claimed to be exempt is in excess of the amount provided in the applicable exemption.

(b) A statement of the facts necessary to support the allegation.

703.570.

(a) The hearing on the motion shall be held not later than 30 days from the date the notice of motion was filed with the court unless continued by the court for good cause.

(b) Not less than 10 days prior to the hearing, the judgment creditor shall serve a notice of the hearing and a copy of the notice of opposition to the claim of exemption on the claimant and on the judgment debtor, if other than the claimant. Service shall be made personally or by mail.

703.580.

(a) The claim of exemption and notice of opposition to the claim of exemption constitute the pleadings, subject to the power of the court to permit amendments in the interest of justice.

(b) At a hearing under this section, the exemption claimant has the burden of proof.

(c) The claim of exemption is deemed controverted by the notice of opposition to the claim of exemption and both shall be received in evidence. If no other evidence is offered, the court, if satisfied that sufficient facts are shown by the claim of exemption (including the financial statement if one is required) and the notice of opposition, may make its determination thereon. If not satisfied, the court shall order the hearing continued for the production of other evidence, oral or documentary.

(d) At the conclusion of the hearing, the court shall determine by order whether or not the property is exempt in whole or in part. Subject to Section 703.600, the order is determinative of the right of the judgment creditor to apply the property to the satisfaction of the judgment. No findings are required in a proceeding under this section.

(e) The court clerk shall promptly transmit a certified copy of the order to the levying officer. Subject to Section 703.610, the levying officer shall, in compliance with the order, release the property or apply the property to the satisfaction of the money judgment.

(f) Unless otherwise ordered by the court, if an exemption is not determined within the time provided by Section 703.570, the property claimed to be exempt shall be released.

* * *

Article 3. Exempt Property 704.010–704.210

704.010.

(a) Any combination of the following is exempt in the amount of two thousand three hundred dollars ($2,300) [**$3325**]:

(1) The aggregate equity in motor vehicles.

(2) The proceeds of an execution sale of a motor vehicle.

(3) The proceeds of insurance or other indemnification for the loss, damage, or destruction of a motor vehicle.

(b) Proceeds exempt under subdivision (a) are exempt for a period of 90 days after the time the proceeds are actually received by the judgment debtor.

(c) For the purpose of determining the equity, the fair market value of a motor vehicle shall be determined by reference to used car price guides customarily used by California automobile dealers unless the motor vehicle is not listed in such price guides. * * *

704.020.

(a) Household furnishings, appliances, provisions, wearing apparel, and other personal effects are exempt in the following cases:

(1) If ordinarily and reasonably necessary to, and personally used or procured for use by, the judgment debtor and members of the judgment debtor's family at the judgment debtor's principal place of residence.

(2) Where the judgment debtor and the judgment debtor's spouse live separate and apart, if ordinarily and reasonably necessary to, and personally used or procured for use by, the spouse and members of the spouse's family at the spouse's principal place of residence.

(b) In determining whether an item of property is "ordinarily and reasonably necessary" under subdivision (a), the court shall take into account both of the following:

(1) The extent to which the particular type of item is ordinarily found in a household.

(2) Whether the particular item has extraordinary value as compared to the value of items of the same type found in other households.

(c) If an item of property for which an exemption is claimed pursuant to this section is an item of the type ordinarily found in a household but is determined not to be exempt because the item has extraordinary value as compared to the value of items of the same type found in other households, the proceeds obtained at an execution sale of the item are exempt in the amount determined by the court to be a reasonable amount sufficient to purchase a replacement of ordinary value if the court determines that a replacement is reasonably necessary. Proceeds exempt under this subdivision are exempt for a period of 90 days after the proceeds are actually received by the judgment debtor.

* * *

704.040.

Jewelry, heirlooms, and works of art are exempt to the extent that the aggregate equity therein does not exceed six thousand seventy-five dollars ($6,075) [**$8725**].

704.050.

Health aids reasonably necessary to enable the judgment debtor or the spouse or a dependent of the judgment debtor to work or sustain health, and prosthetic and orthopedic appliances, are exempt.

704.060.

(a) Tools, implements, instruments, materials, uniforms, furnishings, books, equipment, one commercial motor vehicle, one vessel, and other personal property are exempt to the extent that the aggregate equity therein does not exceed:

(1) Six thousand seventy-five dollars ($6,075) [**$8725**], if reasonably necessary to and actually used by the judgment debtor in the exercise of the trade, business, or profession by which the judgment debtor earns a livelihood.

(2) Six thousand seventy-five dollars ($6,075) [**$8725**], if reasonably necessary to and actually used by the spouse of the judgment debtor in the exercise of the trade, business, or profession by which the spouse earns a livelihood.

(3) Twice the amount of the exemption provided in paragraph (1) [**$17,450**], if reasonably necessary to and actually used by the judgment debtor and by the spouse of the judgment debtor in the exercise of the same trade, business, or profession by which both earn a livelihood. In the case covered by this paragraph, the exemptions provided in paragraphs (1) and (2) are not available.

(b) If property described in subdivision (a) is sold at an execution sale, or if it has been lost, damaged, or destroyed, the proceeds of the execution sale or of insurance or other indemnification are exempt for a period of 90 days after the proceeds are actually received by the judgment debtor or the judgment debtor's spouse. The amount exempt under this subdivision is the amount specified in subdivision (a) that applies to the particular case less the aggregate equity of any other property to which the exemption provided by subdivision (a) for the particular case has been applied.

(c) Notwithstanding subdivision (a), a motor vehicle is not exempt under subdivision (a) if there is a motor vehicle exempt under Section 704.010 which is reasonably adequate for use in the trade, business, or profession for which the exemption is claimed under this section.

(d) Notwithstanding subdivisions (a) and (b):

(1) The amount of the exemption for a commercial motor vehicle under paragraph (1) or (2) of subdivision (a) is limited to four thousand eight hundred fifty dollars ($4,850).

(2) The amount of the exemption for a commercial motor vehicle under paragraph (3) of subdivision (a) is limited to twice the amount of the exemption provided in paragraph (1) of this subdivision.

704.070.

(a) As used in this section:

(1) "Earnings withholding order" means an earnings withholding order under Chapter 5 (commencing with Section 706.010) (Wage Garnishment Law).

(2) "Paid earnings" means earnings as defined in Section 706.011 that were paid to the employee during the 30-day period ending on the date of the levy. For the purposes of this paragraph, where earnings that have been paid to the employee are sought to be subjected to the enforcement of a money judgment other than by a levy, the date of levy is deemed to be the date the earnings were otherwise subjected to the enforcement of the judgment.

* * *

(b) Paid earnings that can be traced into deposit accounts or in the form of cash or its equivalent as provided in Section 703.080 are exempt in the following amounts:

(1) All of the paid earnings are exempt if prior to payment to the employee they were subject to an earnings withholding order....

(2) Seventy-five percent of the paid earnings that are levied upon or otherwise sought to be subjected to the enforcement of a money judgment are exempt if prior to payment to the employee they were not subject to an earnings withholding order....

704.080.

(a) For the purposes of this section:

(1) "Deposit account" means a deposit account in which payments of public benefits or social security benefits are directly deposited by the government or its agent.

(2) "Social security benefits" means payments authorized by the Social Security Administration for regular retirement and survivors' benefits, supplemental security income benefits, coal miners' health benefits, and disability insurance benefits. "Public benefits" means aid payments authorized pursuant to subdivision (a) of Section 11450 of the Welfare and Institutions Code, payments for supportive services as described in Section 11323.2 of the Welfare and Institutions Code, and general assistance payments made pursuant to Section 17000.5 of the Welfare and Institutions Code.

(b) A deposit account is exempt without making a claim in the following amount:

(1) One thousand two hundred twenty-five dollars ($1,225) [**$1750**] where one depositor is the designated payee of the directly deposited public benefits payments.

(2) Two thousand four hundred twenty-five dollars ($2,425) [**$3500**] where one depositor is the designated payee of directly deposited social security payments.

(3) One thousand eight hundred twenty-five dollars ($1,825) [**$2600**] where two or more depositors are the designated payees of the directly deposited public benefits payments, unless those depositors are joint payees of directly deposited payments that represent a benefit to only one of the depositors, in which case the exemption under paragraph (1) applies.

(4) Three thousand six hundred fifty dollars ($3,650) [**$5250**] where two or more depositors are the designated payees of directly deposited social security payments, unless those depositors are joint payees of directly deposited payments that represent a benefit to only one of the depositors, in which case the exemption under paragraph (2) applies.

(c) The amount of a deposit account that exceeds the exemption provided in subdivision (b) is exempt to the extent that it consists of payments of public benefits or social security benefits.

(d) Notwithstanding Article 5 (commencing with Section 701.010) of Chapter 3, when a deposit account is levied upon or otherwise sought to be subjected to the enforcement of a money judgment, the financial institution that holds the deposit account shall either place the amount that exceeds the exemption provided in subdivision (b) in a suspense account or otherwise prohibit withdrawal of that amount pending notification of the failure of the judgment creditor to file the affidavit required by this section or the judicial determination of the exempt status of the amount. Within 10 business days after the levy, the financial institution shall provide the levying officer with a written notice stating (1) that the deposit account is one in which payments of public benefits or social security benefits are directly deposited by the government or its agent and (2) the balance of the deposit account that exceeds the exemption provided by subdivision (b). Promptly upon receipt of the notice, the levying officer shall serve the notice on the judgment creditor. Service shall be made personally or by mail.

(e) Notwithstanding the procedure prescribed in Article 2 (commencing with Section 703.510), whether there is an amount exempt under subdivision (c) shall be determined as follows:

(1) Within five days after the levying officer serves the notice on the judgment creditor under subdivision (d), a judgment creditor who desires to claim that the amount is not exempt shall file with the court an affidavit alleging that the amount is not exempt and file a copy with the levying officer. The affidavit shall be in the form of the notice of opposition provided by Section 703.560, and a hearing shall be set and held, and notice given, as provided by Sections 703.570 and 703.580. For the purpose of this subdivision, the "notice of opposition to the claim of exemption" in Sections 703.570 and 703.580 means the affidavit under this subdivision.

(2) If the judgment creditor does not file the affidavit with the levying officer and give notice of hearing pursuant to Section 703.570 within the time provided in paragraph (1), the levying officer shall release the deposit account and shall notify the financial institution.

(3) The affidavit constitutes the pleading of the judgment creditor, subject to the power of the court to permit amendments in the interest of justice. The affidavit is deemed controverted and no counteraffidavit is required.

(4) At a hearing under this subdivision, the judgment debtor has the burden of proving that the excess amount is exempt.

(5) At the conclusion of the hearing, the court by order shall determine whether or not the amount of the deposit account is exempt pursuant to subdivision (c) in whole or in part and shall make an

appropriate order for its prompt disposition. No findings are required in a proceeding under this subdivision.

(6) Upon determining the exemption claim for the deposit account under subdivision (c), the court shall immediately transmit a certified copy of the order of the court to the financial institution and to the levying officer. If the order determines that all or part of the excess is exempt under subdivision (c), with respect to the amount of the excess which is exempt, the financial institution shall transfer the exempt excess from the suspense account or otherwise release any restrictions on its withdrawal by the judgment debtor. The transfer or release shall be effected within three business days of the receipt of the certified copy of the court order by the financial institution.

(f) If the judgment debtor claims that a portion of the amount is exempt other than pursuant to subdivision (c), the claim of exemption shall be made pursuant to Article 2 (commencing with Section 703.510). If the judgment debtor also opposes the judgment creditor's affidavit regarding an amount exempt pursuant to subdivision (c), both exemptions shall be determined at the same hearing, provided the judgment debtor has complied with Article 2 (commencing with Section 703.510).

* * *

704.100.

(a) Unmatured life insurance policies (including endowment and annuity policies), but not the loan value of such policies, are exempt without making a claim.

(b) The aggregate loan value of unmatured life insurance policies (including endowment and annuity policies) is subject to the enforcement of a money judgment but is exempt in the amount of nine thousand seven hundred dollars ($9,700) [**$13,975**]. If the judgment debtor is married, each spouse is entitled to a separate exemption under this subdivision, and the exemptions of the spouses may be combined, regardless of whether the policies belong to either or both spouses and regardless of whether the spouse of the judgment debtor is also a judgment debtor under the judgment. The exemption provided by this subdivision shall be first applied to policies other than the policy before the court and then, if the exemption is not exhausted, to the policy before the court.

(c) Benefits from matured life insurance policies (including endowment and annuity policies) are exempt to the extent reasonably necessary for the support of the judgment debtor and the spouse and dependents of the judgment debtor.

704.110.

(a) As used in this section:

(1) "Public entity" means the state, or a city, city and county, county, or other political subdivision of the state, or a public trust, public corporation, or public board, or the governing body of any of them, but does not include the United States except where expressly so provided.

(2) "Public retirement benefit" means a pension or an annuity, or a retirement, disability, death, or other benefit, paid or payable by a public retirement system.

(3) "Public retirement system" means a system established pursuant to statute by a public entity for retirement, annuity, or pension purposes or payment of disability or death benefits.

(b) All amounts held, controlled, or in process of distribution by a public entity derived from contributions by the public entity or by an officer or employee of the public entity for public retirement benefit purposes, and all rights and benefits accrued or accruing to any person under a public retirement system, are exempt without making a claim.

* * *

(d) All amounts received by any person, a resident of the state, as a public retirement benefit or as a return of contributions and interest thereon from the United States or a public entity or from a public retirement system are exempt.

* * *

704.115.

(a) As used in this section, "private retirement plan" means:

(1) Private retirement plans, including, but not limited to, union retirement plans.

(2) Profit-sharing plans designed and used for retirement purposes.

(3) Self-employed retirement plans and individual retirement annuities or accounts provided for in the Internal Revenue Code of 1986, as amended, including individual retirement accounts qualified under Section 408 or 408A of that code, to the extent the amounts held in the plans, annuities, or accounts do not exceed the maximum amounts exempt from federal income taxation under that code.

(b) All amounts held, controlled, or in process of distribution by a private retirement plan, for the payment of benefits as an annuity, pension, retirement allowance, disability payment, or death benefit from a private retirement plan are exempt.

* * *

(d) After payment, the amounts described in subdivision (b) and all contributions and interest thereon returned to any member of a private retirement plan are exempt.

(e) Notwithstanding subdivisions (b) and (d), except as provided in subdivision (f), the amounts described in paragraph (3) of subdivision (a) are exempt only to the extent necessary to provide for the support of the judgment debtor when the judgment debtor retires and for the support of the spouse and dependents of the judgment debtor, taking into account all resources that are likely to be available for the support of the judgment debtor when the judgment debtor retires. In determining the amount to be exempt under this subdivision, the court shall allow the judgment debtor such additional amount as is necessary to pay any federal and state income taxes payable as a result of the applying of an amount described in paragraph (3) of subdivision (a) to the satisfaction of the money judgment.

(f) Where the amounts described in paragraph (3) of subdivision (a) are payable periodically, the amount of the periodic payment that may be applied to the satisfaction of a money judgment is the amount that may be withheld from a like amount of earnings under Chapter 5 (commencing with Section 706.010) (Wage Garnishment Law). To the extent a lump-sum distribution from an individual retirement account is treated differently from a periodic distribution under this subdivision, any lump-sum distribution from an account qualified under Section 408A of the Internal Revenue Code shall be treated the same as a lump-sum distribution from an account qualified under Section 408 of the Internal Revenue Code for purposes of determining whether any of that payment may be applied to the satisfaction of a money judgment.

* * *

704.140.

(a) Except as provided in Article 5 (commencing with Section 708.410) of Chapter 6, a cause of action for personal injury is exempt without making a claim.

(b) Except as provided in subdivisions (c) and (d), an award of damages or a settlement arising out of personal injury is exempt to the extent necessary for the support of the judgment debtor and the spouse and dependents of the judgment debtor.

* * *

(d) Where an award of damages or a settlement arising out of personal injury is payable periodically, the amount of such periodic payment that may be applied to the satisfaction of a money judgment is the amount that may be withheld from a like amount of earnings under Chapter 5 (commencing with Section 706.010) (Wage Garnishment Law).

704.150.

(a) Except as provided in Article 5 (commencing with Section 708.410) of Chapter 6, a cause of action for wrongful death is exempt without making a claim.

(b) Except as provided in subdivision (c), an award of damages or a settlement arising out of the wrongful death of the judgment debtor's spouse or a person on whom the judgment debtor or the judgment debtor's spouse was dependent is exempt to the extent reasonably necessary for support of the judgment debtor and the spouse and dependents of the judgment debtor.

(c) Where an award of damages or a settlement arising out of the wrongful death of the judgment debtor's spouse or a person on whom the judgment debtor or the judgment debtor's spouse was dependent is payable periodically, the amount of such a periodic payment that may be applied to the satisfaction of a money judgment is the amount that may be withheld from a like amount of earnings under Chapter 5 (commencing with Section 706.010) (Wage Garnishment Law).

* * * [public benefits, workers' comp, and student aid exemptions omitted]

704.200.

(a) As used in this section:

(1) "Cemetery" has the meaning provided by Section 7003 of the Health and Safety Code.

(2) "Family plot" is a plot that satisfies the requirements of Section 8650 of the Health and Safety Code.

(3) "Plot" has the meaning provided by Section 7022 of the Health and Safety Code.

(b) A family plot is exempt without making a claim.

(c) Except as provided in subdivision (d), a cemetery plot for the judgment debtor and the spouse of the judgment debtor is exempt.

(d) Land held for the purpose of sale or disposition as cemetery plots or otherwise is not exempt.

704.210.

Property that is not subject to enforcement of a money judgment is exempt without making a claim.

Article 4. Homestead Exemption 704.710–704.850

704.710.

As used in this article:

(a) "Dwelling" means a place where a person resides and may include but is not limited to the following:

- (1) A house together with the outbuildings and the land upon which they are situated.
- (2) A mobilehome together with the outbuildings and the land upon which they are situated.
- (3) A boat or other waterborne vessel.
- (4) A condominium, as defined in Section 783 of the Civil Code.
- (5) A planned development, as defined in Section 11003 of the Business and Professions Code.
- (6) A stock cooperative, as defined in Section 11003.2 of the Business and Professions Code.
- (7) A community apartment project, as defined in Section 11004 of the Business and Professions Code.

(b) "Family unit" means any of the following:

- (1) The judgment debtor and the judgment debtor's spouse if the spouses reside together in the homestead.
- (2) The judgment debtor and at least one of the following persons who the judgment debtor cares for or maintains in the homestead:
  - (A) The minor child or minor grandchild of the judgment debtor or the judgment debtor's spouse or the minor child or grandchild of a deceased spouse or former spouse.
  - (B) The minor brother or sister of the judgment debtor or judgment debtor's spouse or the minor child of a deceased brother or sister of either spouse.

(C) The father, mother, grandfather, or grandmother of the judgment debtor or the judgment debtor's spouse or the father, mother, grandfather, or grandmother of a deceased spouse.

(D) An unmarried relative described in this paragraph who has attained the age of majority and is unable to take care of or support himself or herself.

(3) The judgment debtor's spouse and at least one of the persons listed in paragraph (2) who the judgment debtor's spouse cares for or maintains in the homestead.

(c) "Homestead" means the principal dwelling (1) in which the judgment debtor or the judgment debtor's spouse resided on the date the judgment creditor's lien attached to the dwelling, and (2) in which the judgment debtor or the judgment debtor's spouse resided continuously thereafter until the date of the court determination that the dwelling is a homestead. Where exempt proceeds from the sale or damage or destruction of a homestead are used toward the acquisition of a dwelling within the six-month period provided by Section 704.720, "homestead" also means the dwelling so acquired if it is the principal dwelling in which the judgment debtor or the judgment debtor's spouse resided continuously from the date of acquisition until the date of the court determination that the dwelling is a homestead, whether or not an abstract or certified copy of a judgment was recorded to create a judgment lien before the dwelling was acquired.

(d) "Spouse" does not include a married person following entry of a judgment decreeing legal separation of the parties, unless such married persons reside together in the same dwelling.

* * *

704.730.

(a) The amount of the homestead exemption is one of the following:

(1) Seventy-five thousand dollars ($75,000) unless the judgment debtor or spouse of the judgment debtor who resides in the homestead is a person described in paragraph (2) or (3).

(2) One hundred thousand dollars ($100,000) if the judgment debtor or spouse of the judgment debtor who resides in the homestead is at the time of the attempted sale of the homestead a member of a family unit, and there is at least one member of the family unit who owns no interest in the homestead or whose only interest in the homestead is a community property interest with the judgment debtor.

(3) One hundred seventy-five thousand dollars ($175,000) if the judgment debtor or spouse of the judgment debtor who resides in the homestead is at the time of the attempted sale of the homestead any one of the following:

(A) A person 65 years of age or older.

(B) A person physically or mentally disabled who as a result of that disability is unable to engage in substantial gainful employment. There is a rebuttable presumption affecting the burden of proof that a person receiving disability insurance benefit payments under Title II or supplemental security income payments under Title XVI of the federal Social Security Act satisfies the requirements of this paragraph as to his or her inability to engage in substantial gainful employment.

(C) A person 55 years of age or older with a gross annual income of not more than twenty-five thousand dollars ($25,000) or, if the judgment debtor is married, a gross annual income, including the gross annual income of the judgment debtor's spouse, of not more than thirty-five thousand dollars ($35,000) and the sale is an involuntary sale.

(b) Notwithstanding any other provision of this section, the combined homestead exemptions of spouses on the same judgment shall not exceed the amount specified in paragraph (2) or (3), whichever is applicable, of subdivision (a), regardless of whether the spouses are jointly obligated on the judgment and regardless of whether the homestead consists of community or separate property or both. Notwithstanding any other provision of this article, if both spouses are entitled to a homestead exemption, the exemption of proceeds of the homestead shall be apportioned between the spouses on the basis of their proportionate interests in the homestead.

* * *

Chapter 5. Wage Garnishment 706.010–706.154

Article 1. Short Title; Definitions 706.010–706.011

706.010.

This chapter shall be known and may be cited as the "Wage Garnishment Law."

706.011.

As used in this chapter:

(a) "Disposable earnings" means the portion of an individual's earnings that remains after deducting all amounts required to be withheld by law.

(b) "Earnings" means compensation payable by an employer to an employee for personal services performed by such employee, whether denominated as wages, salary, commission, bonus, or otherwise.

* * *

(e) "Employee" means a public officer and any individual who performs services subject to the right of the employer to control both what shall be done and how it shall be done.

(f) "Employer" means a person for whom an individual performs services as an employee.

* * *

Article 2. General Provisions 706.020–706.034

706.020.

Except for [family support orders], the earnings of an employee shall not be required to be withheld by an employer for payment of a debt by means of any judicial procedure other than pursuant to this chapter.

706.021.

Notwithstanding any other provision of this title, a levy of execution upon the earnings of an employee shall be made by service of an earnings withholding order upon the employer in accordance with this chapter.

706.022.

(a) As used in this section, "withholding period" means the period which commences on the 10th day after service of an earnings withholding order upon the employer and which continues until the earliest of the following dates:

(1) The date the employer has withheld the full amount required to satisfy the order.

(2) The date of termination specified in a court order served on the employer.

(3) The date of termination specified in a notice of termination served on the employer by the levying officer.

(4) The date of termination of a dormant or suspended earnings withholding order as determined pursuant to Section 706.032.

(b) Except as otherwise provided by statute, an employer shall withhold the amounts required by an earnings withholding order from all earnings of the employee payable for any pay period of the employee which ends during the withholding period.

* * *

706.024.

(a) The amount required to satisfy an earnings withholding order is the total amount required to satisfy the writ of execution on the date the order is issued, with the following additions and subtractions:

(1) The addition of the statutory fee for service of the order and any other statutory fees for performing duties under the order.

(2) The addition of costs added to the order pursuant to Section 685.090.

(3) The subtraction of the amount of any partial satisfactions.

(4) The addition of daily interest accruing after issuance of the order, as adjusted for partial satisfactions.

(b) From time to time the levying officer, in the levying officer's discretion, may give written notice to the employer of the amount required to satisfy the earnings withholding order and the employer shall determine the total amount to withhold based upon the levying officer's notice, notwithstanding a different amount stated in the order originally served on the employer.

(c) If the full amount required to satisfy the earnings withholding order as stated in the order or in the levying officer's notice under subdivision (b) is withheld from the judgment debtor's earnings, interest ceases to accrue on that amount.

706.025.

(a) Except as provided in subdivision (b), the amount required to be withheld pursuant to an earnings withholding order shall be paid monthly to the levying officer not later than the 15th day of each month....

(b) The employer may elect to pay the amounts withheld to the levying officer more frequently than monthly. If the employer so elects, payment of the amount withheld from the employee's earnings for each pay period shall be made not later than 10 days after the close of the pay period.

706.026.

(a) The levying officer shall receive and account for all amounts paid by the employer pursuant to Section 706.025 and shall pay the amounts so received over to the person entitled thereto at least once every 30 days.

(b) At least once every two years, the levying officer shall file an accounting with the court, as provided by Section 699.560, for all amounts collected under the earnings withholding order, including costs and interest added to the amount due....

706.027.

If the judgment pursuant to which the earnings withholding order is issued is satisfied before the order otherwise terminates pursuant to Section 706.022, the judgment creditor shall promptly notify the levying officer who shall promptly terminate the order by serving a notice of termination on the employer.

706.028.

(a) "Final earnings withholding order for costs and interest" means an earnings withholding order for the collection only of unsatisfied costs and interest, which is issued after an earlier earnings withholding order has been returned satisfied.

(b) After the amount stated as owing in a prior earnings withholding order is paid, the judgment creditor may obtain a final earnings withholding order for costs and interest to collect amounts of costs and interest that were not collected under the prior earnings withholding order.

(c) A final earnings withholding order for costs and interest shall be enforced in the same manner as other earnings withholding orders.

(d) Satisfaction of the amount stated as owing in a final earnings withholding order for costs and interest is equivalent to satisfaction of the money judgment. For this purpose, interest ceases to accrue on the date of issuance of the final earnings withholding order and no additional costs may be added after that date, except for the statutory fee for service of the order and any other statutory fees for performing duties under the order.

706.029.

Service of an earnings withholding order creates a lien upon the earnings of the judgment debtor that are required to be withheld pursuant to the order and upon all property of the employer subject to the enforcement of a money judgment in the amount required to be withheld pursuant to such order. The lien continues for a period of one year from the date the earnings of the judgment debtor become payable unless the amount required to be withheld pursuant to the order is paid as required by law.

* * *

706.034.

The employer may deduct from the earnings of the employee the sum of one dollar and fifty cents ($1.50) for each payment made in accordance with an earnings withholding order issued pursuant to this chapter.

Article 3. Restrictions on Earnings Withholding 706.050–706.052

706.050.

(a) Except as otherwise provided in this chapter, the maximum amount of disposable earnings of an individual judgment debtor for any workweek that is subject to levy under an earnings withholding order shall not exceed the lesser of the following:

(1) Twenty-five percent of the individual's disposable earnings for that week.

(2) Fifty percent of the amount by which the individual's disposable earnings for that week exceed 40 times the state minimum hourly wage in effect at the time the earnings are payable. If a judgment debtor works in a location where the local minimum hourly wage is greater than the state minimum hourly wage, the local minimum hourly wage in effect at the time the earnings are payable shall be used for the calculation made pursuant to this paragraph.

(b) For any pay period other than weekly, the following multipliers shall be used to determine the maximum amount of disposable earnings subject to levy under an earnings withholding order that is proportional in effect to the calculation described in paragraph (2) of subdivision (a), except as specified in paragraph (1):

(1) For a daily pay period, the amounts shall be identical to the amounts described in subdivision (a).

(2) For a biweekly pay period, multiply the applicable hourly minimum wage by 80 work hours.

(3) For a semimonthly pay period, multiply the applicable hourly minimum wage by 862/3 work hours.

(4) For a monthly pay period, multiply the applicable hourly minimum wage by 1731/3 work hours.

(c) This section shall become operative on July 1, 2016.

706.051.

(a) For the purposes of this section, "family of the judgment debtor" includes the spouse or former spouse of the judgment debtor.

(b) Except as provided in subdivision (c), the portion of the judgment debtor's earnings that the judgment debtor proves is necessary for the support of the judgment debtor or the judgment debtor's family supported in whole or in part by the judgment debtor is exempt from levy under this chapter.

* * *

Article 5. Procedure for Earnings Withholding Orders and Exemption Claims 706.100–706.109

* * *

706.102.

(a) If a writ of execution has been issued to the county where the judgment debtor's employer is to be served and the time specified in subdivision (b) of Section 699.530 for levy on property under the writ has not expired, a judgment creditor may apply for the issuance of an earnings withholding order by filing an application with a levying officer in such county who shall promptly issue an earnings withholding order.

* * *

706.103.

(a) The levying officer shall serve upon the designated employer all of the following:

(1) The original and one copy of the earnings withholding order.

(2) The form for the employer's return.

(3) The notice to employee of earnings withholding order.

(4) A copy of the form that the judgment debtor may use to make a claim of exemption.

(5) A copy of the form the judgment debtor may use to provide a financial statement.

(b) At the time the levying officer makes service pursuant to subdivision (a), the levying officer shall provide the employer with a copy of the employer's instructions referred to in Section 706.127. The Judicial Council may adopt rules prescribing the circumstances when compliance with this subdivision is not required.

(c) No earnings withholding order shall be served upon the employer after the time specified in subdivision (b) of Section 699.530.

706.104.

Any employer who is served with an earnings withholding order shall:

(a) Deliver to the judgment debtor a copy of the earnings withholding order, the notice to employee of earnings withholding, a copy of the form that the judgment debtor may use to make a claim of exemption, and a copy of the form the judgment debtor may use to provide a financial statement within 10 days from the date of service. If the judgment debtor is no longer employed by the employer and the employer does not owe the employee any earnings, the employer is not required to make such delivery. The employer is not subject to any civil liability for failure to comply with this subdivision. Nothing in this subdivision limits the power of a court to hold the employer in contempt of court for failure to comply with this subdivision.

(b) Complete the employer's return on the form provided by the levying officer and mail it by first-class mail, postage prepaid, to the levying officer within 15 days from the date of service. If the earnings withholding order is ineffective, the employer shall state in the employer's return that the order will not be complied with for this reason and shall return the order to the levying officer with the employer's return.

706.105.

(a) A judgment debtor may claim an exemption under Section 706.051....

(b) A claim of exemption shall be made by filing with the levying officer an original and one copy of (1) the judgment debtor's claim of exemption and (2) the judgment debtor's financial statement.

(c) Upon filing of the claim of exemption, the levying officer shall promptly send to the judgment creditor, at the address stated in the application for the earnings withholding order, by first-class mail, postage prepaid, all of the following:

(1) A copy of the claim of exemption.

(2) A copy of the financial statement.

(3) A notice of claim of exemption. The notice shall state that the claim of exemption has been filed and that the earnings withholding order will be terminated, or modified to reflect the amount of earnings claimed to be exempt in the claim of exemption, unless a notice of opposition to the claim of exemption is filed with the levying officer by the judgment creditor within 10 days after the date of the mailing of the notice of claim of exemption.

(d) A judgment creditor who desires to contest a claim of exemption shall, within 10 days after the date of the mailing of the notice of claim of exemption, file with the levying officer a notice of opposition to the claim of exemption.

(e) If a notice of opposition to the claim of exemption is filed with the levying officer within the 10-day period, the judgment creditor is entitled to a hearing on the claim of exemption. If the judgment creditor desires a hearing on the claim of exemption, the judgment creditor shall file a notice of motion for an order determining the claim of exemption with the court within 10 days after the date the levying officer mailed the notice of claim of exemption. If the notice of motion is so filed, the hearing on the motion shall be held not later than 30 days from the date the notice of motion was filed unless continued by the court for good cause. At the time prescribed by subdivision (b) of Section 1005, the judgment creditor shall give written notice of the hearing to the levying officer and shall serve a notice of the hearing and a copy of the notice of opposition to the claim of exemption on the judgment debtor and, if the claim of exemption so requested, on the attorney for the judgment debtor. Service is deemed made when the notice of the hearing and a copy of the notice of opposition to the claim of exemption are deposited in the mail, postage prepaid, addressed to the judgment debtor at the address stated in the claim of exemption and, if service on the attorney for the judgment debtor was requested in the claim of exemption, to the attorney at the address stated in the claim of exemption. The judgment creditor shall file proof of the service with the court. After receiving the notice of the hearing and before the date set for the hearing, the levying officer shall file the claim of exemption and the notice of opposition to the claim of exemption with the court.

(f) If the levying officer does not receive a notice of opposition to the claim of exemption within the 10-day period after the date of mailing of the notice of claim of exemption and a notice of the hearing not later than 10 days after the filing of the notice of opposition to the claim of exemption, the levying officer shall serve on the employer one of the following:

(1) A notice that the earnings withholding order has been terminated if all of the judgment debtor's earnings were claimed to be exempt.

(2) A modified earnings withholding order that reflects the amount of earnings claimed to be exempt in the claim of exemption if only a portion of the judgment debtor's earnings was claimed to be exempt.

(g) If, after hearing, the court orders that the earnings withholding order be modified or terminated, the clerk shall promptly transmit a certified copy of the order to the levying officer who shall promptly serve on the employer of the judgment debtor (1) a copy of the modified earnings withholding order or (2) a notice that the earnings withholding order has been terminated. The court may order that the earnings withholding order be terminated as of a date that precedes the date of hearing. If the court determines that any amount withheld pursuant to the earnings withholding order shall be paid to the judgment debtor, the court shall make an order directing the person who holds that amount to pay it promptly to the judgment debtor.

(h) If the earnings withholding order is terminated by the court, unless the court otherwise orders or unless there is a material change of circumstances since the time of the last prior hearing on the earnings withholding order, the judgment creditor may not apply for another earnings withholding order directed to the same employer with respect to the same judgment debtor for a period of 100 days following the date of service of the earnings withholding order or 60 days after the date of the termination of the order, whichever is later.

(i) If an employer has withheld and paid over amounts pursuant to an earnings withholding order after the date of termination of the order but prior to the receipt of notice of its termination, the judgment debtor may recover those amounts only from the levying officer if the levying officer still holds those amounts or, if those amounts have been paid over to the judgment creditor, from the judgment creditor. If the employer has withheld amounts pursuant to an earnings withholding order after termination of the order but has not paid over those amounts to the levying officer, the employer shall promptly pay those amounts to the judgment debtor.

(j) An appeal lies from any court order under this section denying a claim of exemption or modifying or terminating an earnings withholding order. An appeal by the judgment creditor from an order modifying or terminating the earnings withholding order does not stay the order from which the appeal is taken. Notwithstanding the appeal, until the order modifying or terminating the earnings withholding order is set aside or modified, the order allowing the claim of exemption in whole or in part shall be given the same effect as if the appeal had not been taken.

* * *

706.108.

(a) If a writ of execution has been issued to the county where the judgment debtor's employer is to be served and the time specified in subdivision (b) of Section 699.530 for levy on property under the writ has not expired, a judgment creditor may deliver an application for issuance of an earnings withholding order to a registered process server who may then issue an earnings withholding order. * * *

* * *

706.154.

(a) If an employer fails to withhold or to pay over the amount the employer is required to withhold and pay over pursuant to this chapter, the judgment creditor may bring a civil action against the employer to recover such amount. The remedy provided by this subdivision is not exclusive. * * *

Chapter 6. Miscellaneous Creditors' Remedies 708.010–709.030

Article 1. Written Interrogatories to Judgment Debtor 708.010–708.030

708.010.

(a) Except as provided in this section and in subdivision (b) of Section 708.020, the procedure in this article may be used at any time a money judgment is enforceable.

* * *

708.020.

(a) The judgment creditor may propound written interrogatories to the judgment debtor, in the manner provided in Chapter 13 (commencing with Section 2030.010) of Title 4 of Part 4, requesting information to aid in enforcement of the money judgment. The judgment debtor shall answer the interrogatories in the manner and within the time provided by Chapter 13 (commencing with Section 2030.010) of Title 4 of Part 4.

(b) The judgment creditor may not serve interrogatories pursuant to this section within 120 days after the judgment debtor has responded to interrogatories previously served pursuant to this section or within 120 days after the judgment debtor has been examined pursuant to Article 2 (commencing with Section 708.110), and the judgment debtor is not required to respond to any interrogatories so served.

(c) Interrogatories served pursuant to this section may be enforced, to the extent practicable, in the same manner as interrogatories in a civil action.

(d) The limitation provided by Chapter 13 (commencing with Section 2030.010) of Title 4 of Part 4 on the number of interrogatories that may be propounded applies to each set of interrogatories propounded from time to time pursuant to this section, but does not apply cumulatively to interrogatories propounded by the judgment creditor to the judgment debtor.

708.030.

(a) The judgment creditor may demand that any judgment debtor produce and permit the party making the demand, or someone acting on that party's behalf, to inspect and to copy a document that is in the possession, custody, or control of the party on whom the demand is made in the manner provided in Chapter 14 (commencing with Section 2031.010) of Title 4 of Part 4, if the demand requests information to aid in enforcement of the money judgment. The judgment debtor shall respond and comply with the demand in the manner and within the time provided by Chapter 14 (commencing with Section 2031.010) of Title 4 of Part 4.

(b) The judgment creditor may not serve interrogatories or inspection demands pursuant to this section or Section 708.020 within 120 days after the judgment debtor has responded to the interrogatories or demands previously served pursuant to this section or Section 708.020, or within 120 days after the judgment debtor has been examined pursuant to Article 2 (commencing with Section 708.110), and the judgment debtor is not required to respond to any discovery so served.

(c) Inspection demands served pursuant to this section may be enforced to the extent practicable, in the same manner as inspection demands in a civil action.

Article 2. Examination Proceedings 708.110–708.205

708.110.

(a) The judgment creditor may apply to the proper court for an order requiring the judgment debtor to appear before the court, or before a referee appointed by the court, at a time and place specified in the order, to furnish information to aid in enforcement of the money judgment.

(b) If the judgment creditor has not caused the judgment debtor to be examined under this section during the preceding 120 days, the court shall make the order upon ex parte application of the judgment creditor.

(c) If the judgment creditor has caused the judgment debtor to be examined under this section during the preceding 120 days, the court shall make the order if the judgment creditor by affidavit or otherwise shows good cause for the order. The application shall be made on noticed motion if the court so directs or a court rule so requires. Otherwise, it may be made ex parte.

(d) The judgment creditor shall personally serve a copy of the order on the judgment debtor not less than 10 days before the date set for the examination. Service shall be made in the manner specified in Section 415.10. Service of the order creates a lien on the personal property of the judgment debtor for a period of one year from the date of the order unless extended or sooner terminated by the court.

(e) The order shall contain the following statement in 14-point boldface type if printed or in capital letters if typed: "NOTICE TO JUDGMENT DEBTOR. If you fail to appear at the time and place specified in this order, you may be subject to arrest and punishment for contempt of court and the court may make an order requiring you to pay the reasonable attorney's fees incurred by the judgment creditor in this proceeding."

708.120.

(a) Upon ex parte application by a judgment creditor who has a money judgment and proof by the judgment creditor by affidavit or otherwise to the satisfaction of the proper court that a third person has possession or control of property in which the judgment debtor has an interest or is indebted to the judgment debtor in an amount exceeding two hundred fifty dollars ($250), the court shall make an order directing the third person to appear before the court, or before a referee appointed by the court, at a time and place specified in the order, to answer concerning such property or debt. The affidavit in support of the judgment creditor's application may be based on the affiant's information and belief.

(b) Not less than 10 days prior to the date set for the examination, a copy of the order shall be:

(1) Served personally on the third person.

(2) Served personally or by mail on the judgment debtor.

(c) If the property in the third person's possession or control in which the judgment debtor has an interest or the debt owed by the third person to the judgment debtor is described in the affidavit or application for an order under subdivision (a) in a manner reasonably adequate to permit it to be identified, service of the order on the third person creates a lien on the judgment debtor's interest in the property or on the debt for a period of one year from the date of the order unless extended or sooner terminated by the court.

(d) The judgment debtor may claim that all or any portion of the property or debt is exempt from enforcement of a money judgment by application to the court on noticed motion, filed with the court and personally served on the judgment creditor not later than three days before the date set for the examination. The judgment debtor shall execute an affidavit in support of the application that includes all of the matters set forth in subdivision (b) of Section 703.520. If a claim of exemption is made pursuant to this section, a notice of opposition to the claim of exemption is not required. The court shall determine any claim of exemption made pursuant to this section. Failure of the judgment debtor to make a claim of exemption does not preclude the judgment debtor from later claiming the exemption unless the property or debt is described in the order in a manner reasonably adequate to permit it to be identified and the judgment debtor receives notice of the examination proceeding at least 10 days before the date set for the examination.

(e) An order made pursuant to subdivision (a) shall contain the following statements in 14-point boldface type if printed or in capital letters if typed:

> (1) "NOTICE TO PERSON SERVED. If you fail to appear at the time and place specified in this order, you may be subject to arrest and punishment for contempt of court and the court may make an order requiring you to pay the reasonable attorney's fees incurred by the judgment creditor in this proceeding."
> (2) "NOTICE TO JUDGMENT DEBTOR. The person in whose favor the judgment was entered in this action claims that the person to be examined pursuant to this order has possession or control of property which is yours or owes you a debt. This property or debt is as follows: (Description of property or debt).
> If you claim that all or any portion of this property or debt is exempt from enforcement of the money judgment, you must file your exemption claim in writing with the court and personally serve a copy on the judgment creditor not later than three days before the date set for the examination. You must appear at the time and place set for this examination to establish your claim of exemption or your exemption may be waived."

(f) An order made pursuant to subdivision (a) is not effective unless, at the time it is served on the third person, the person serving the order tenders to the third person fees for the mileage necessary to be traveled from the third person's residence to the place of examination. The mileage fees shall be in the same amount generally provided for witnesses when legally required to attend civil proceedings in the court where the examination proceeding is to be conducted.

708.130.

(a) Witnesses may be required to appear and testify before the court or referee in an examination proceeding under this article in the same manner as upon the trial of an issue.

(b) The privilege prescribed by Article 4 (commencing with Section 970) of Chapter 4 of Division 8 of the Evidence Code does not apply in an examination proceeding under this article.

* * *

708.170.

(a) If an order requiring a person to appear for an examination was served by a sheriff, marshal, a person specially appointed by the court in the order, or a registered process server, and the person fails to appear:

(1) The court may do either of the following:

(A) Pursuant to a warrant, have the person brought before the court to answer for the failure to appear and may punish the person for contempt.

(B) Issue a warrant for the arrest of the person who failed to appear as required by the court order, pursuant to Section 1993.

(2) If the person's failure to appear is without good cause, the judgment creditor shall be awarded reasonable attorney's fees incurred in the examination proceeding. Attorney's fees awarded against the judgment debtor shall be added to and become part of the principal amount of the judgment.

(b) A person who willfully makes an improper service of an order for an examination which subsequently results in the arrest pursuant to subdivision (a) of the person who fails to appear is guilty of a misdemeanor.

708.180.

(a) Subject to subdivision (b), if a third person examined pursuant to Section 708.120 claims an interest in the property adverse to the judgment debtor or denies the debt, the court may, if the judgment creditor so requests, determine the interests in the property or the existence of the debt. The determination is conclusive as to the parties to the proceeding and the third person, but an appeal may be taken from the determination. The court may grant a continuance for a reasonable time for discovery proceedings, the production of evidence, or other preparation for the hearing.

* * *

(c) Upon application of the judgment creditor made ex parte, the court may make an order forbidding transfer of the property to the judgment debtor or payment of the debt to the judgment debtor until the interests in the property or the existence of the debt is determined pursuant to subdivision (a) or until a creditor's suit may be commenced and an order obtained pursuant to Section 708.240. An undertaking may be required in the discretion of the court. The court may modify or vacate the order at any time with or without a hearing on such terms as are just.

(d) Upon application of the judgment creditor upon noticed motion, the court may, if it determines that the judgment debtor probably owns an interest in the property or that the debt probably is owed to the judgment debtor, make an order forbidding the transfer or other disposition of the property to any person or forbidding payment of the debt until the interests in the property or the existence of the debt is determined pursuant to subdivision (a) or until a creditor's suit may be commenced and an order obtained pursuant to Section 708.240. The court shall require the judgment creditor to furnish an undertaking as provided in Section 529. The court may modify or vacate the order at any time after notice and hearing on such terms as are just.

* * *

708.205.

(a) Except as provided in subdivision (b), at the conclusion of a proceeding pursuant to this article, the court may order the judgment debtor's interest in the property in the possession or under the control of the judgment debtor or the third person or a debt owed by the third person to the judgment debtor to be applied toward the satisfaction of the money judgment if the property is not exempt from enforcement of a money judgment. Such an order creates a lien on the property or debt.

(b) If a third person examined pursuant to Section 708.120 claims an interest in the property adverse to the judgment debtor or denies the debt and the court does not determine the matter as provided in subdivision (a) of Section 708.180, the court may not order the property or debt to be applied toward the satisfaction of the money judgment but may make an order pursuant to subdivision (c) or (d) of Section 708.180 forbidding transfer or payment to the extent authorized by that section.

Article 3. Creditor's Suit 708.210–708.290

708.210.

If a third person has possession or control of property in which the judgment debtor has an interest or is indebted to the judgment debtor, the judgment creditor may bring an action against the third person to have the interest or debt applied to the satisfaction of the money judgment.

708.220.

The judgment debtor shall be joined in an action brought pursuant to this article but is not an indispensable party. The residence of the judgment debtor may not be considered in the determination of proper venue unless otherwise provided by contract between the judgment debtor and the third person.

* * *

708.240.

The judgment creditor may apply to the court in which an action under this article is pending for either or both of the following:

(a) An order restraining the third person from transferring to the judgment debtor the property in which the judgment debtor is claimed to have an interest or from paying to the judgment debtor the alleged debt. The order shall be made on noticed motion if the court so directs or a court rule so requires. Otherwise, the order may be made on ex parte application. The order shall remain in effect until judgment is entered in the action or until such earlier time as the court may provide in the order. An undertaking may be required in the discretion of the court. The court may modify or vacate the order at any time with or without a hearing on such terms as are just.

(b) A temporary restraining order or a preliminary injunction or both, restraining the third person from transferring to any person or otherwise disposing of the property in which the judgment debtor is claimed to have an interest, pursuant to Chapter 3 (commencing with Section 525) of Title 7, and the court may make, dissolve, and modify such orders as provided therein.

708.250.

Service of summons on the third person creates a lien on the interest of the judgment debtor in the property or on the debt owed to the judgment debtor that is the subject of an action under this article.

708.260.

(a)In an action brought pursuant to this article, the judgment debtor may claim that all or any portion of the property or debt is exempt from enforcement of a money judgment. The claim shall be made by application to the court on noticed motion, filed with the court and served on the judgment creditor not later than 30 days before the date set for trial. Service shall be made personally or by mail. The judgment debtor shall execute an affidavit in support of the application that includes all of the matters set forth in subdivision (b) of Section 703.520. No notice of opposition to the claim of exemption is required. If the judgment debtor has not been named as a party to the action, the judgment debtor may obtain an order under Section 389 that the judgment debtor be made a party. Except as provided in subdivision (b), failure of the judgment debtor to make a claim of exemption is a waiver of the exemption.

* * *

708.280.

(a) The court shall determine any exemption claim made in the action. If the judgment debtor establishes to the satisfaction of the court that the property or debt is exempt from enforcement of a money judgment, the court shall so adjudge and may not make the orders referred to in subdivisions (b), (c), and (d).

(b) If the judgment creditor establishes that the third person has property in which the judgment debtor has an interest or is indebted to the judgment debtor, the court shall render judgment accordingly. The property or debt may be applied to the satisfaction of the judgment creditor's judgment against the judgment debtor as ordered by the court.

(c) If the court determines that the third person has property in which the judgment debtor has an interest, the court may order the third person not to transfer the property until it can be levied upon or otherwise applied to the satisfaction of the judgment.

(d) If the court determines that the third person has transferred property that was subject to a lien in favor of the judgment creditor or, contrary to court order of which the third person has notice, has paid the debt to the judgment debtor or has transferred the property, the court shall render judgment against the third person in an amount equal to the lesser of the following:

(1) The value of the judgment debtor's interest in the property or the amount of the debt.

(2) The amount of the judgment creditor's judgment against the judgment debtor remaining unsatisfied.

* * *

Article 4. Charging Orders 708.310–708.320

708.310.

If a money judgment is rendered against a partner or member but not against the partnership or limited liability company, the judgment debtor's interest in the partnership or limited liability company may be applied toward the satisfaction of the judgment by an order charging the judgment debtor's interest pursuant to Section 15907.3, 16504, or 17705.03 of the Corporations Code.

* * *

Article 6. Assignment Order 708.510–708.560

708.510.

(a)Except as otherwise provided by law, upon application of the judgment creditor on noticed motion, the court may order the judgment debtor to assign to the judgment creditor or to a receiver appointed pursuant to Article 7 (commencing with Section 708.610) all or part of a right to payment due or to become due, whether or not the right is conditioned on future developments, including but not limited to the following types of payments:

(1) Wages due from the federal government that are not subject to withholding under an earnings withholding order.

(2) Rents.

(3) Commissions.

(4) Royalties.

(5) Payments due from a patent or copyright.

(6) Insurance policy loan value.

(b) The notice of the motion shall be served on the judgment debtor. Service shall be made personally or by mail.

(c) Subject to subdivisions (d), (e), and (f), in determining whether to order an assignment or the amount of an assignment pursuant to subdivision (a), the court may take into consideration all relevant factors, including the following:

(1) The reasonable requirements of a judgment debtor who is a natural person and of persons supported in whole or in part by the judgment debtor.

(2) Payments the judgment debtor is required to make or that are deducted in satisfaction of other judgments and wage assignments, including earnings assignment orders for support.

(3) The amount remaining due on the money judgment.

(4) The amount being or to be received in satisfaction of the right to payment that may be assigned.

(d) A right to payment may be assigned pursuant to this article only to the extent necessary to satisfy the money judgment.

(e) When earnings or periodic payments pursuant to a pension or retirement plan are assigned pursuant to subdivision (a), the amount of the earnings or the periodic payments assigned shall not exceed the amount that may be withheld from a like amount of earnings under Chapter 5 (commencing with Section 706.010) (Wage Garnishment Law).

(f) Where a specific amount of the payment or payments to be assigned is exempt by another statutory provision, the amount of the payment or payments to be assigned pursuant to subdivision (a) shall not exceed the amount by which the payment or payments exceed the exempt amount.

708.520.

(a)When an application is made pursuant to Section 708.510 or thereafter, the judgment creditor may apply to the court for an order restraining the judgment debtor from assigning or otherwise disposing of the right to payment that is sought to be assigned. The application shall be made on noticed motion if the court so directs or a court rule so requires. Otherwise, it may be made ex parte.

(b) The court may issue an order pursuant to this section upon a showing of need for the order. The court, in its discretion, may require the judgment creditor to provide an undertaking.

(c) The court may modify or vacate the order at any time with or without a hearing on such terms as are just.

(d) The order shall be personally served upon the judgment debtor and shall contain a notice to the judgment debtor that failure to comply with the order may subject the judgment debtor to being held in contempt of court.

* * *

Article 7. Receiver to Enforce Judgment 708.610–708.630

* * *

708.620.

The court may appoint a receiver to enforce the judgment where the judgment creditor shows that, considering the interests of both the judgment creditor and the judgment debtor, the appointment of a receiver is a reasonable method to obtain the fair and orderly satisfaction of the judgment.

708.630.

(a) The judgment debtor's interest in an alcoholic beverage license may be applied to the satisfaction of a money judgment only as provided in this section.

(b) The court may appoint a receiver for the purpose of transferring the judgment debtor's interest in an alcoholic beverage license that is transferable under Article 5 (commencing with Section 24070) of Chapter 6 of Division 9 of the Business and Professions Code, unless the judgment debtor shows in the proceeding to appoint a receiver that the amount of delinquent taxes described in Section 24049 of the Business and Professions Code and claims of creditors with priority over the judgment creditor pursuant to Section 24074 of the Business and Professions Code exceed the probable sale price of the license.

(c) The receiver may exercise the powers of the licensee as necessary and in exercising such powers shall comply with the applicable provisions of Division 9 (commencing with Section 23000) of the Business and Professions Code and applicable regulations of the Department of Alcoholic Beverage Control. An application shall be filed to transfer the license to the receiver and a temporary retail permit shall be obtained during the pendency of the transfer.

* * *

Appendix C

Illinois Code of Civil Procedure (735 ILCS 5/) & Supreme Court Rule 277

735 ILCS 5/2-1402. Supplementary proceedings.

(a) A judgment creditor, or his or her successor in interest ... is entitled to prosecute supplementary proceedings for the purposes of examining the judgment debtor or any other person to discover assets or income of the debtor not exempt from the enforcement of the judgment, a deduction order or garnishment, and of compelling the application of non-exempt assets or income discovered toward the payment of the amount due under the judgment. A supplementary proceeding shall be commenced by the service of a citation issued by the clerk. The procedure for conducting supplementary proceedings shall be prescribed by rules. It is not a prerequisite to the commencement of a supplementary proceeding that a certified copy of the judgment has been returned wholly or partly unsatisfied. All citations issued by the clerk shall have the following language, or language substantially similar thereto, stated prominently on the front, in capital letters: "IF YOU FAIL TO APPEAR IN COURT AS DIRECTED IN THIS NOTICE, YOU MAY BE ARRESTED AND BROUGHT BEFORE THE COURT TO ANSWER TO A CHARGE OF CONTEMPT OF COURT, WHICH MAY BE PUNISHABLE BY IMPRISONMENT IN THE COUNTY JAIL." The court shall not grant a continuance of the supplementary proceeding except upon good cause shown.

(b) Any citation served upon a judgment debtor or any other person shall include a certification by the attorney for the judgment creditor or the judgment creditor setting forth the amount of the judgment, the date of the judgment, or its revival date, the balance due thereon, the name of the court, and the number of the case, and a copy of the citation notice required by this subsection. Whenever a citation is served upon a person or party other than the judgment debtor, the officer or person serving the citation shall send to the judgment debtor, within three business days of the service upon the cited party, a copy of the citation and the citation notice, which may be sent by regular first-class mail to the judgment debtor's last known address. In no event shall a citation hearing be held sooner than five business days after the mailing of the citation and citation notice to the judgment debtor, except by agreement of the parties. The citation notice need not be mailed to a corporation, partnership, or association. The citation notice shall be in substantially the following form:

"CITATION NOTICE

(Name and address of Court)
Name of Case: (Name of Judgment Creditor), Judgment Creditor v. (Name of Judgment Debtor), Judgment Debtor.
Address of Judgment Debtor: (Insert last known address)
Name and address of Attorney for Judgment Creditor or of Judgment Creditor (If no attorney is listed): (Insert name and address)
Amount of Judgment: $ (Insert amount)
Name of Person Receiving Citation: (Insert name)
Court Date and Time: (Insert return date and time specified in citation)

NOTICE: The court has issued a citation against the person named above. The citation directs that person to appear in court to be examined for the purpose of allowing the judgment creditor to discover income and assets belonging to the judgment debtor or in which the judgment debtor has an interest. The citation was issued on the basis of a judgment against the judgment debtor in favor of the judgment creditor in the amount stated above. On or after the court date stated above, the court may compel the application of any discovered income or assets toward payment on the judgment.

The amount of income or assets that may be applied toward the judgment is limited by federal and Illinois law. The JUDGMENT DEBTOR HAS THE RIGHT TO ASSERT STATUTORY EXEMPTIONS AGAINST CERTAIN INCOME OR ASSETS OF THE JUDGMENT DEBTOR WHICH MAY NOT BE USED TO SATISFY THE JUDGMENT IN THE AMOUNT STATED ABOVE:

(1) Under Illinois or federal law, the exemptions of personal property owned by the debtor include the debtor's equity interest, not to exceed

$4,000 in value, in any personal property as chosen by the debtor; Social Security and SSI benefits; public assistance benefits; unemployment compensation benefits; worker's compensation benefits; veteran's benefits; circuit breaker property tax relief benefits; the debtor's equity interest, not to exceed $2,400 in value, in any one motor vehicle, and the debtor's equity interest, not to exceed $1,500 in value, in any implements, professional books, or tools of the trade of the debtor.

(2) Under Illinois law, every person is entitled to an estate in homestead, when it is owned and occupied as a residence, to the extent in value of $15,000, which homestead is exempt from judgment.

(3) Under Illinois law, the amount of wages that may be applied toward a judgment is limited to the lesser of (i) 15% of gross weekly wages or (ii) the amount by which disposable earnings for a week exceed the total of 45 times the federal minimum hourly wage or, under a wage deduction summons served on or after January 1, 2006, the Illinois minimum hourly wage, whichever is greater.

(4) Under federal law, the amount of wages that may be applied toward a judgment is limited to the lesser of (i) 25% of disposable earnings for a week or (ii) the amount by which disposable earnings for a week exceed 30 times the federal minimum hourly wage.

(5) Pension and retirement benefits and refunds may be claimed as exempt under Illinois law.

The judgment debtor may have other possible exemptions under law.

THE JUDGMENT DEBTOR HAS THE RIGHT AT THE CITATION HEARING TO DECLARE EXEMPT CERTAIN INCOME OR ASSETS OR BOTH. The judgment debtor also has the right to seek a declaration at an earlier date, by notifying the clerk in writing at (insert address of clerk). When so notified, the Clerk of the Court will obtain a prompt hearing date from the court and will provide the necessary forms that must be prepared by the judgment debtor or the attorney for the judgment debtor and sent to the judgment creditor and the judgment creditor's attorney regarding the time and location of the hearing. This notice may be sent by regular first class mail."

(b-1) Any citation served upon a judgment debtor who is a natural person shall be served by personal service or abode service as provided in Supreme Court Rule 105 and shall include a copy of the Income and Asset Form set forth in subsection (b-5).

(b-5) The Income and Asset Form required to be served by the judgment creditor in subsection (b-1) shall be in substantially the following form:

INCOME AND ASSET FORM

To Judgment Debtor: Please complete this form and bring it with you to the hearing referenced in the enclosed citation notice. You should also bring to the hearing any documents you have to support the information you provide in this form, such as pay stubs and account statements. The information you provide will help the court determine whether you have any property or income that can be used to satisfy the judgment entered against you in this matter. The information you provide must be accurate to the best of your knowledge.

If you fail to appear at this hearing, you could be held in contempt of court and possibly arrested.

In answer to the citation and supplemental proceedings served upon the judgment debtor, he or she answers as follows:

Name: ______________________
Home Phone Number: ______________________
Home Address: ______________________
Date of Birth: ______________________
Marital Status: ______________________
I have ____________ dependents.
Do you have a job? YES NO
Company's name I work for: ______________________
Company's address: ______________________

Job:
I earn $_________ per _________
If self employed, list here your business name and address:
____
Income from self employment is $________________per year.
I have the following benefits with my employer:
____

I do not have a job, but I support myself through:
Government Assistance $_________________ per month
Unemployment $______________________ per month
Social Security $_____________________ per month
SSI $______________________ per month
Pension $______________________ per month
Other $______________________ per month

Real Estate:

Do you own any real estate? YES NO

I own real estate at ______________________, with names of other owners ____________________________________

Additional real estate I own: ______________________________

I have a beneficial interest in a land trust. The name and address of the trustee is: ______________________

The beneficial interest is listed in my name and ______________

There is a mortgage on my real estate. State the mortgage company's name and address for each parcel of real estate owned:

____

An assignment of beneficial interest in the land trust was signed to secure a loan from ______________________

I have the following accounts:

Checking account at ______; account balance $______

Savings account at ______; account balance $______

Money market or certificate of deposit at ____________________

Safe deposit box at __________________________________

Other accounts (please identify): ______________________

I own:

A vehicle (state year, make, model, and VIN): ______________

Jewelry (please specify): ______________________

Other property described as: ______________________

Stocks/Bonds ______________________

Personal computer ______________________________________

DVD player ______________________

Television ______________________

Stove ______________________

Microwave ______________________

Work tools ______________________

Business equipment ______________________

Farm equipment ______________________

Other property (please specify):

____

Signature: ____

* * *

(c) When assets or income of the judgment debtor not exempt from the satisfaction of a judgment, a deduction order or garnishment are discovered, the court may, by appropriate order or judgment:

(1) Compel the judgment debtor to deliver up, to be applied in satisfaction of the judgment, in whole or in part, money, choses in action, property or effects in his or her possession or control, so discovered, capable of delivery and to which his or her title or right of possession is not substantially disputed.

(2) Compel the judgment debtor to pay to the judgment creditor or apply on the judgment, in installments, a portion of his or her income, however or whenever earned or acquired, as the court may deem proper, having due regard for the reasonable requirements of the judgment debtor and his or her family, if dependent upon him or her, as well as any payments required to be made by prior order of court or under wage assignments outstanding; provided that the judgment debtor shall not be compelled to pay income which would be considered exempt as wages under the Wage Deduction Statute....

(3) Compel any person cited, other than the judgment debtor, to deliver up any assets so discovered, to be applied in satisfaction of the judgment, in whole or in part, when those assets are held under such circumstances that in an action by the judgment debtor he or she could recover them in specie or obtain a judgment for the proceeds or value thereof as for conversion or embezzlement. A judgment creditor may recover a corporate judgment debtor's property on behalf of the judgment debtor for use of the judgment creditor by filing an appropriate petition within the citation proceedings.

(4) Enter any order upon or judgment against the person cited that could be entered in any garnishment proceeding.

(5) Compel any person cited to execute an assignment of any chose in action or a conveyance of title to real or personal property or resign memberships in exchanges, clubs, or other entities....

(6) Authorize the judgment creditor to maintain an action against any person or corporation that, it appears upon proof satisfactory to the court, is indebted to the judgment debtor, for the recovery of the debt, forbid the transfer or other disposition of the debt until an action can be commenced and prosecuted to judgment, direct that the papers or proof in the possession or control of the debtor and necessary in the prosecution of the action be delivered to the creditor or impounded in court, and provide for the disposition of any moneys in excess of the sum required to pay the judgment creditor's judgment and costs allowed by the court.

(c-5) If a citation is directed to a judgment debtor who is a natural person, no payment order shall be entered under subsection (c) unless the Income and

Asset Form was served upon the judgment debtor as required by subsection (b-1), the judgment debtor has had an opportunity to assert exemptions, and the payments are from non-exempt sources.

(d) No order or judgment shall be entered under subsection (c) in favor of the judgment creditor unless there appears of record a certification of mailing showing that a copy of the citation and a copy of the citation notice was mailed to the judgment debtor as required by subsection (b).

(d-5) If upon examination the court determines that the judgment debtor does not possess any non-exempt income or assets, then the citation shall be dismissed.

(e) All property ordered to be delivered up shall, except as otherwise provided in this Section, be delivered to the sheriff to be collected by the sheriff or sold at public sale and the proceeds thereof applied towards the payment of costs and the satisfaction of the judgment. If the judgment debtor's property is of such a nature that it is not readily delivered up to the sheriff for public sale or if another method of sale is more appropriate to liquidate the property or enhance its value at sale, the court may order the sale of such property by the debtor, third party respondent, or by a selling agent other than the sheriff upon such terms as are just and equitable. The proceeds of sale, after deducting reasonable and necessary expenses, are to be turned over to the creditor and applied to the balance due on the judgment.

(f) (1) The citation may prohibit the party to whom it is directed from making or allowing any transfer or other disposition of, or interfering with, any [nonexempt] property … belonging to the judgment debtor or to which he or she may be entitled or which may thereafter be acquired by or become due to him or her, and from paying over or otherwise disposing of any moneys not so exempt which are due or to become due to the judgment debtor, until the further order of the court or the termination of the proceeding, whichever occurs first. The third party may not be obliged to withhold the payment of any moneys beyond double the amount of the balance due sought to be enforced by the judgment creditor. The court may punish any party who violates the restraining provision of a citation as and for a contempt, or if the party is a third party may enter judgment against him or her in the amount of the unpaid portion of the judgment and costs allowable under this Section, or in the amount of the value of the property transferred, whichever is lesser.

(2) The court may enjoin any person, whether or not a party to the supplementary proceeding, from making or allowing any transfer or other disposition of, or interference with, [non-exempt] property of the judgment debtor …

(g) If it appears that any property, chose in action, credit or effect discovered, or any interest therein, is claimed by any person, the court shall, as in garnishment proceedings, permit or require the claimant to appear and maintain his or her right....

(h) Costs in proceedings authorized by this Section shall be allowed, assessed and paid in accordance with rules, provided that if the court determines, in its discretion, that costs incurred by the judgment creditor were improperly incurred, those costs shall be paid by the judgment creditor.

(i) This Section is in addition to and does not affect enforcement of judgments or proceedings supplementary thereto, by any other methods now or hereafter provided by law.

(j) This Section does not grant the power to any court to order installment or other payments from, or compel the sale, delivery, surrender, assignment or conveyance of any property exempt by statute from the enforcement of a judgment thereon, a deduction order, garnishment, attachment, sequestration, process or other levy or seizure.

* * *

(k-5) If the court determines that any property held by a third party respondent is wages pursuant to Section 12-801, the court shall proceed as if a wage deduction proceeding had been filed and proceed to enter such necessary and proper orders as would have been entered in a wage deduction proceeding including but not limited to the granting of the statutory exemptions allowed by Section 12-803....

(k-10) If a creditor discovers personal property of the judgment debtor that is subject to the lien of a citation to discover assets, the creditor may have the court impress a lien against a specific item of personal property, including a beneficial interest in a land trust. The lien survives the termination of the citation proceedings and remains as a lien against the personal property in the same manner that a judgment lien recorded against real property pursuant to Section 12-101 remains a lien on real property. If the judgment is revived before dormancy, the lien shall remain. A lien against personal property may, but need not, be recorded in the office of the recorder or filed as an informational filing pursuant to the Uniform Commercial Code.

(*l*) At any citation hearing at which the judgment debtor appears and seeks a declaration that certain of his or her income or assets are exempt, the court shall proceed to determine whether the property which the judgment debtor declares to be exempt is exempt from judgment. At any time before the return date specified on the citation, the judgment debtor may request, in writing, a hearing to declare exempt certain income and assets by notifying the clerk of the court before that time, using forms as may be provided by the clerk of the court. The clerk of the court will obtain a prompt hearing date from the court and will provide the necessary forms that must be prepared by the judgment debtor or the attorney for the judgment debtor and sent to the judgment creditor, or the judgment creditor's attorney, regarding the time and location of the hearing....

(m) The judgment or balance due on the judgment becomes a lien when a citation is served in accordance with subsection (a) of this Section. The lien binds nonexempt personal property, including money, choses in action, and effects of the judgment debtor as follows:

(1) When the citation is directed against the judgment debtor, upon all personal property belonging to the judgment debtor in the possession or control of the judgment debtor or which may thereafter be acquired or come due to the judgment debtor to the time of the disposition of the citation.

(2) When the citation is directed against a third party, upon all personal property belonging to the judgment debtor in the possession or control of the third party or which thereafter may be acquired or come due the judgment debtor and comes into the possession or control of the third party to the time of the disposition of the citation.

The lien established under this Section does not affect the rights of citation respondents in property prior to the service of the citation upon them and does not affect the rights of bona fide purchasers or lenders without notice of the citation. The lien is effective for the period specified by Supreme Court Rule....

* * *

Illinois Supreme Court Rule 277. Supplementary Proceedings

(a) **When Proceeding May be Commenced and Against Whom; Subsequent Proceeding Against Same Party.** A supplementary proceeding authorized by section 2-1402 of the Code of Civil Procedure may be commenced at any time with respect to a judgment which is subject to enforcement. The proceeding may be against the judgment debtor or any third party the judgment creditor believes has property of or is indebted to the judgment debtor. If there has been a prior supplementary proceeding with respect to the same judgment against the party, whether he is the judgment debtor or a third party, no further proceeding shall be commenced against him except by leave of court. The leave may be granted upon *ex parte* motion of the judgment creditor, but only upon a finding of the court, based upon affidavit of the judgment creditor or some other person, having personal knowledge of the facts, (1) that there is reason to believe the party against whom the proceeding is sought to be commenced has property or income the creditor is entitled to reach, or, if a third party, is indebted to the judgment debtor, (2) that the existence of the property, income or indebtedness was not known to the judgment creditor during the pendency of any prior supplementary proceeding, and (3) that the additional supplementary proceeding is sought in good faith to discover assets and not to harass the judgment debtor or third party.

(b) How Commenced. The supplementary proceeding shall be commenced by the service of a citation on the party against whom it is brought. The clerk shall issue a citation upon oral request. In cases in which an order of court is prerequisite to the commencement of the proceeding, a copy of the order shall be served with the citation.

(c) Citation—Form, Contents, and Service. The citation by which a supplementary proceeding is commenced:

(1) shall be captioned in the cause in which the judgment was entered;
(2) shall state the date the judgment was entered or revived, and the amount thereof remaining unsatisfied;
(3) shall require the party to whom it is directed, or if directed to a corporation or partnership, a designated officer or partner thereof, to appear for examination at a time (not less than 5 days from the date of service of the citation) and place to be specified therein, concerning the property or income of or indebtedness due the judgment debtor; and
(4) may require, upon reasonable specification thereof, the production at the examination of any books, documents, or records in his or its possession or control which have or may contain information concerning the property or income of the debtor.

The citation shall be served and returned in the manner provided by rule for service, otherwise than by publication, of a notice of additional relief upon a party in default.

(d) When Proceeding May Be Commenced. A supplementary proceeding against the judgment debtor may be commenced in the court in which the judgment was entered. A supplementary proceeding against a third party must, and against the judgment debtor may, be commenced in a county of this State in which the party against whom it is brought resides, or, if an individual, is employed or transacts business in person, upon the filing of a transcript of the judgment in the court in that county. If the party to be cited neither resides nor is employed nor transacts his business in person in this State, the proceeding may be commenced in any county in the State, upon the filing of a transcript of the judgment in the court in the county in which the proceeding is to be commenced.

(e) **Hearing.** The examination of the judgment debtor, third party or other witnesses shall be before the court, or, if the court so orders, before an officer authorized to administer oaths designated by the court, unless the judgment creditor elects ... to conduct all or a part of the hearing by deposition as provided by the rules of this court for discovery depositions. The court at any time may terminate the deposition or order that proceedings be conducted before the court or officer designated by the court, and otherwise control and direct the proceeding to the end that the rights and interests of all parties and persons involved may be protected and harassment avoided. Any interested party may subpoena witnesses and adduce evidence as upon the trial of any civil action. Upon the request of either party or the direction of the court, the officer before whom the proceeding is conducted shall certify to the court any evidence taken or other proceedings had before him.

(f) **When Proceeding Terminated.** A proceeding under this rule continues until terminated by motion of the judgment creditor, order of the court, or satisfaction of the judgment, but terminates automatically 6 months from the date of (1) the respondent's first personal appearance pursuant to the citation or (2) the respondent's first personal appearance pursuant to subsequent process issued to enforce the citation, whichever is sooner. The court may, however, grant extensions beyond the 6 months, as justice may require. Orders for the payment of money continue in effect notwithstanding the termination of the proceedings until the judgment is satisfied or the court orders otherwise.

(g) **Concurrent and Consecutive Proceedings.** Supplementary proceedings against the debtor and third parties may be conducted concurrently or consecutively. The termination of one proceeding does not affect other pending proceedings not concluded.

(h) **Sanctions.** Any person who fails to obey a citation, subpoena, or order or other direction of the court issued pursuant to any provision of this rule may be punished for contempt. Any person who refuses to obey any order to deliver up or convey or assign any personal property or in an appropriate case its proceeds or value or title to lands, or choses in action, or evidences of debt may be committed until he has complied with the order or is discharged by due course of law. The court may also enforce its order against the real and personal property of that person.

(i) **Costs.** The court may tax as costs a sum for witness', stenographer's, and officer's fees, and the fees and outlays of the sheriff, and direct the payment thereof out of any money which may come into the hands of the sheriff or the judgment creditor as a result of the proceeding. If no property applicable to the payment of the judgment is discovered in the course of the proceeding, the court may tax as costs a sum for witness', stenographer's, and officer's fees incurred by any person subpoenaed, to be paid to him by the person who subpoenaed him, and unless paid within the time fixed, enforcement may be had in the manner provided by law for the collection of a judgment for the payment of money.

* * *

735 ILCS 5/12-101. Lien of judgment. With respect to the creation of liens on real estate by judgments, ... a judgment is a lien on the real estate of the person against whom it is entered in any county in this State ... only from the time a transcript, certified copy or memorandum of the judgment is filed in the office of the recorder in the county in which the real estate is located. The lien may be foreclosed by an action ... under Article XV in the same manner as a mortgage of real property, except that ... the real estate homestead exemption under Section 12-901 shall apply.... A judgment is not a lien on real estate for longer than 7 years from the time it is entered or revived, unless the judgment is revived within 7 years after its entry or last revival and a memorandum of judgment is filed before the expiration of the prior memorandum of judgment.

* * *

735 ILCS 5/12-108. Limitation on enforcement. (a) Except as herein provided, no judgment shall be enforced after the expiration of 7 years from the time the same is rendered, except upon the revival of the same by a proceeding provided by Section 2-1601 of this Act; but real estate, levied upon within the 7 years, may be sold to enforce the judgment at any time within one year after the expiration of the 7 years.

* * *

735 ILCS 5/12-112. What liable to enforcement.... Any real property ... held in tenancy by the entirety shall not be liable to be sold upon judgment entered ... against only one of the tenants * * *.

* * *

735 ILCS 5/12-801. Definitions. As used in Part 8 of Article XII of this Act:
* * *

"Employer" means the person named as employer in [a citation to discover assets].

* * *

"Judgment creditor" means the recipient of any judgment....

"Judgment debtor" means a person against whom a judgment has been obtained.

"Wages" means any hourly pay, salaries, commissions, bonuses, or other compensation owed by an employer to a judgment debtor.

* * *

735 ILCS 5/12-803. Wages subject to collection. The wages, salary, commissions and bonuses subject to collection under a deduction order, for any work week shall be the lesser of (1) 15% of such gross amount paid for that week or (2) the amount by which disposable earnings for a week exceed 45 times the Federal Minimum Hourly Wage prescribed by Section 206(a)(1) of Title 29 of the United States Code, as amended, or ... the minimum hourly wage prescribed by Section 4 of the Minimum Wage Law, whichever is greater, in effect at the time the amounts are payable. This provision (and no other) applies irrespective of the place where the compensation was earned or payable and the State where the employee resides. No amounts required by law to be withheld may be taken from the amount collected by the creditor. The term "disposable earnings" means that part of the earnings of any individual remaining after the deduction from those earnings of any amounts required by law to be withheld.

735 ILCS 5/12-804. Exemptions from deduction orders. Benefits and refunds payable by pension or retirement funds or systems and any assets of employees held by such funds or systems, and any monies an employee is required to contribute to such funds or systems are exempt and are not subject to a deduction order under Part 8 of Article XII of this Act. A plan governed by the Employee Retirement Income Security Act of 1974 shall be considered a retirement fund for purposes of this Part 8.

* * *

735 ILCS 5/12-807. Failure of employer to appear. (a) If an employer fails to appear and answer as required by Part 8 of Article XII of this Act, the court may enter a conditional judgment against the employer for the amount due upon the judgment against the judgment debtor. * * *

735 ILCS 5/12-808. Duty of employer.

(a) An employer served as herein provided shall pay the employee the amount of his or her exempt wages.

(b) To the extent of the amount due upon the judgment and costs, the employer shall hold, subject to order of court, any non-exempt wages due or which subsequently come due. The judgment or balance due thereon is a lien on wages due at the time of the service of summons, and such lien shall continue as to subsequent earnings until the total amount due upon the judgment and costs is paid, except that such lien on subsequent earnings shall terminate sooner if the employment relationship is terminated or if the underlying judgment is vacated or modified.

* * *

(e) Pursuant to answer under oath to the interrogatories by the employer, an order shall be entered compelling the employer to deduct [the "wages subject to collection," determined pursuant to section 12-803] from wages of the judgment debtor.... The order shall further provide that deducted wages shall be remitted to the creditor or creditor's attorney on a monthly basis.

(f) If after the entry of a deduction order, the employer ceases to remit funds to the plaintiff pursuant to the order without a lawful excuse (which would terminate the employer's obligation under the deduction order such as the debtor having filed a bankruptcy, the debtor having left employment or the employer having received service of a support order against the judgment debtor having priority over the wage deduction proceedings), the court shall, upon plaintiff's motion, enter a conditional judgment against the employer for the balance due on the judgment. * * *.

735 ILCS 5/12-808.5. Certification of judgment balance. Whenever a wage deduction order has not been fully satisfied by the end of the first full calendar quarter following the date of service of the wage deduction summons:

(1) The judgment creditor or his attorney shall prepare a certification that states the amount of the judgment remaining unsatisfied as of the last calendar day of each full calendar quarter for which the wage deduction order continues in effect.

(2) The certification shall be mailed or delivered to the employer by the judgment creditor or his or her attorney within 15 days after the end of each calendar quarter for which the wage deduction order continues in effect. The employer shall hand deliver or mail by first class mail a copy of the certification to the judgment debtor at the judgment debtor's last known address.

(3) In the event that the plaintiff fails to provide the certification required by this Section, the employer must continue to withhold funds from the defendant's wages but may hold the funds without remitting to the plaintiff until

such time as it receives a certification required by this Section. A certification of judgment balance need not be filed with the court.

(4) Any party to the wage deduction proceeding may, upon motion with notice to all other parties, ask the court to review the balance due claimed by the judgment creditor.

735 ILCS 5/12-809. Offsetting claims. The employer is entitled to assert against indebtedness due to the judgment debtor offsetting claims against either or both the judgment creditor and the judgment debtor.

* * *

735 ILCS 5/12-814. Costs and fees.

(a) The costs of obtaining a deduction order shall be charged to the judgment debtor, unless the court determines, in its discretion, that costs incurred by the judgment creditor were improperly incurred, in which case those costs shall be paid by the judgment creditor.

(b) No fee shall be paid by an employer for filing his or her appearance, answer or satisfaction of judgment against him or her.

(c) A fee consisting of 2% of the amount required to be deducted by any deduction order shall be allowed and paid to the employer, and the amount so paid shall be charged to the judgment debtor.

* * *

735 ILCS 5/12-818. Discharge or suspension of employee prohibited.

No employer may discharge or suspend any employee by reason of the fact that his or her earnings have been subjected to a deduction order for any one indebtedness. Any person violating this Section shall be guilty of a Class A misdemeanor.

* * *

735 ILCS 5/12-901. [Homestead exemption] Amount. Every individual is entitled to an estate of homestead to the extent in value of $15,000 of his or her interest in a farm or lot of land and buildings thereon, a condominium, or personal property, owned or rightly possessed by lease or otherwise and occupied by him or her as a residence, or in a cooperative that owns property that the individual uses as a residence. That homestead and all right in and title to that homestead is exempt from attachment, judgment, levy, or each individual may not exceed his or her proportionate share of $30,000 based upon percentage of ownership.

* * *

735 ILCS 5/12-1001. Personal property exempt. The following personal property, owned by the debtor, is exempt from judgment, attachment, or distress for rent:

(a) The necessary wearing apparel, bible, school books, and family pictures of the debtor and the debtor's dependents;
(b) The debtor's equity interest, not to exceed $4,000 in value, in any other property;
(c) The debtor's interest, not to exceed $2,400 in value, in any one motor vehicle;
(d) The debtor's equity interest, not to exceed $1,500 in value, in any implements, professional books, or tools of the trade of the debtor;
(e) Professionally prescribed health aids for the debtor or a dependent of the debtor;
(f) All proceeds payable because of the death of the insured and the aggregate net cash value of any or all life insurance and endowment policies and annuity contracts payable to a wife or husband of the insured, or to a child, parent, or other person dependent upon the insured, or to a revocable or irrevocable trust [naming one of these people primary beneficiary];
(g) The debtor's right to receive:

(1) a social security benefit, unemployment compensation, or public assistance benefit;
(2) a veteran's benefit;
(3) a disability, illness, or unemployment benefit; and
(4) alimony, support, or separate maintenance, to the extent reasonably necessary for the support of the debtor and any dependent of the debtor.

(h) The debtor's right to receive, or property that is traceable to:

(1) an award under a crime victim's reparation law;
(2) a payment on account of the wrongful death of an individual of whom the debtor was a dependent, to the extent reasonably necessary for the support of the debtor;

(3) a payment under a life insurance contract that insured the life of an individual of whom the debtor was a dependent, to the extent reasonably necessary for the support of the debtor or a dependent of the debtor;

(4) a payment, not to exceed $15,000 in value, on account of personal bodily injury of the debtor or an individual of whom the debtor was a dependent; and

(5) any restitution payments made to persons pursuant to the federal Civil Liberties Act of 1988 and the Aleutian and Pribilof Island Restitution Act, P.L. 100-383.

For purposes of this subsection (h), a debtor's right to receive an award or payment shall be exempt for a maximum of 2 years after the debtor's right to receive the award or payment accrues; property traceable to an award or payment shall be exempt for a maximum of 5 years after the award or payment accrues; and an award or payment and property traceable to an award or payment shall be exempt only to the extent of the amount of the award or payment, without interest or appreciation from the date of the award or payment.

(i) The debtor's right to receive an award under Part 20 of Article II of this Code relating to crime victims' awards.

(j) Moneys held in an account invested in the Illinois College Savings Pool of which the debtor is a participant or donor ***.

Money due the debtor from the sale of any personal property that was exempt from judgment, attachment, or distress for rent at the time of the sale is exempt from attachment and garnishment to the same extent that the property would be exempt had the same not been sold by the debtor.

If a debtor owns property exempt under this Section and he or she purchased that property with the intent of converting nonexempt property into exempt property or in fraud of his or her creditors, that property shall not be exempt from judgment, attachment, or distress for rent ...

The personal property exemptions set forth in this Section shall apply only to individuals and only to personal property that is used for personal rather than business purposes....

735 ILCS 5/12-1006. Exemption for retirement plans.

(a) A debtor's interest in or right, whether vested or not, to the assets held in or to receive pensions, annuities, benefits, distributions, refunds of contributions, or other payments under a retirement plan is exempt from judgment, attachment, execution, distress for rent, and seizure for the satisfaction of debts if the plan (i) is intended in good faith to qualify as a retirement plan under applicable provisions of the Internal Revenue Code of 1986 … or (ii) is a public employee pension plan created under the Illinois Pension Code….

(b) "Retirement plan" includes the following:

(1) a stock bonus, pension, profit sharing, annuity, or similar plan or arrangement, including a retirement plan for self-employed individuals or a simplified employee pension plan;
(2) a government or church retirement plan or contract;
(3) an individual retirement annuity or … account; and
(4) a public employee pension plan created under the Illinois Pension Code, as now or hereafter amended. * * *

Index

abstract of judgment, 81
aid to families and children, 64
alias writ, 10
alter ego, 61, 62
American Rule, 25
animals, 67
appeal, 23
appraisal, 70
arbitral awards, 21, 22
arbitration, 22
arrest, 10, 30, 31
asset protection, 58, 63, 74–76
asset-protection trust, 76
assignment order, 54, 77
attachment, 80
attorney's fees, 25, 26, 74
auction, 8, 9, 13, 57, 58, 70
authenticated, 19, 20
automatic stay, 89, 90
avoidable preferences, 92
bank accounts, 43, 44, 58, 68, 69
bankruptcy, 7, 11, 14, 61, 85, 87–93
bankruptcy stay, 89, 90
bench warrant, 30
bible, 65
bill in equity, 15
bill of discovery, 11
branch, 43–45, 52
broker, 52
business associations, 50, 61
capable of delivery, 40, 42, 85
capias, 10
cause of action, 53, 54, 59
cellphone, 67
central location for service, 45
certificated security, 52
Chancellor, 9, 11, 12
chapter 11, 87–89, 92
chapter 13, 88, 89, 91
chapter 7, 88, 89, 91
charging order, 52, 53, 82
Charles Schwab, 52
citation to discover assets, 29, 35, 38, 54, 55, 58, 71, 83, 84
clawback, 92
clean hands, 62
closely held company, 52
cloud title, 37
comity, 21
commissions, 42, 45, 46
common law lien, 80
computer, 67
confession judgment, 20
confirmation, 22
consent directive, 77

contempt, 3, 14, 30, 31, 34, 35, 41, 55, 77
Cook, David, 31
Cook Islands, 75
copyright, 54
corporation, 50, 51, 62, 76
costs, 11, 23, 25, 26, 28, 47, 58
courthouse door, 57
courthouse steps, 57
credit report, 27, 28
creditor's bill, 15
DAPT, 76
debtors' prison, 10
debts due, 39, 42, 43, 53, 72
denial of discharge, 91
deposit account, 43
deposition, 12, 29
disability insurance, 64
discharge, 88, 90, 91
discovery, 3, 11, 12, 15, 26, 28–31, 33–36, 39, 42, 46, 54, 55, 60, 61, 73, 76
disposable income, 48, 49, 88, 89
distractio bonorum, 9
docketing, 25, 36, 79, 81
domestic asset protection trust, 76
dormancy, 24
dormant, 24, 25
duces tecum, 29
Dunn & Bradstreet, 27
E*Trade, 52
earnings withholding order, 47, 56, 82
electronic deposit, 64
elegit, 10, 13
encumbrance, 67
Equifax, 27
Equifax Small Business, 27
equity, 11–15, 52, 53, 66, 67, 69–71, 81
exceptions from discharge, 91
execution, 10, 11, 13–16, 18, 19, 24, 34, 38–43, 46, 47, 51–54, 56–59, 64, 68, 70, 73, 80–85
execution lien, 40, 80, 81, 85
execution writ, 10, 13, 14, 16, 24, 38, 40, 42, 43, 82, 84
exemption, 34, 58, 64–71, 74, 75, 81
Experian, 27, 28
Experian Business, 27
extraordinary cognition, 8, 9
Fair Credit Reporting Act, 27
Fair Debt Collection Practices Act (FDCPA), 54, 72–74
Federal Arbitration Act, 22
federal benefits, 64, 71
Federal Debt Collection Procedures Act, 18, 72
Federal Rules of Civil Procedure, 18
federalism, 17
fee shifting, 26
Fidelity, 52
Field Code, 15
Field, David Dudley, 15
Field, Stephen J., 15
fieri facias, 10–15, 38
fire sale, 57
firearms, 65
Florida, 5, 16, 25, 28, 30, 37, 39, 55, 59, 83, 84, 86
foreclosure, 13, 37, 56, 57
foreign judgment, 20
foreign-country money judgment, 21
fraud, 59, 60, 62, 75, 91
fraudulent conveyance, 76
fraudulent transfer, 59, 60, 91
fresh start, 88
full faith and credit, 19, 21
furnishings, 65, 70

garnishee, 41, 42
garnishee's memorandum, 42
garnishment, 14, 15, 24, 40–49, 51–56, 58, 71, 77, 84
harassment, 30
headquarters, 43, 44
health aids, 65, 71
heirlooms, 65
homestead, 65–67, 69, 70
implements, 65
imprisonment for debt, 10, 11, 17, 30
income and asset form, 29
income execution, 34, 46
indirect holding system, 52
inflation, 66, 69–71
insurance, 3, 26, 62, 64–66, 71
intangibles, 40, 42, 53, 80
intellectual property, 3, 42, 54, 92
intentional tort, 92
interrogatories, 12, 29, 48
investment security, 52
Iowa, 9, 16, 37
jail, 10, 30
jewelry, 65
judgment lien, 20, 36, 37, 40, 79, 80, 82–86
judgment roll, 25
judgment-proof, 58
Judicial Council, 47, 70
keeper, 51
levari facias, 10
levy, 10–12, 37–45, 51–53, 56, 58, 67, 69, 85
license, 54, 56
lien, 13, 20, 23, 25, 35–37, 40, 79–86, 92
limited liability company (LLC), 28, 50, 51, 53, 72, 74, 75
marshal, 38
means test, 88, 89
memberships, 55
military, 64
milk, 67
mortgage, 36, 37, 66, 67, 80
NASDAQ, 52
New York Stock Exchange, 52, 55
non-dischargeable claim, 92
non-US money judgment, 21
nulla bona, 11, 15
objection to discharge, 91
OEX, 30, 83
offshore, 56
ORAP, 30, 83
order for appearance and examination, 30
order of priority, 67, 79, 81
partnership, 50, 52, 53, 74, 75
patent, 54
Paynet, 27
Pennsylvania, 5, 15, 16, 30, 46, 59, 66, 67, 70
perfection, 81, 84
personal property recording statute, 84
personal services, 42, 45
pets, 65
piercing the corporate veil, 61
pluries writ, 10
post-judgment interest, 23, 25
poundage, 38
preference, 92
preference avoidance, 92
preferential transfer, 92
priority, 37, 67, 79–82, 84
private place, 40
proceedings supplementary, 15, 16, 18, 26, 29, 55, 60, 83
process server, 38

public assistance, 64
public auction, 8, 9, 13, 57, 58
public policy, 22
rank [**of lien**], 82, 84–85
real estate, 25, 81
real property, 23, 36, 37, 56, 65, 81
realty, 13, 36, 37, 39, 57, 79, 81–84
receiver, 14, 51, 54, 83
receivership, 14, 15, 50, 51, 53, 85
redemption, 57
registration, 18, 19, 21, 23, 27
religious, 65–67
residence, 67, 70
restraining notice, 34, 37, 68
retirement, 49, 64–67, 70, 71
return [**of writ**], 11, 15, 39
revenue rule, 22
revival, 24
Roman procedure, 7, 8
Rome, 7, 9, 87
royal law courts, 9
salaries, 14, 42, 45, 46
scire facias, 10, 24
Scottrade, 52
securities, 34, 50, 52, 58, 74
securities intermediary, 52
security entitlement, 52
security interest, 80, 85
self-settled, 75, 76
selling agent, 58
separate entity, 44, 52, 62
settlor, 74
sewing machines, 66, 67
sheriff, 10, 11, 13, 15, 19, 38–43, 46–48, 51, 52, 54–58, 67, 71, 82, 84, 90
Simpson, O. J., 31
sister-state judgment, 20, 21
social security, 49, 64
spendthrift trust, 75
statute of limitations, 60, 76
statutorily exempt payment, 68
statutory lien, 80
stock, 14, 52, 55
subpoena, 34, 73
supersedeas, 23
supersedeas bond, 23
supplemental proceedings, 15
supplementary proceedings, 15, 16, 18, 26, 29, 55, 60, 83
tax lien, 82
tax return, 30, 31
TD Ameritrade, 52
tenancy by the entirety, 70
teste, 39
Texas, 5, 15, 16, 19, 23, 24, 26, 28, 39–41, 46, 51, 55, 64–66
till tap, 51
tools, 65, 71
trademark, 54
TransUnion, 27
turnover order, 53–57, 76, 82–84
uncertificated security, 52
undercapitalization, 62
unemployment benefits, 64
Uniform Commercial Code (UCC), 37, 52, 53, 56, 76, 80, 83, 84, 86
Uniform Enforcement of Foreign Judgments Act, 19
Uniform Foreign-Country Money Judgments Recognition Act, 21
Uniform Fraudulent Transfer Act (UFTA), 59–61
Uniform Voidable Transactions Act (UVTA), 59, 61, 76
validation notice, 73
vehicle, 65, 67, 69, 71, 91
veil piercing, 51, 61, 62

venditio bonorum, 8
veterans, 64
wage deduction order, 47, 48
wage garnishment, 24, 45, 46, 48, 55, 71, 77
wages, 14, 42, 45–49, 56, 58, 68, 69, 71, 90
waiting period, 23
wearing apparel, 65, 66, 71
wildcard, 66, 67, 71
willful or malicious, 91
workers compensation, 64
writ, 9–16, 24, 38–44, 46, 51–53, 73, 82, 84, 90
writ of execution, 13, 38, 39, 41, 43, 51, 73, 82